STUDY GUIDE

to accompany

FINANCIAL ACCOUNTING

TOOLS FOR BUSINESS DECISION-MAKING

CANADIAN EDITION

PAUL D. KIMMEL Ph.D., C.P.A.
University of Wisconsin—Milwaukee
Milwaukee, Wisconsin

JERRY J. WEYGANDT Ph.D., C.P.A.
Arthur Andersen Alumni Professor of Accounting
University of Wisconsin
Madison, Wisconsin

DONALD E. KIESO Ph.D., C.P.A.
KPMG Peat Marwick Emeritus Professor of Accountancy
North Illinois University
DeKalb, Illinois

BARBARA TRENHOLM M.B.A., F.C.A.
University of New Brunswick
Fredericton, New Brunswick

PREPARED BY:

CECELIA M. FEWOX
College of Charleston
Carleston, South Carolina

ANN CLARKE-OKAH, C.A.
Carleton University
Ottawa, Ontario

JOHN WILEY AND SONS CANADA, LTD
Toronto • New York • Chichester • Weinheim • Brisbane • Singapore

Canadian Cataloguing in Publication Data
Clarke-Okah, Ann
    Study Guide to accompany Financial accounting, tools for business decision-making, first Canadian edition

ISBN 0-471-64632-6

1. Accounting.   2. Accounting—Problems, exercises etc. I. Title.
II. Title: Financial accounting: tools for business decision-making

HF5635.F44 2000 Suppl.   657'. 044   C2001-930443-9

Production Credits
Publisher: John Horne
Publishing Services Director: Karen Bryan
Editorial Manager: Karen Staudinger
Sr. Marketing Manager: Janine Daoust
Design & Typesetting: Lakshmi Gosyne
Printing & Binding: Tri-Graphic Printing Limited

Printed and bound in Canada
10 9 8 7 6 5 4 3 2 1

John Wiley & Sons Canada, Ltd.
22 Worcester Road
Etobicoke, Ontario M9W 1L1
Visit our website at: www.wiley.com/canada/kimmel

CONTENTS

Chapter

CHAPTER

1

INTRODUCTION TO FINANCIAL STATEMENTS

CHAPTER OVERVIEW

Chapter 1 introduces you to a variety of financial accounting topics. You will learn about the primary forms of business organization and the three principal types of business activity. You will also learn about users of accounting information and how that information is delivered. You will learn about the basic financial statements and their components, the assumptions and principles underlying these statements, and items that supplement the financial statements in an annual report.

REVIEW OF SPECIFIC STUDY OBJECTIVES

- A **proprietorship** is a business owned by one person. It is *simple to set up*, and the *owner has control over the business*. Because they are so simple to organize, there are many thousands of proprietorships operating in the business world.

- A **partnership** is a business owned by more than one person. It provides strength in numbers: Each *partner may bring economic resources, or unique talents or skills* to the combination.

- A **corporation** is a separate legal entity owned by shareholders. *Advantages* include the fact that *share capital is easy to sell* and that the *raising of funds is simple*. While there are many more proprietorships and partnerships than there are corporations, corporations produce far more revenue.

The **purpose of financial information** is to *provide data for decision-making*. **Accounting is the information system that identifies, records, and communicates the economic events of an organization to interested users**.

- **Internal users** are people who work for the business, and *managers who plan, organize, and run a business*. Accounting information helps to answer questions such as, "Does the business have enough resources to build a new manufacturing plant?" *Internal reports* help to provide the required information.
- **External users** work outside of the business and include *investors*, who use accounting information for their share capital decisions; *creditors*, who evaluate the risk of lending to, and the credit-worthiness of business borrowers; *taxing authorities*, which review compliance with tax laws; *regulatory agencies*, which review compliance with prescribed rules; *customers*; *labour unions*; and *economic planners*.

There are **three types of business activity** which the accounting information system tracks: *financing, investing*, and *operating*.

- **Financing activities** deal with the ways a business *raises funds for operations*. The **two primary sources of outside funds** are *borrowing money and issuing shares*.
- A business may **borrow money** by taking out a loan at a bank, issuing debt securities, or purchasing goods on credit. A **creditor** is a person or entity to which a business owes money, and a **liability** is a debt or other obligation, which represents creditors' claims on the business. Examples of liabilities are *accounts payable*, resulting from purchases on credit; *notes payable*, resulting from direct borrowing or purchasing on credit; *wages payable*, representing wages owed to employees; *sales and real estate taxes payable* to local governments; and *bonds payable*, sold to investors and usually due several years in the future. A creditor has a legal right to be paid at an agreed-upon time and must be paid before an owner (shareholder) is paid.
- A corporation may also **issue shares** to investors. Share capital is the term which describes the total amount paid into the corporation by shareholders for the shares purchased. *A shareholder is an owner of the business* and receives payments in the form of dividends. (Please note that there are companies which do not pay dividends to shareholders). As noted above, shareholder claims are secondary to creditor claims.
- **Investing activities** deal with what a corporation does with the financing it receives. Certainly a new business must *purchase assets* with which to operate. An **asset** is a resource owned by a business. Examples of assets are property, plant, and equipment, such as buildings, and trucks, and accounts receivable, which is someone's or some entity's promise to pay the business money in the future.
- **Operating activities** are just that: *operations of the business*. Different businesses have different operations, of course. A paper company produces and sells paper, while a dairy company produces and sells milk. When a company operates, it earns revenues. **Revenues** are the *increase in assets arising from the sale of a product or service*. When a company operates, it also incurs costs. **Expenses** are *the cost of assets consumed, or services used in the process of generating revenues*. If revenues exceed expenses (hopefully!), then a business earns *net earnings*. If expenses exceed revenues, then a business incurs a *net loss*.

Various users desire information to help them make decisions, and this financial **information is provided in the form of financial statements**, which form the backbone of financial accounting. There are *four financial statements*: the *statement of earnings (also commonly known as income statement)*, the *statement of retained earnings*, the *balance sheet*, and the *statement of cash flows*.

STUDY OBJECTIVE

Describe the content and purpose of each of the financial statements.

- The **statement of earnings** *reports the success or failure of the company's operations during the period*. Only **revenues and expenses** appear on the statement of earnings, along with their difference, either net earnings (revenues exceed expenses) or net loss (expenses exceed revenues). New accounting students often want to put the "Cash" account on the statement of earnings, but this is incorrect because cash is an asset (a resource owned by a business). Only revenues and expenses appear on the statement of earnings.

- The **statement of retained earnings** shows the *amounts and causes of changes in the retained earnings balance during the period*. Net earnings are added to beginning retained earnings, (or, if there is a net loss, that amount is deducted) and then dividends are deducted. (Remember that a business will have either net earnings or net loss; it can't have both at the same time.) *Users of financial statements can find out about management's dividend policy by analysing this statement*. To summarize, the Retained Earnings account is the total of all the net earnings that the company has earned, all the net losses it has incurred, and all the dividends it has paid. The statement of retained earnings documents this activity for the current period.

- The **balance sheet** *reports assets and claims to those assets at a specific point in time*. There are **two types of claims**: *claims of creditors (liabilities)* and *claims of owners (shareholders' equity)*. The balance sheet is an expanded expression of the **basic accounting equation**, which is:

STUDY OBJECTIVE

Explain the meaning of assets, liabilities, and shareholders' equity, and state the basic accounting equation.

$$\text{Assets} = \text{Liabilities} + \text{Shareholders' Equity}$$

Please note that this is a mathematical equation and must be in balance at all times. It can be used to answer questions such as: If assets total $100 and liabilities total $20, what is the total of shareholders' equity? (Answer: $80. Because $20 plus something must equal $100, and the something must be $80.)

Shareholders' equity consists of **two parts**: *Share capital* (often just one class of shares, common shares, is issued) and *retained earnings*.

- The **statement of cash flows** *provides financial information about the cash receipts and cash payments of a business for a specific period of time*. Here a user will find information about the *financing, investing, and operating activities* of the business.

- Note the **interrelationships between statements**:
  1. Net earnings or net loss from the statement of earnings appears on the statement of retained earnings.
  2. The ending balance of retained earnings is the same number reported on the balance sheet for retained earnings.
  3. The ending balance of cash must be the same, both on the balance sheet and on the statement of cash flows.

- Companies usually present **comparative statements**, which are *statements reporting information for more than one period*.

- Please be aware of the following when you **prepare financial statements**:
  1. All statements **must have a heading**. The *company name* appears on the first line, the *name of the document* appears on the second line, and the *date* appears on the third line. With respect to **dates**, the **balance sheet date** is for *one point in time* (June 30, 2001, or December 31, 2002), while the date **on the statement of earnings, the statement of retained earnings**, and the **statement of cash flows** is for a *period of time* ("For the month ended June 30, 2001" or "For the year ended December 31, 2002").

2. The number at the top of a column should have a dollar sign: This indicates that it is the first number in that column. The final number on a statement, such as Net Earnings or Total Assets, should have a dollar sign and be double-underlined. This indicates that it is the "answer." If there is a negative number, such as Net Loss, then it should be presented in parentheses or brackets. These are parts of a type of shorthand used by people who prepare statements and understood by users of statements.

Companies provide their shareholders with an **annual report**, which includes the *financial statements*, *notes to the financial statements*, an *independent auditor's report*, and a *management discussion and analysis section*.

- The **notes to the financial statements** provide *additional details about the items presented in the main body of the statements*. Examples of notes are one explaining which methods a company uses for its inventory and one explaining the progress of a lawsuit against the company.
- The **independent auditor's report** is prepared by an auditor, a professional who conducts an independent examination of a company's accounting data. The most desirable opinion is the *unqualified opinion*, which states that the financial statements are in accordance with generally accepted accounting principles.
- The **management discussion and analysis (MD&A) section** covers management's goals and objectives, observations about past performance, and key financial statistics.

There are various assumptions and principles, which **form a foundation for financial reporting**. The Canadian Institute of Chartered Accountants (CICA) sets accounting standards in Canada.

- The **assumptions** are:
  1. the **monetary unit assumption** which requires that *only those things that can be expressed in money are included in the accounting records*. Customer satisfaction and a loyal, competent workforce are extremely important but will not appear on a financial statement.
  2. the **economic entity assumption** which states that *every economic entity can be separately identified and accounted for*. If an individual owns a business, that individual must have two sets of records: one for his individual transactions and one for the business.
  3. the **time period assumption** which states that the *life of a business can be divided into artificial time periods and that useful reports covering those periods can be prepared for the business*.
  4. the **going concern assumption** which states that the *business will remain in operation for the foreseeable future*. This principle underlies much of what we do in accounting. If it seems likely that a company will go out of business in the near future, then different assumptions will govern preparation of the financial statements.
- The **principles** are:
  1. the **cost principle** which dictates that *assets are recorded at their cost*, not only at the time of their acquisition, but also for the entire time that they are held. There is much discussion about the relevance of this principle, but for now accountants adhere to it for various reasons, one of which is that cost is easy to measure.
  2. the **full disclosure principle** which requires that *all circumstances and events that would make a difference to financial statement users should be disclosed*, either in the statements themselves or in the notes and supporting schedules that accompany the statements.

CHAPTER SELF-TEST

As you work through the exercises and problems, remember to use the **Decision Toolkit** discussed and used in the text:

1. *Decision Checkpoints*: At this point you ask a question.
2. *Info Needed for Decision*: You make a choice regarding the information needed to answer the question.
3. *Tool to Use for Decision*: At this point you review just what the information chosen in step 2 does for the decision-making process.
4. *How to Evaluate Results*: You perform evaluation of information for answering the question.

Note: The notation (SO1) means that the question was drawn from study objective number one.

Completion

Please write in the word or words, which will complete the sentence.

(SO1) 1. A _____ is a separate legal entity owned by shareholders.

(SO2) 2. A(n) _____ _____ is a manager who plans, organizes, and runs a business.

(SO3) 3. An example of a(n) _____ activity is a corporation's sale of shares to investors.

(SO4) 4. The purpose of the _____ _____ _____ is to report the success or failure of the company's operations during the period.

(SO4) 5. The statement of _____ _____ includes an addition of net earnings and a deduction of dividends.

(SO5) 6. Claims of creditors on the assets of the business are called _____; claims of owners are called _____ _____.

(SO5) 7. If liabilities total $6,000 and shareholders' equity totals $10,000, then assets must total _____.

(SO6) 8. Only an independent public accountant may perform an _____ of a company's financial statements.

(SO7) 9. The _____ _____ assumption requires that only those things that can be expressed in money are included in the accounting records.

(SO7) 10. An asset was purchased for $5,000 and is now worth $7,000. The _____ _____ dictates that the asset continues to be recorded on the books at $5,000.

Multiple Choice

Please circle the correct answer.

(SO1) 1. Which of the following statements is correct?
   a. A proprietor has no personal liability for debts of their business.
   b. There are far more corporations than there are proprietorships and partnerships.
   c. Revenue produced by corporations is generally greater than that produced by proprietorships and partnerships.
   d. It is very difficult for a corporation to raise capital.

(SO2)   2. Which of the following is an example of an external user of accounting information?
   a. Marketing manager of the business
   b. President of the labour union
   c. Officer of the corporation
   d. Production supervisor of the business

(SO3)   3. Which of the following is an investing activity?
   a. Borrowing money from a bank
   b. Earning revenue from the sale of products
   c. Incurring salaries expense
   d. The purchase of a delivery truck

(SO3)   4. A business's earning of revenues is considered to be a(n):
   a. operating activity.
   b. investing activity.
   c. financing activity.
   d. balance sheet activity.

(SO3)   5. Borrowing money from a bank is considered to be a(n):
   a. operating activity.
   b. investing activity.
   c. financing activity.
   d. balance sheet activity.

(SO4)   6. Which of the following accounts will be found on a statement of earnings?
   a. Revenues, expenses, and dividends
   b. Revenues and expenses
   c. Revenues, expenses, and cash
   d. Expenses, dividends, and cash

(SO4)   7. If revenues are $20,000 and expenses are $5,000, then the business:
   a. incurred a net loss of $25,000.
   b. had net earnings of $20,000.
   c. had net earnings of $15,000.
   d. incurred a net loss of $15,000.

(SO4)   8. If beginning retained earnings is $10,000, net loss is $3,000, and dividends are $1,000, then
   the ending retained earnings shown on the statement of retained earnings is:
   a. $14,000.
   b. $12,000.
   c. $ 8,000.
   d. $ 6,000.

(SO5)   9. Which of the following is an appropriate date for a balance sheet?
   a. December 31, 2003
   b. For the month ending December 31, 2003
   c. For the quarter ending December 31, 2003
   d. For the year ending December 31, 2003

(SO5)   10. Which of the following is the correct expression of the basic accounting equation?
   a. Liabilities = Assets + Shareholders' Equity
   b. Shareholders' Equity = Assets + Liabilities
   c. Assets = Liabilities + Shareholders' Equity
   d. Assets = Liabilities – Shareholders' Equity

(SO5)   11. Assets total $14,000, shareholders' equity totals $9,000, and revenues total $6,000. What is the dollar amount of liabilities?
    a. $23,000
    b. $17,000
    c. $11,000
    d. $ 5,000

(SO5)   12. The statement which shows the operating, investing, and financing activities of a business is the:
    a. statement of retained earnings.
    b. statement of cash flows.
    c. statement of earnings.
    d. balance sheet.

(SO7)   13. Which of the following assumptions states that every business must be separately identified and accounted for?
    a. Monetary unit assumption
    b. Economic entity assumption
    c. Time period assumption
    d. Going concern assumption

(SO7)   14. Which of the following assumes that a business will remain in operation for the foreseeable future?
    a. Monetary unit assumption
    b. Economic entity assumption
    c. Time period assumption
    d. Going concern assumption

(SO7)   15. Which of the following requires that all circumstances and events, that would make a difference to financial statement users, should be disclosed?
    a. Full disclosure principle
    b. Economic entity assumption
    c. Time period assumption
    d. Cost principle

(SO7)   16. The _____ _____ assumption states that the life of a business can be divided into artificial time periods and that useful reports covering those periods can be prepared for the business.
    a. monetary unit
    b. going concern
    c. time period
    d. economic entity

(SO6)   17. In which section of the annual report does management highlight favourable or unfavourable trends and identify significant events and uncertainties affecting its ability to pay near-term obligations, ability to fund operations and expansion, and results of operations?
    a. Financial statements
    b. Management discussion and analysis
    c. Notes to the financial statements
    d. Auditor's report

(SO6)   18. Which of the following provides additional details about the items presented in the main body of the financial statements?
a. Management discussion and analysis
b. Auditor's report
c. Notes to the financial statements
d. None of the above is correct

(SO6)   19. Which of the following gives the results of the independent examination of the company's financial data?
a. Financial statements
b. Management discussion and analysis
c. Notes to the financial statements
d. Auditor's report

Problems

(SO5)   1. From the appropriate accounts given below, please prepare a balance sheet for Jerome Corporation on September 30, 2001:

Accumulated Amortization	$ 3,000
Common Shares	15,000
Service Revenue	20,000
Note Payable	5,000
Salaries Expense	10,000
Accounts Receivable	7,000
Dividends	2,000
Unearned Revenue	3,000
Retained Earnings, September 30, 2001	24,000
Supplies	2,000
Insurance Expense	1,500
Prepaid Insurance	3,000
Utilities Expense	4,000
Office Equipment	17,000
Accounts Payable	1,000
Cash	22,000

Jerome Corporation
Balance Sheet
September 30, 2001

2. Please refer to Cognos Incorporated financial statements at the end of this study guide for information for answering the following questions. Don't forget to use the **Decision Toolkit** approach for help in the problem-solving.

(SO5)   a. What is the total dollar amount of the company's assets in 2000? What are the three asset classes and their dollar amount, again in 2000?

(SO5)   b. Which class of liabilities has the largest total dollar amount in 2000?

(SO4)   c. Was the company profitable in 2000? What has been the trend in company earnings over the three years shown?

(SO4)   d. What was the biggest expense in 2000?

(SO4)   e. What was the company's income tax expense in 2000?

SOLUTIONS TO SELF-TEST

Completion

1. corporation
2. internal user
3. financing
4. statement of earnings
5. retained earnings
6. liabilities; shareholders' equity
7. $16,000
8. audit
9. monetary unit
10. cost principle

Multiple Choice

1. c Proprietors are liable for debts of their businesses, there are more proprietorships and partnerships than there are corporations, and corporations can raise capital through selling of shares and bonds.
2. b The marketing manager, corporation officer, and production supervisor all work for the business, and are therefore internal users.
3. d Borrowing money is a financing activity, and earning revenue and incurring expense are operating activities.
4. a Investing activities deal with the purchase of assets, and financing activities deal with the borrowing of money and selling of shares.
5. c
6. b Dividends appear on the statement of retained earnings, and cash is an asset on the balance sheet.
7. c $20,000 – $5,000
8. d $10,000 – $3,000 – $1,000
9. a The balance sheet shows balances at a specific date, not for a period of time.
10. c
11. d $14,000 – $9,000
12. b The statement of retained earnings shows changes in the retained earnings account over the period, the statement of earnings summarizes revenue and expense activity, and the balance sheet shows assets, liabilities, and shareholders' equity items.
13. b The monetary unit assumption requires that only those things which can be expressed in money are included in the accounting records; the time period assumption states that the life of a business can be divided into artificial time periods; and the going concern assumption assumes that a business will remain in operation for the foreseeable future.
14. d
15. a The economic entity assumption states that every business must be separately identified and accounted for; the time period assumption states that the life of a business can be divided into artificial time periods; and the cost principle dictates that assets are recorded at their cost.
16. c

17. b The financial statements report results and balances, the notes give more details about items in the financial statements, and the auditor's report gives the auditor's opinion about whether the statements are presented in accordance with generally accepted accounting principles.
18. c
19. d

Problems

1.

Jerome Corporation
Balance Sheet
September 30, 2001

Assets

Cash		$22,000
Accounts Receivable		7,000
Supplies		2,000
Prepaid Insurance		3,000
Office Equipment	$17,000	
Less: Accumulated Amortization	3,000	14,000
Total Assets		$48,000

Liabilities and Shareholders' Equity

Liabilities		
Note Payable	$ 5,000	
Accounts Payable	1,000	
Unearned Revenue	3,000	
Total Liabilities		$ 9,000
Shareholders' Equity		
Common Shares	$15,000	
Retained Earnings	24,000	
Total Shareholders'Equity		39,000
Total Liabilities and Shareholders' Equity		$48,000

2.
a. $379,886, Current Assets ($313,188), Fixed Assets ($44,835), Intangible Assets ($21,863).
b. Current Liabilities.
c. Yes, the company's income has increased over the three years.
d. Selling, general and administrative expenses at $238,147.
e. $22,873.

NOTES

NOTES

2

A FURTHER LOOK AT FINANCIAL STATEMENTS

CHAPTER OVERVIEW

Chapter 2 explains "generally accepted accounting principles" and the basic objective of financial reporting. You will learn about the qualitative characteristics of accounting information, as well as the two constraints in accounting. You will look further at financial statements, learning how to construct ratios using a company's financial statements and how to use those ratios to analyse the company's strengths and weaknesses.

REVIEW OF SPECIFIC STUDY OBJECTIVES

- The term **"financial reporting"** includes *all the financial information presented by a company, both in its financial statements and in additional disclosures,* such as notes to the statements.
- The **primary objective of financial reporting** is to *provide information useful for decision-making.*
- **Generally accepted accounting principles** are accounting *rules that have substantial authoritative support and are recognized as a general guide for financial reporting purposes.* Standard-setting bodies determine these rules. In Canada the primary standard-set-

ting body is the **Canadian Institute of Chartered Accountants (CICA)**. The CICA's **over-riding criterion** is that an accounting rule should *generate financial information that is most useful for making a decision*.

<table>
<tr><td>

STUDY OBJECTIVE

2

Discuss the qualitative characteristics of accounting information.
</td></tr>
</table>

To be useful, information should have the following **qualitative characteristics:** *understandability, relevance, reliability,* and *comparability*.

- Accounting information is **understandable** if the **average user is able to study the information intelligently**.
- Accounting information is **relevant** if it **makes a difference in a business decision**. If relevant, accounting information provides a *basis for forecasting, confirms or corrects prior expectations,* and is presented on a *timely basis*.
- Accounting information is **reliable** if it **can be depended on**. If reliable, accounting information is *verifiable* (free of error), is a *faithful representation* of what it purports to be, and is *neutral* (does not favour one set of users over another).
- Accounting information is **comparable** when *different companies use the same accounting principles*, or when *one company uses the same accounting principles and methods from year to year*. This does not mean that a company must use the same principles forever after making the initial selection. If it changes in order to produce more meaningful information, then it must disclose the change in the notes to the financial statements.

<table>
<tr><td>

STUDY OBJECTIVE

3

Identify the two constraints in accounting.
</td></tr>
</table>

Constraints *permit a company to modify generally accepted accounting principles without jeopardizing the usefulness of the reported information*. The **two constraints are cost-benefit and materiality**.

- The **cost-benefit** constraint ensures that the value of the information exceeds the cost of providing it.
- An item is **material** if it *influences the decision of an investor or creditor*. It is important to note that what is material for one company may be immaterial for another. Assume that companies A and B each have a $1,000 error in the financial statements. Company A's net earnings are $10,000, while company B's net earnings are $100,000. The $1,000 error will likely will be material for A since it is 10% of net earnings, while it will likely be immaterial for B since it is only 1% of net earnings.

<table>
<tr><td>

STUDY OBJECTIVE

4

Identify the sections of a classified balance sheet.
</td></tr>
</table>

The **balance sheet** of a company presents a *snapshot of its financial position at a point in time*. A **classified balance sheet** breaks the statement components into several classifications, usually having *three asset categories, two liability categories,* and the *two shareholders' equity categories*.

The following are the **three common asset categories**:

1. **Current assets** are assets *expected to be converted into cash or used in the business within a relatively short period of time*, usually within one year. Please note that some companies use a period longer than one year to classify assets and liabilites as current because they have a longer *operating cycle* (the average time that it takes to spend cash to obtain or manufacture a product to sell, then to sell the product, and then to collect cash from the customer). The operating cycle is sometimes called the cash-to-cash cycle. Current assets are *listed in the order in which they are expected to be converted into cash* and include **cash, short-term investments, receivables, inventories, and prepaid expenses**.

2. **Long-term investments** are *investments in shares and bonds of other corporations that are normally held for many years*.

3. **Capital assets** may be *tangible* or *intangible*. **Tangible capital assets** are *assets with physical substance that have relatively long useful lives and are used in the operations of the business*. Examples include **land, building, machinery and equipment, and natural resources**.

These assets lose some of their value, or wear out with the passage of time, and their cost must be allocated to expense over the useful life of the asset. On the balance sheet, they are *shown at their cost less total accumulated amortization*. (The one exception is land: Instead of decreasing in value, land normally appreciates.)

Intangible capital assets are *capital assets which have no physical substance*. They are essentially long-lived rights; examples include **patents, copyrights, and trademarks or trade names**. New accounting students often say that a patent has physical substance, and that a piece of paper can be held in a hand. The piece of paper does have physical substance but is not the patent itself, it is only evidence that a patent exists. The patent is protection of the invention granted by the federal government for a period of 20 years from the date of application.

The following are the two common liability categories:

1. **Current liabilities** are *obligations that are to be paid within one year*. Examples include **accounts payable, notes payable, salaries payable, interest payable, taxes payable, and current maturities of long-term obligations**. Notes payable are usually listed first, followed by accounts payable and other current liabilities.

2. **Long-term liabilities** are *expected to be paid after one year from the balance sheet date*. If the balance sheet date is December 31, 2000, and an obligation is due on June 30, 2002, then the obligation is long-term. Examples include **bonds payable, mortgages payable, long-term notes payable, lease liabilities, and pension liabilities**. There is no particular guidance for listing these long-term obligations, and companies simply choose a way of disclosing them, which is most useful for the users of their financial statements.

- As you learned in Chapter 1, **shareholders' equity** has *two components: share capital and retained earnings*. Share capital consists of shareholders' investments of assets in the business, while retained earnings are just that—earnings retained for use in the business.

- Financial statements are used to gauge the strength or weakness of a company. To make numbers in the statements more useful and meaningful, users conduct **ratio analysis**, a *technique for expressing relationships among selected financial statement data*.

- **Profitability ratios** *measure the operating success of a company for a given period of time*. Two such ratios are the **return on assets ratio** and the **profit margin ratio**.

- The **return on assets ratio** is an *overall measure of profitability*, calculated by *dividing net earnings by average assets*. (To calculate average assets, add together the beginning and ending asset values for the period and then divide by 2.) A **high ratio is preferable** because the ratio *indicates the amount of net earnings generated by each dollar invested in assets*.

- The **profit margin ratio** *measures the percentage of each dollar of sales that results in net earnings*. It is calculated by *dividing net earnings by net sales* for the period. High volume stores usually have low profit margins, while low volume stores have high profit margins.

- Please note that one ratio by itself doesn't convey very much. The ratio must be compared with something, either with the ratios from prior years of the company, or with the ratios of other companies in the same industry, or with the particular industry's averages.

- The **statement of retained earnings** describes the *changes in retained earnings* for the period. These changes usually involve net earnings or net loss and dividends.

- A **statement of earnings** reports the *changes in revenues and expenses* for the period. The result, net earnings or net loss for the period, is incorporated into the statement of retained earnings.

- The **balance sheet** reports the *financial position of the company's assets, liabilities, and shareholders' equity* at the end of the period. Ending retained earnings, determined on the statement of retained earnings, is included in the shareholders' equity section of the balance sheet.

STUDY OBJECTIVE

Identify and calculate ratios for analysing a company's profitability.

STUDY OBJECTIVE

Explain the relationship between a statement of retained earnings, a statement of earnings, and a balance sheet.

STUDY OBJECTIVE

7

Identify and calculate ratios for analysing a company's liquidity and solvency.

Just as you have performed ratio analysis using numbers from the statement of earnings, so, too, can you calculate **ratios using numbers from the classified balance sheet**.

Liquidity refers to a *company's ability to pay obligations expected to come due within the next year or operating cycle.*

- One measure of liquidity is **working capital**, which is the *difference between current assets and current liabilities.* It is certainly preferable to have a positive number (current assets exceed current liabilities) because this indicates that a company has a good likelihood of being able to pay its liabilities. If current assets are $300 and current liabilities are $100, then working capital is $200.

- Another measure of liquidity is the **current ratio**, calculated by *dividing current assets by current liabilities.* Referring to the numbers just above, dividing $300 by $100 yields a current ratio of 3:1, meaning that the company has $3 of current assets for every $1 of current liabilities. Remember that a ratio by itself does not convey very much information: It must be compared to something.

Solvency deals with a company's *ability to survive over a long period of time, with its ability to pay its long-term obligations and the interest due on them.*

- The **debt to total assets ratio** is one source of information about a company's solvency and *measures the percentage of assets financed by creditors rather than invested by shareholders.* It is calculated by *dividing total debt (both current and long-term) by total assets.* The higher the percentage of debt financing, the greater the risk that the company may be unable to pay its debts as they mature. If total debt is $3,000,000 and total assets are $5,000,000, then the ratio is 60%, meaning that of every dollar invested in company assets, creditors have provided $0.60. A creditor does not like to see a high debt to total assets ratio for a company.

- The **statement of cash flows can be used to calculate measures of liquidity and solvency**. The **cash current debt coverage ratio** is a measure of liquidity and is calculated by *dividing cash provided by operating activities, by average current liabilities.* The **cash total debt coverage ratio** is a measure of solvency and is calculated by *dividing cash provided by operating activities, by average total liabilities.*

CHAPTER SELF-TEST

As you work through the exercises and problems, remember to use the **Decision Toolkit** discussed and used in the text:

1. *Decision Checkpoints*: At this point you ask a question.
2. *Info Needed for Decision*: You make a choice regarding the information needed to answer the question.
3. *Tool to Use for Decision*: At this point you review just what the information chosen in step 2 does for the decision-making process.
4. *How to Evaluate Results*: You perform evaluation of information for answering the question.

Note: The notation (SO1) means that the question was drawn from study objective number one.

Matching

Please write the letters of the following terms in the spaces to the left of the definitions.

a. Cost-benefit
b. Consistency
c. Current assets
d. Current liabilities
e. Generally accepted accounting principles
f. Intangible assets
g. Liquidity
h. Long-term investments
i. Materiality
j. Operating cycle
k. Solvency

(SO7) _____ 1. The ability of a company to pay interest as it comes due and to repay the face value of debt at maturity.

(SO3) _____ 2. The constraint of determining whether an item is important enough to influence the decision of a reasonably prudent investor or creditor.

(SO3) _____ 3. The value of information should exceed the cost of obtaining it.

(SO4) _____ 4. Obligations to be paid within the next year or operating cycle, whichever is longer.

(SO1) _____ 5. A set of rules and practices recognized as a general guide for financial reporting purposes.

(SO4) _____ 6. Resources expected to be realized in cash or sold, or consumed within one year, or the operating cycle, whichever is longer.

(SO4) _____ 7. Resources not expected to be realized or cashed within the next year, or operating cycle.

(SO2) _____ 8. Use of the same accounting principles and methods from year to year within a company.

(SO4) _____ 9. The average time required to go from cash to cash in producing revenues.

(SO4) _____ 10. Capital assets that do not have physical substance.

Multiple Choice

Please circle the correct answer.

(SO1)   1. The primary accounting standard-setting body in Canada is the:
   a. Federal Government.
   b. Canadian Institute of Chartered Accountants.
   c. Ontario Securities Commission.
   d. Accounting Principles Board.

(SO1)   2. Accounting rules having substantial authoritative support and recognized as a general guide for financial reporting purposes are called:
   a. general accounting principles.
   b. generally accepted auditing principles.
   c. generally accepted accounting standards.
   d. generally accepted accounting principles.

(SO2)   3. Accounting information is _____ if it would make a difference in a business decision.
   a. reliable
   b. relevant
   c. comparable
   d. understandable

(SO2)   4. _____ results when different companies use the same accounting principles.
   a. Relevance
   b. Understandability
   c. Comparability
   d. Reliability

(SO3)   5. An item is _____ if it is likely to influence the decision of an investor or creditor.
   a. consistent
   b. reliable
   c. conservative
   d. material

(SO3)   6. The constraint, which says "Make sure the information is worth it", is:
   a. cost-benefit.
   b. materiality.
   c. relevance.
   d. reliability.

(SO5)   7. Net earnings are $100,000, average assets are $800,000, and net sales are $1,000,000. The return on assets ratio is:
   a. 10 times.
   b. 8 times.
   c. 10.0%.
   d. 12.5%.

(SO5)   8. Net earnings are $100,000, average assets are $800,000, and net sales are $1,000,000. The profit margin ratio is:
   a. 10 times.
   b. 8 times.
   c. 10.0%.
   d. 12.5%.

(SO6)   9. Which of the following statements report the ending balance of the retained earnings account?
  a. Statement of retained earnings and balance sheet
  b. Statement of retained earnings only
  c. Balance sheet only
  d. Statement of cash flows

(SO4)   10. Which of the following is considered a current asset on a classified balance sheet?
  a. Short-term investments
  b. Land
  c. Building
  d. Patent

(SO4)   11. Which of the following is considered a tangible capital asset on a classified balance sheet?
  a. Supplies
  b. Investment in Cognos Inc. shares
  c. Land
  d. Copyright

(SO4)   12. Current liabilities are $10,000, long-term liabilities are $20,000, common shares is $50,000, and retained earnings total $70,000. Total shareholders' equity is:
  a. $150,000.
  b. $140,000.
  c. $120,000.
  d. $ 70,000.

(SO7)   13. The ability to pay obligations that are expected to become due within the next year or operating cycle is called:
  a. working capital.
  b. profitability.
  c. solvency.
  d. liquidity.

(SO7)   14. Current assets are $60,000, total assets are $180,000, current liabilities are $30,000, and total liabilities are $50,000. The current ratio is:
  a. 2 to 1.
  b. 1.2 to 1.
  c. 0.5 to 1.
  d. 0.33 to 1.

(SO7)   15. Which ratio measures the percentage of assets financed by creditors rather than by shareholders?
  a. Current ratio
  b. Debt to total assets ratio
  c. Cash current debt coverage ratio
  d. Profit margin ratio

(SO7)   16. Which of the following statements provides information about the operating, investing, and financing activities of a company?
  a. Statement of cash flows
  b. Balance sheet
  c. Statement of earnings
  d. Statement of retained earnings

(SO7)   17. Which of the following is a measure of liquidity calculated as cash provided by operating activities, divided by average current liabilities?
a. Current ratio
b. Cash total debt coverage ratio
c. Cash current debt coverage ratio
d. Profit margin ratio

Problems

1. Consider the following data from Meadows Corporation:

	2003	2002
Current assets	$ 61,000	$ 50,000
Total assets	108,000	85,000
Current liabilities	47,000	39,000
Total liabilities	80,000	62,000
Net sales	200,000	180,000
Net earnings	39,000	28,000

After calculating the following, please explain what the results mean:

(SO7)   a. Working capital for 2003 and 2002.

(SO7)   b. Current ratio for 2003 and 2002.

(SO7)   c. Debt to total assets ratio for 2003 and 2002.

(SO5)　　d. Return on assets ratio for 2003.

(SO5)　　e. Profit margin ratio for 2003 and 2002.

2. Please refer to JetForm Corporation's financial statements at the end of this study guide for information for answering the following questions. Don't forget to use the **Decision Toolkit** approach for help in the problem-solving.

(SO4)　　a. What classes of assets does JetForm show on its balance sheet?

(SO7)　　b. Can JetForm meet its near-term obligations in 2000 and 1999? Please comment on the trend that you see.

(SO6)　　c. Does JetForm present a statement of retained earnings or a statement of shareholders' equity? What is the advantage of the company's choice?

(SO8)　　d. What is JetForm's source of cash in 2000?

SOLUTIONS TO SELF-TEST

Matching

1. k
2. i
3. a
4. d
5. e
6. c
7. h
8. b
9. j
10. f

Multiple Choice

1. b The Federal Government has given the statutory right to set accounting standards to the Canadian Institute of Chartered Accountants.
2. d
3. b Reliability means that information can be depended on, comparability results when different companies use the same accounting principles, and understandable means that the average user is able to study the information.
4. c
5. d Conservatism means that when preparing financial statements, a company should choose the accounting method that will be least likely to overstate assets and earnings.
6. a An item is material when its size makes it likely to influence the decision of an investor or creditor.
7. d $100,000 ÷ $800,000
8. c $100,000 ÷ $1,000,000
9. a The statement of retained earnings reports the ending balance of the retained earnings account. So too does the balance sheet, in its shareholders' equity items.
10. a Land, Building, and Patent are all capital assets.
11. c Supplies is a current asset, Investments is a noncurrent asset, and Copyright is an intangible captial asset.
12. c $50,000 + $70,000
13. d Working capital is the difference between current assets and current liabilities, profitability refers to the operating success of an enterprise during a period, and solvency is the ability of a company to pay interest as it comes due and to repay the face value of the debt at maturity.
14. a $60,000 ÷ $30,000
15. b The current ratio measures the ability of a company to pay its near-term obligations, the cash current debt coverage ratio measures liquidity on a cash basis, and the profit margin ratio measures the percentage of each dollar of sales that results in net earnings.
16. a The balance sheet reports assets, liabilities, and shareholders' equity items; the statement of earnings reports revenues and expenses; and the statement of retained earnings reports changes in the retained earnings account.
17. c The cash total debt coverage ratio is a measure of solvency calculated as cash provided by operating activities, divided by average *total* liabilities.

Problems

1. a. Current assets – current liabilities = working capital

    2003: $61,000 – $47,000 = $14,000
    2002: $50,000 – $39,000 = $11,000
    Working capital is a measure of liquidity. Since this company's working capital is positive, there is a greater likelihood that it will pay its liabilities.

   b. Current assets ÷ current liabilities = current ratio

    2003: $61,000 ÷ $47,000 = 1.30 (rounded) to 1
    2002: $50,000 ÷ $39,000 = 1.28 (rounded) to 1
    The current ratio is another measure of liquidity. In 2003 the company had $1.30 of current assets for every dollar of current liabilities. In 2002 it had $1.28 of current assets for every dollar of current liabilities.

   c. Total debt ÷ total assets = debt to total assets ratio

    2003: $80,000 ÷ $108,000 = 74%
    2002: $62,000 ÷ $85,000 = 73% (rounded)
    This ratio measures the percentage of assets financed by creditors rather than by shareholders. In 2003, $0.74 of every dollar invested in assets was provided by creditors. In 2002 $0.73 of every dollar was provided by creditors. The higher the percentage of debt financing, the riskier the company.

   d. Net earnings ÷ average assets = return on assets ratio

    2003: $39,000 ÷ ($108,000 + $85,000)/2 = 40.4%
    This ratio is a measure of profitability. It indicates the amount of net earnings generated by each dollar invested in assets. For every dollar invested in assets, this company generated approximately $0.40 of net earnings. The higher the return on assets, the more profitable the company.

   e. Net earnings ÷ net sales – profit margin ratio

    2003: $39,000 ÷ $200,000 = 19.5%
    2002: $28,000 ÷ $180,000 = 15.5%
    This ratio measures the percentage of each dollar of sales that results in net earnings. In 2003 each dollar of sales generated $0.195 of net earnings; in 2002 each dollar of sales generated $0.155 of net earnings.

2. a. Current Assets, Term Accounts Receivable, Deferred Income taxes, Fixed Assets, Other Assets.
   b. Yes, in both 2000 and 1999 current assets exceed current liabilities.
   c. JetForm presents a statement of shareholders' equity which provides the user with more detailed information about transactions affecting equity.
   d. Cash provided in Operating Activities.

<u>NOTES</u>

<u>NOTES</u>

CHAPTER

3

THE ACCOUNTING INFORMATION SYSTEM

CHAPTER OVERVIEW

Chapter 3 shows you how to analyse transactions and their effect on the accounting equation. You will learn about accounts, debits and credits, and how to perform the basic steps in the recording process: journalizing, posting transactions to the ledger, and preparing a trial balance.

REVIEW OF SPECIFIC STUDY OBJECTIVES

- The **accounting information system** is the *system of collecting and processing transaction data and communicating financial information to interested parties*.
- **Accounting transactions** are *economic events that require recording in the financial statements*. An accounting transaction occurs *when assets, liabilities, or shareholders' equity items change as a result of an economic event*.
- **Transaction analysis** is the *process of identifying the specific effects of economic events on the accounting equation*. The **accounting equation must always be in balance** after a transaction is recorded. Remember, it is a mathematical equation. If a shareholder invests cash in the business, then cash on the left side of the equation increases while shareholders' equity on the right side of the equation increases, by the same amount.

- Please remember the following with respect to specific parts of the accounting equation:
  1. If a company receives cash for work to be performed in the future, then it should not record revenue. It records an increase in cash on the left side of the equation and an increase in liabilities on the right side of the equation: It owes performance of that work in the future.
  2. Revenues increase shareholders' equity.
  3. Expenses decrease shareholders' equity.
  4. Some events in the life of a corporation are not transactions and are not to be recorded. The hiring of an employee and the beginning of an employees' strike are two such events.

STUDY OBJECTIVE

2

Explain what an account is and how it helps in the recording process.

- **An accounting information system uses accounts** that are *individual accounting records of increases and decreases in a specific asset, liability, or shareholders' equity item.*
- The simplest form of an account is the **T account**, so named because of its shape. T accounts have *account titles, a left side (called the debit side)*, and *a right side (called the credit side)*.

STUDY OBJECTIVE

3

Define debits and credits and explain how they are used to record business transactions.

Debit, abbreviated Dr., means left, while credit, abbreviated Cr., means right. These terms simply denote position: They do not mean good or bad, increase or decrease. The *important thing is to know what a debit does to a particular account and what a credit does to that same account.*
- **To debit an account** means to enter an *amount on the left side of the account.* **To credit an account** means to *enter an amount on the right side of the account.* If an account has $300 on the debit side and $100 on the credit side, then that account has a $200 overall debit balance. If an account has $500 on the credit side and $200 on the debit side, then that account has a $300 overall credit balance. **Debits are always added together, and credits are always added together, but a debit and a credit are subtracted one from the other.**
- The **dollar amount of the debits and the dollar amount of the credits must be equal in each transaction**. This provides the *basis of the double-entry accounting system.* Double-entry simply means that each accounting transaction has equal debits and credits made in the accounts.
- The following is a summary of the **debit/credit procedures for the accounts that you know** ("+" means "increase, while "−" means "decrease):

	Debit	Credit		Debit	Credit
Assets	+	−	Liabilities	−	+
Dividends	+	−	Shareholders' Equity	−	+
Expenses	+	−	Revenues	−	+

Remember that **shareholders' equity has two components: share capital and retained earnings**. *Both follow the procedures indicated for "Shareholders' Equity"* above.
- **Dividends**, which are distributions by a corporation to its shareholders in an amount proportional to each investor's percentage ownership, **and expenses both reduce shareholders' equity**; therefore, they follow procedures opposite from those followed by equity. **Common shares (and preferrred shares, if any), retained earnings, and revenues all increase shareholders' equity**.
- **Share capital (including common and preferred shares, if any) and retained earnings** are reported in the shareholders' equity section of the *balance sheet*. **Dividends** are reported on the *statement of retained earnings*. **Revenues and expenses** are reported on the *statement of earnings*.
- Since assets are on the left side of the accounting equation and liabilities and shareholders' equity are on the right side, the procedures for assets are opposite from the procedures for liabilities and equity items.
- The **normal balance** is the balance expected to be in an account. Please note that the normal balance is *found on the side that increases a particular account*. Dividends are increased by

debits, and the normal balance is a debit. Revenues are increased by credits, and the normal balance is a credit. Occasionally an account may have a balance other than its normal balance. As your text points out, the Cash account will have a credit balance when the cash account is overdrawn at the bank.

- The **recording process begins with a source document**.
- Each **transaction is analysed and entered in a journal**. The **journal information is then transferred to** the appropriate accounts in **the ledger**.

STUDY OBJECTIVE

Identify the basic steps in the recording process.

- A **journal** is a *place where a transaction is initially recorded before it is transferred to the accounts*. It may be in the form of paper or it may be a file on a computer disk or hard drive. **Transactions are entered in chronological order**.
- **Journalizing** is the *process of entering transaction data in the journal*. A **complete journal entry** consists of the following:
  1. The *date* of the transaction;
  2. The *accounts and amounts* to be debited and credited; and
  3. An *explanation* of the transaction.

STUDY OBJECTIVE

Explain what a journal is and how it helps in the recording process.

- A typical journal entry has the following format:

May 12	Supplies	500	
	Cash		500
	(Purchased supplies for cash)		

Please note that the credit account title is indented. This decreases the possibility of switching the debit and credit amounts. It also makes it easy to see that the account Cash is credited without having to have eyes glance right to see in which column the Cash amount is residing. It is fatiguing to have your eyes continually scan back and forth across a page.

- The **ledger** is the *entire group of accounts maintained by a company*. It keeps all the information about changes in specific account balances in one place. A **general ledger** contains all the assets, liabilities, and shareholders' equity accounts.
- As is true for the journal, a general ledger may be in the form of paper or may be an electronic file on a computer.
- The **chart of accounts** is a *listing of all the ledger accounts used in the business*.

STUDY OBJECTIVE

Explain what a ledger is and how it helps in the recording process.

- **Posting** is the *procedure of transferring journal entries to ledger accounts*. Posting accumulates the effects of journalized transactions in the individual accounts.
- To **illustrate posting**, consider the entry from study objective 5 above in which Supplies was debited and Cash was credited for $500 on May 12. In the ledger account Supplies, the date is recorded and $500 is written in the debit column. In the ledger account Cash, the date is again recorded and $500 is written in the credit column.

STUDY OBJECTIVE

Explain what posting is and how it helps in the recording process.

STUDY OBJECTIVE

Explain the purposes of a trial balance.

- A **trial balance** is a *list of accounts and their balances at a given time*. A trial balance is usually prepared at the end of an accounting period. Accounts are listed in their ledger order with the balances listed in the appropriate column, debit or credit. The **dollar amount of the debits must equal the dollar amount of the credits**; otherwise, there is an error that must be corrected. The **primary purpose** of a trial balance is to *prove the mathematical equality of debits and credits in the ledger*. It also *helps to uncover errors in journalizing and posting* and is *useful in preparation of financial statements*.

- It is, of course, possible that **a trial balance have equal debits and credits, but mistakes can still be present**. If a *journal entry has not been posted*, then an error has occurred, but the trial balance will be in balance. If a *journal entry is posted twice*, then the same is true. If a *journal entry is recorded as $500 instead of $5,000 on both the debit and the credit side*, then an error has occurred, but once again, the trial balance will be in balance. If a $200 *debit is posted to Cash instead of to another asset*, then an error is present, but the trial balance will be in balance.

CHAPTER SELF-TEST

As you work through the exercises and problems, remember to use the **Decision Toolkit** discussed and used in the text:

1. *Decision Checkpoints*: At this point you ask a question.
2. *Info Needed for Decision*: You make a choice regarding the information needed to answer the question.
3. *Tool to Use for Decision*: At this point you review just what the information chosen in step 2 does for the decision-making process.
4. *How to Evaluate Results*: You perform evaluation of information for answering the question.

Note: The notation (SO1) means that the question was drawn from study objective number one.

Completion

Please write in the word or words which will complete the sentence.

(SO1)   1. Economic events that require recording in the financial statements are called _____ _____.

(SO2)   2. A(n) _____ is an individual accounting record of increases and decreases in a specific asset, liability, or shareholders' equity item.

(SO3)   3. Under the _____ - _____ system, the dual effect of each transaction is recorded in appropriate accounts.

(SO3)   4. A debit _____ the Common Shares account.

(SO4)   5. Evidence of an accounting transaction comes in the form of a _____ _____.

(SO5)   6. A complete journal entry consists of a date, accounts and amounts, and a brief _____ of the transaction.

(SO6)   7. A complete listing of a company's accounts is called a _____ of accounts.

(SO6)   8. The procedure of transferring journal entries to ledger accounts is called _____.

(SO8)   9. A _____ _____ is a list of accounts and their balances at a given time.

(SO8)   10. Even though the debit total may equal the credit total on a trial balance, a(n) _____ may have occurred.

Multiple Choice

Please circle the correct answer.

(SO1)   1. If a company receives cash from a customer before performing services for the customer, then:
   a. assets increase and liabilities decrease.
   b. assets increase and shareholders' equity increases.
   c. assets decrease and liabilities increase.
   d. assets increase and liabilities increase.

(SO1)   2. If a company performs services for a customer and receives cash for the services, then:
   a. assets increase and liabilities decrease.
   b. assets increase and shareholders' equity increases.
   c. assets decrease and liabilities increase.
   d. assets increase and liabilities increase.

(SO3)   3. An account has $600 on the debit side and $400 on the credit side. The overall balance in the account is a:
   a. debit of $200.
   b. credit of $200.
   c. debit of $600.
   d. credit of $400.

(SO3)   4. Which of the following statements is correct?
   a. A debit decreases an asset.
   b. A credit decreases a liability.
   c. A credit increases shareholders' equity.
   d. A credit decreases a revenue account.

(SO3)   5. Which of the following statements is incorrect?
   a. A debit increases the Dividends account.
   b. A debit increases an expense account.
   c. A credit increases a revenue account.
   d. A credit increases the Dividends account.

(SO4)   6. Which of the following is the correct sequence of events?
   a. Analyse a transaction; record it in the ledger; record it in the journal.
   b. Analyse a transaction; record it in the journal; record it in the ledger.
   c. Record a transaction in the journal; analyse the transaction; record it in the ledger.
   d. None of the above is the correct sequence.

(SO5)   7. Transactions are initially recorded in chronological order in a _____ before they are transferred to the accounts.
   a. journal
   b. register
   c. ledger
   d. T account

(SO5)   8. If a corporation borrows money and issues a 3-month note in exchange, then the journal entry requires a:
a. debit to Notes Payable and a credit to Cash.
b. debit to Notes Payable and a credit to Unearned Revenue.
c. debit to Cash and a credit to Notes Payable.
d. debit to Cash and a credit to Unearned Revenue.

(SO5)   9. If a company pays its employees their weekly salaries, then the journal entry requires a:
a. debit to Unearned Revenue and a credit to Cash.
b. debit to Retained Earnings and a credit to Cash.
c. debit to Cash and a credit to Salaries Expense.
d. debit to Salaries Expense and a credit to Cash.

(SO6)   10. A general ledger of a company contains:
a. only asset and liability accounts.
b. all the asset, liability, and shareholders' equity accounts.
c. only shareholders' equity accounts.
d. only asset and shareholders' equity accounts.

(SO6)   11. The entire group of accounts maintained by a company is referred to collectively as the:
a. ledger.
b. journal.
c. register.
d. T accounts.

(SO6)   12. If a corporate accountant wanted to know the balance in the company's Cash account, then she would look in:
a. the journal.
b. the ledger.
c. both the journal and the ledger.
d. neither the journal nor the ledger.

(SO7)   13. When an accountant posts, he is transferring amounts from:
a. the ledger to the journal.
b. T accounts to the ledger.
c. the journal to the ledger.
d. the ledger to T accounts.

(SO7)   14. If an account is debited in the journal entry, then:
a. that account will be debited in the ledger.
b. that account will be credited in the ledger.
c. that account will be both debited and credited in the ledger.
d. None of the above is correct.

(SO8)   15. Which of the following is the correct sequence of events?
a. Prepare a trial balance; journalize; post
b. Journalize; post; prepare a trial balance
c. Post; journalize; prepare a trial balance
d. Prepare a trial balance; post; journalize

(SO8)   16. The primary purpose of a trial balance is to:
      a. get a total of all accounts with a debit balance.
      b. get a total of all accounts with a credit balance.
      c. prove the mathematical equality of debits and credits after posting.
      d. get a list of all accounts used by a company.

Problems

1. The following is an alphabetical listing of accounts for Davis Corporation. Please prepare a trial balance on September 30, 2002, assuming that all accounts have their normal balance. List the accounts in their proper order.

Accounts Payable	$ 4,000
Advertising Expense	5,000
Cash	35,000
Common Shares	20,000
Dividends	2,000
Equipment	15,000
Prepaid Insurance	3,000
Rent Expense	6,000
Retained Earnings	30,000
Salaries Expense	8,000
Service Revenue	15,000
Unearned Revenue	5,000

Davis Corporation
Trial Balance
September 30, 2002

2. Please refer to both Cognos' and JetForm's financial statements for information for answering the following questions. Don't forget to use the **Decision Tooklit** approach for help in the problem-solving.

(SO3)   a. What does each company call its equity section on the balance sheet? What does each company call the earnings retained in business?

(SO3)   b. What are the normal balances of the following accounts JetForm Corporation lists on its balance sheet: Inventories, Unearned Revenue and Common Shares?

(SO3)   c. What does Cognos call its statement of earnings? What are the normal balances of the following accounts Cognos lists on this statement: Product License and Cost of Product License?

SOLUTIONS TO SELF-TEST

Completion

1. accounting transactions
2. account
3. double-entry
4. decreases
5. source document
6. explanation
7. chart
8. posting
9. trial balance
10. error

Multiple Choice

1. d Cash, an asset, increases, and Unearned Revenue, a liability, increases.
2. b Cash, an asset, increases, and Equity increases because one of its components, Revenue, increases.
3. a $600 Dr. – $400 Cr. = $200 Dr.
4. c A debit increases an asset, a credit increases a liability, and a credit increases a revenue account.
5. d A debit increases the Dividends account.
6. b
7. a The ledger is a collection of accounts, and a T account is a form of account.
8. c The company receives an asset (Cash is increased by the debit), and its liabilities increase (Notes Payable is increased by the credit).
9. d Expenses increase with the debit, and cash decreases with the credit to Cash.
10. b
11. a The journal is the book of original entry, and T accounts are simply a form of account.
12. b The easiest place to find the information is the ledger. She could find it in the journal, but would have to add and subtract all the entries to Cash, which would be very time-consuming.
13. c
14. a Whatever is done to an account in the journal entry is done to that account in the ledger.
15. b
16. c While the trial balance may give a list of all accounts (an account with a zero balance may not be listed) and certainly lists debit and credit balances, these are not the primary purpose of the document.

Problems

1.

Davis Corporation
Trial Balance
September 30, 2000

	Debit	Credit
Cash	$35,000	
Prepaid Insurance	3,000	
Equipment	15,000	
Accounts Payable		$ 4,000
Unearned Revenue		5,000
Common Shares		20,000
Retained Earnings		30,000
Dividends	2,000	
Service Revenue		15,000
Advertising Expense	5,000	
Salaries Expense	8,000	
Rent Expense	6,000	
	$74,000	$74,000

2.
   a. Cognos: Stockholders' Equity, Retained Earnings.
      JetForm: Shareholders' Equity, Deficit.
   b. In order to determine the normal balance you have to know the type of account it is. Inventory is a current asset and would normally be a debit balance. Unearned Revenue is a current liability. Common Shares are an Equity account and both common shares and Unearned Revenue would normally be credit balances.
   c. Consolidated Statements of Income. Product license is a revenue account and would normally be a credit balance. Cost of Product License is an expense account and would normally be a debit balance.

NOTES

NOTES

4

ACCRUAL ACCOUNTING CONCEPTS

CHAPTER OVERVIEW

In Chapter 4 you will learn about two generally accepted accounting principles; the revenue recognition principle and the matching principle. You will learn the differences between the cash and the accrual bases of accounting. The chapter will explain what adjusting journal entries are, why they are needed, and how to prepare them. You will learn how to prepare an adjusted trial balance and closing journal entries, as well as the different steps in the accounting cycle.

REVIEW OF SPECIFIC STUDY OBJECTIVES

- **Accounting divides the economic life of a business into artificial time periods,** such as a month, a quarter, or a year. Some business transactions affect more than one accounting period, and it is necessary to consider a transaction's impact on the affected periods.

- The **revenue recognition principle** states that *revenue is to be recognized in the accounting period in which it is earned.* (To "recognize" means to record in a journal entry.) For a service firm, revenue is earned *at the time the service is performed*, which may or may not be the time at which cash is received. A firm may perform services for a client and receive in return the client's promise to pay the firm in the future.

- The **matching principle** states that *(efforts) expenses must be matched with (accomplishments) revenues.* This means the following: If a company performs services and, thus, earns revenue in a given accounting period, then any expenses which helped the company earn the revenue must be recorded in that same accounting period. The **critical issue** is *determining when the expense makes its contribution to revenue.* The principle is easy to state, but sometimes difficult to implement.

STUDY OBJECTIVE

2

Differentiate between the cash basis and the accrual basis of accounting.

- **Accrual basis accounting,** resulting from application of the revenue recognition and matching principles, means that *transactions that change a company's financial statements are recorded in the periods in which the events occur,* rather than in the periods in which the company receives or pays cash.
- With **cash basis accounting,** *revenue is recorded only when cash is received, and an expense is recorded only when cash is paid.* Because of its potential for violating the revenue recognition and matching principles, the *cash basis* of accounting *does not satisfy generally accepted accounting principles.*
- A new business often uses the cash basis of accounting because of its simplicity, but eventually it will have to change to the accrual basis. The change requires extensive adjustment to the business's accounting records.

STUDY OBJECTIVE

3

Explain why adjusting entries are needed and identify the major types of adjusting entries.

- **Adjusting entries** are *needed to ensure that the revenue recognition and matching principles are followed.* Before adjusting entries are recorded, some accounts may have incorrect balances because some events are not journalized daily. Some events are not journalized during the accounting period because these costs expire with the passage of time rather than as a result of recurring daily transactions. Some items may simply be unrecorded for a variety of reasons.
- **Adjusting entries** are *required every time financial statements are prepared.* Sometimes students will comment that adjusting entries are simply "cooking the books," but the opposite is actually true. Because of the reasons noted above, some accounts may have incorrect balances, and adjusting entries will correct them.
- There are **two broad groups of adjusting entries: prepayments and accruals.**
- **Prepayments** include *prepaid expenses* (expenses paid in cash and recorded as assets before they are used) and *unearned revenues* (cash received and recorded as liabilities before revenue is earned). **Accruals** include *accrued revenues* (revenues earned but not yet received in cash or recorded) and *accrued expenses* (expenses incurred but not yet paid in cash or recorded).
- There are **two important items** to note before we look at the specifics of adjusting entries:
  1. The *adjusting entries* you will learn, will *always involve one statement of earnings account and one balance sheet account.* Please note that this does *not* say that the statement of earnings account is always increased and the balance sheet account is always decreased, or vice versa. The utility of this fact lies in the following: If you prepare an adjusting entry and know that the debit to an expense, a statement of earnings account, is correct, then the credit must be to a balance sheet account.
  2. The account *Cash is never used in an adjusting entry.* If cash is involved, then the event is simply a transaction, not an adjustment to the accounts.

STUDY OBJECTIVE

4

Prepare adjusting entries for prepayments.

- **Prepaid expenses** (or prepayments) are *payments of expenses that will benefit more than one accounting period.* They are initially recorded as assets and expire either with the passage of time or through use. An adjusting entry for a prepaid expense *results in an increase (debit) to an expense account and a decrease (credit) to an asset account.* A good general rule to remember is: *as an asset is used up or consumed, its cost becomes an expense.*

- **Supplies** are one example of a prepaid expense. A company purchases $800 of supplies at the beginning of the accounting period. At the end of the period a physical count shows that only $200 of supplies are left. Therefore, $600 of supplies were used. The asset account Supplies still has the $800 balance, and if that number is recorded on the balance sheet, then the statement will not be correct. An accountant may not record $200, the correct number, on the balance sheet if the ledger account for Supplies shows a balance of $800. So, an adjusting entry is required:

  Supplies Expense   600
      Supplies   600
  (To show supplies used)

  After the entry is recorded and posted, the Supplies account will show the correct balance, $200, and that number will then correctly be shown on the balance sheet. **If the entry had not been made**, *expenses would have been understated, net earnings would have been overstated, and assets and shareholders' equity would have each been overstated by $600.*

- **Insurance** and **rent** are two more examples of a prepaid expense. A company pays six months' of rent, $2,400, at the beginning of March and wants to prepare financial statements at the end of March. The asset account Prepaid Rent shows a balance of $2,400, but this is no longer correct because the company has used up one month of rent. The balance sheet should show Prepaid Rent of $2,000, but this number may not be recorded if the ledger account for Prepaid Rent shows a balance of $2,400. Again, an adjusting entry is required:

  Rent Expense   400
      Prepaid Rent   400
  (To record expired rent)

  After the entry is recorded and posted, the Prepaid Rent account will show the correct balance, $2,000, and that number will then correctly be shown on the balance sheet. **If the entry had not been made**, *expenses would have been understated, net earnings would have been overstated, and assets and shareholders' equity would have been overstated by $400.*

- The adjusting entry for **amortization** is another example of a prepayment. Long-lived assets, such as vehicles, equipment, and buildings are recorded at cost. Their acquisition is basically a long-term prepayment for services. As their *useful life* progresses, part of the cost should be recorded as an expense. **Amortization** is the *process of allocating the cost of an asset to expense over its useful life in a rational and systematic manner.* It is important to remember that **amortization is an allocation concept**, not a valuation concept. It does not attempt to reflect the actual change in the value of the asset. Assume that amortization on a vehicle that cost $18,000 is $3,600 per year, or $300 per month. The following entry records one month of amortization:

  Amortization Expense   300
      Accumulated Amortization—Vehicle   300
  (To record monthly amortization)

  Accumulated Amortization is a *contra asset account*, offset against, or subtracted from, the Vehicle account on the balance sheet. Its normal balance is a credit. The use of this account allows the user to see the original cost of the asset as well as the total cost which has expired to date.

The *balance sheet presentation of this vehicle* after adjustment is:

Vehicle	$18,000
Less: Accumulated amortization—Vehicle	300
	$17,700

The $17,700 is the net **book value** or book value of the asset. Book value is calculated *by sub-tracting the accumulated amortization from the cost of the asset.*

As was true with Supplies and Prepaid Rent, **failure to record this adjusting entry** for amortization would have meant that *expenses would have been understated, net earnings would have been overstated, and assets and shareholders' equity would have each been overstated by $300.*

- **Unearned revenues** occur when *cash is received before revenue is earned.* Magazine sub-scriptions and rent are two examples. Unearned revenues are the *opposite of prepaid expenses*: An unearned revenue on one company's books is a prepaid expense on another company's books. If my company pays your company $6,000 for six months' rent in advance, then my company will have Prepaid Rent of $6,000, while your company will have Unearned Rent of $6,000. After one month has elapsed, your company must write the following adjusting entry to show that it has earned one month of rent revenue:

Unearned Rent	1,000	
Rent Revenue		1,000
(To record revenue earned)		

Please note that the entry involves a *decrease (debit) to the liability account and an increase (credit) to the revenue account.* **If the entry is not recorded**, then *revenues, net earnings, and shareholders' equity will be understated by $1,000, while liabilities will be overstated by $1,000.*

Most liabilities are discharged by the payment of money. Note that **an unearned revenue, a liability, is discharged by the performance of a service**.

STUDY OBJECTIVE

5

Prepare adjusting entries for accruals.

- Adjusting entries for **accruals** are required in order to *record revenues earned and expenses incurred in the current accounting period that have not been recognized through daily entries, and thus are not yet reflected in the accounts.* Accruals occur in the form of **accrued revenues** and **accrued expenses**.
- The adjusting entry for accruals will **increase both a balance sheet and a statement of earnings account.**
- **Accrued revenues** are *revenues earned but not yet received in cash or recorded at the financial statement date.* Examples are interest, rent, and services. They may accrue with the passage of time or may result from services performed but neither billed nor collected. The adjusting entry for an accrued revenue will always involve an **increase in a receivable (debit) and an increase in a revenue (credit)**. A company has earned $300 in interest revenue but has not been paid that amount in cash. If financial statements are to be prepared, then an adjusting entry to recognize that revenue is required:

Interest Receivable	300	
Interest Revenue		300
(To record interest revenue)		

If this entry is not made, then *assets and shareholders' equity on the balance sheet, and revenues and net earnings on the statement of earnings will be understated.* When the company receives that interest in cash, it will record a debit to Cash and a credit to Interest Receivable, not to Interest Revenue.

- **Accrued expenses** are *expenses incurred but not yet paid or recorded at the financial statement date.* Examples include interest, rent, taxes, and salaries. The company which owes the $300 of interest in the above example has an accrued expense of $300. The adjusting entry for an accrued expense will always involve an **increase (debit) to an expense account and an increase (credit) to a liability account.** A company borrows $12,000 at 12% interest for six months on November 1. The principal and all the interest are due on May 1. If financial statements are prepared on December 31, then the company must journalize an adjusting entry for the interest owed but not yet paid. *Interest is calculated by multiplying the face value of the note by the rate by the time*: in our example, $12,000 x 0.12 x 2/12, or $240. The entry is:

Interest Expense	240	
Interest Payable		240
(To record accrued interest)		

  It is **important to note** that the *account Notes Payable is not used in the entry.* Notes Payable was credited when the money was borrowed and will be debited when the note principal of $12,000 is repaid. **If this adjusting entry is not made**, then *liabilities and interest expense will be understated, and net earnings and shareholders' equity will be overstated.*

- A **trial balance is prepared after many journal entries have been journalized and posted.** Just as a trial balance was prepared after journalizing and posting regular transactions, so an **adjusted trial balance** is prepared after adjusting entries have been journalized and posted. The *purpose of an adjusted trial balance is to prove the equality of debits and credits in the general ledger.* Since all account balances have been brought up to date, the *adjusted trial balance is used in the preparation of financial statements.*

STUDY OBJECTIVE

Describe the nature and purpose of the adjusted trial balance.

- One **format** is to put two sets of columns side by side: One is for debits and credits before adjustment, and the other is for debits and credits after adjustment. Remember that it is from the adjusted trial balance columns that the financial statements are prepared.

- **Temporary accounts** relate to only a given accounting period and *include revenues, expenses, and dividends.* **Permanent accounts** have balances which carry forward into future accounting periods and include *assets, liabilities, and shareholders' equity*; the balance sheet accounts.

STUDY OBJECTIVE

Explain the purposes of closing entries.

- At the end of the accounting period, **temporary account balances are closed, or zeroed out,** transferring their balances to the permanent shareholders' equity account, Retained Earnings. **Closing entries** *transfer net earnings or net loss and dividends to Retained Earnings.* Revenues and expenses are closed to another temporary account, Income Summary, and only the resulting net earnings or net loss is then transferred to Retained Earnings.

- **Closing entries accomplish two things:** They *update the Retained Earnings account* and they *zero out the balance in the temporary accounts,* making them ready to accumulate data in the next accounting period.

- **After closing entries have been journalized and posted, a post-closing trial balance is prepared.** Once again, the purpose is to prove the equality of debits and credits in the ledger. It also helps to show all temporary accounts have been closed. If, for example, the accountant prepares a post-closing trial balance and finds a balance of $5,000 in Salaries Expense, then she will know that a temporary account was improperly excluded when closing entries were prepared. *Only permanent accounts should appear on the post-closing trial balance.*

STUDY OBJECTIVE

Describe the required steps in the accounting cycle.

- The following are the steps in the **accounting cycle**:
  1. Analyse business transactions.
  2. Journalize the transactions.
  3. Post to ledger accounts.
  4. Prepare a trial balance.
  5. Journalize and post adjusting entries.
  6. Prepare an adjusted trial balance.
  7. Prepare financial statements.
  8. Journalize and post closing entries.
  9. Prepare a post-closing trial balance.
- These steps are repeated in each accounting period.

STUDY OBJECTIVE

Describe the purpose and basic form of a work sheet (Appendix 4A).

- A **work sheet** is a *multiple-column form used in the adjustment process and in preparing financial statements*. It may be prepared manually or on the computer with electronic spreadsheet software.
- A **work sheet is not a permanent accounting record**. It is used by accountants to make work easier at the end of the accounting period. A work sheet helps by putting all required information in one place, saving the accountant from having to leaf through pages or to look in multiple places for information. It *helps in preparing adjusting entries, closing entries, and financial statements*.
- There are **usually five sets of two columns** on a work sheet. The first two columns are for the trial balance; the next two are for adjustments; the next two are for the adjusted trial balance; the next two correspond to the statement of earnings; and the last two correspond to the balance sheet. *Every number in the Adjusted Trial Balance columns is extended either to the Statement of Earnings or to the Balance Sheet columns.*

CHAPTER SELF-TEST

As you work through the exercises and problems, remember to use the **Decision Toolkit** discussed and used in the text:
1. *Decision Checkpoints*: At this point you ask a question.
2. *Info Needed for Decision*: You make a choice regarding the information needed to answer the question.
3. *Tool to Use for Decision*: At this point you review just what the information chosen in step 2 does for the decision-making process.
4. *How to Evaluate Results*: You perform evaluation of information for answering the question.

Note: The notation (SO1) means that the question was drawn from study objective number one.

Matching

Please write the letters of the following terms in the spaces to the left of the definitions.
   a. Accrual basis accounting
   b. Accrued expenses
   c. Accrued revenues
   d. Adjusted trial balance
   e. Adjusting entries
   f. Cash basis accounting
   g. Closing entries
   h. Permanent accounts

       i.　Post-closing trial balance
       j.　Prepaid expenses
       k.　Temporary accounts
       l.　Unearned revenues

(SO2)　　____　1. An accounting basis in which revenue is recorded only when cash is received, and an expense is recorded only when cash is paid.

(SO3)　　____　2. Expenses paid in cash and recorded as assets before they are used or consumed.

(SO7)　　____　3. A trial balance prepared after closing entries have been journalized and posted.

(SO7)　　____　4. Asset, liability, and shareholders' equity accounts.

(SO3)　　____　5. Revenues earned but not yet received in cash or recorded.

(SO2)　　____　6. Accounting basis in which transactions are recorded in the periods in which the events occur, rather than in the periods in which the company receives or pays cash.

(SO7)　　____　7. Revenue, expense, and dividend accounts whose balances are transferred to retained earnings at the end of an accounting period.

(SO6)　　____　8. A trial balance prepared after adjusting entries have been journalized and posted.

(SO3)　　____　9. Entries made at the end of an accounting period to ensure that the revenue recognition and matching principles are followed.

(SO7)　　____　10. Entries made at the end of an accounting period to transfer the balances of temporary accounts to Retained Earnings.

Multiple Choice

Please circle the correct answer.

(SO1)　　1. The generally accepted accounting principle which dictates that revenue be recognized in the accounting period in which it is earned is the:
    a. time period principle.
    b. matching principle.
    c. revenue recognition principle.
    d. accrued revenues principle.

(SO2)　　2. In 2001, Abbott Company performs work for a customer and bills the customer $10,000 and also pays expenses of $3,000. The customer pays Abbott in 2002. If Abbott uses the *cash* basis of accounting, then Abbott will report:
    a. revenue of $10,000 in 2001.
    b. revenue of $10,000 in 2002.
    c. expenses of $3,000 in 2002.
    d. net earnings of $7,000 in 2001.

(SO2)　　3. In 2001, Abbott Company performs work for a customer and bills the customer $10,000 and also pays expenses of $3,000. The customer pays Abbott in 2002. If Abbott uses the *accrual* basis of accounting, then Abbott will report:
    a. revenue of $10,000 in 2001.
    b. revenue of $10,000 in 2002.
    c. expenses of $3,000 in 2002.
    d. net earnings of $7,000 in 2002.

(SO3)   4. Adjusting journal entries must be prepared:
       a. at the end of every calendar year.
       b. at the end of every month.
       c. when the accountant has time to write them.
       d. whenever financial statements are to be prepared.

(SO3)   5. Cash received and recorded as a liability before revenue is earned is called:
       a. an accrued revenue.
       b. an unearned revenue.
       c. an unrecorded revenue.
       d. None of the above is correct.

(SO4)   6. On October 1, a company paid $6,000 for a one-year insurance policy, debiting Prepaid Insurance and crediting Cash. The adjusting entry on December 31 will require a:
       a. debit to Insurance Expense for $1,500.
       b. debit to Insurance Expense for $4,500.
       c. credit to Prepaid Insurance for $4,500.
       d. credit to Cash for $1,500.

(SO4)   7. At the beginning of an accounting period, a company purchased $800 of supplies, debiting Supplies and crediting Cash. At the end of the accounting period, a physical count of supplies showed that only $100 of supplies were still on hand. The adjusting entry will require a:
       a. credit to Supplies Expense for $700.
       b. debit to Supplies Expense for $100.
       c. debit to Supplies for $700.
       d. credit to Supplies for $700.

(SO4)   8. Little Corporation received $5,000 from a customer for whom it is to perform work in the future, debiting Cash and crediting Unearned Revenue. At the end of the accounting period, Little has earned $2,000 of the revenue. The adjusting entry will require a:
       a. debit to Cash for $2,000.
       b. debit to Service Revenue for $2,000.
       c. credit to Service Revenue for $2,000.
       d. credit to Service Revenue for $3,000.

(SO5)   9. The generally accepted accounting principle which dictates that efforts be matched with accomplishments is the:
       a. accrued expenses principle.
       b. matching principle.
       c. revenue recognition principle.
       d. time period principle.

(SO5)   10. At the end of its accounting period, Pooky Corporation has not billed a customer for $400 of rent. The adjusting entry will require a:
       a. debit to Cash for $400.
       b. credit to Accounts Receivable for $400.
       c. credit to Unearned Revenue for $400.
       d. credit to Rent Revenue for $400.

(SO5)   11. If the adjusting entry for an accrued expense is not written, then:
       a. liabilities and interest expense will be understated.
       b. liabilities and interest expense will be overstated.
       c. net earnings will be understated.
       d. liabilities and shareholders' equity will be overstated.

(SO5)   12. Buddy Corporation pays its employees $1,000 per five-day week on Fridays. The last day of the month falls on a Thursday, and financial statements will be prepared that day. The adjusting entry for salaries will require a:
a. debit to Salaries Payable for $200.
b. credit to Salaries Expense for $200.
c. debit to Salaries Expense for $200.
d. debit to Salaries Expense for $800.

(SO6)   13. Financial statements can be prepared directly from the:
a. trial balance.
b. adjusted trial balance.
c. post-closing trial balance.
d. reversing trial balance.

(SO6)   14. Which of the following is a temporary account?
a. The dividends account
b. An asset account
c. A liability account
d. A shareholders' equity account

(SO7)   15. Which of the following is true?
a. Only permanent accounts are closed.
b. Both permanent and temporary accounts are closed.
c. Neither permanent nor temporary accounts are closed.
d. Only temporary accounts are closed.

(SO7)   16. Which of the following correctly describes the closing process?
a. Net earnings or net loss is transferred to the Cash account.
b. Net earnings or net loss and dividends are transferred to Retained Earnings.
c. Permanent accounts become ready to accumulate data in the next accounting period.
d. Each revenue and each expense account is closed individually to Retained Earnings.

(SO8)   17. Which is the correct order of steps in the accounting cycle?
a. Post transactions, journalize transactions, prepare a trial balance, prepare financial statements.
b. Journalize and post transactions, journalize and post closing entries, journalize and post adjusting entries.
c. Journalize and post transactions, journalize and post adjusting entries, journalize and post closing entries.
d. Prepare financial statements, prepare adjusting entries, prepare closing entries, prepare a post-closing trial balance.

(SO9)   18. A work sheet:
a. is not a permanent accounting record.
b. is a type of journal.
c. is a type of ledger.
d. does not contain columns for adjustments.

Problems

(SO4, SO5) 1. Please write for Cassie Company, as of June 30, adjusting entries for the following situations :

a. The Supplies account shows a balance of $1,500, but a physical count shows only $300 of supplies.

b. The company purchased a one-year insurance policy for $3,600 on May 1, debiting Prepaid Insurance.

c. On June 1 the company received $1,200 from another company, which is renting a small building from Cassie for 6 months. Cassie credited Unearned Rent Revenue.

d. Cassie's accountant discovered that Cassie had performed services for a client totalling $900 but has not yet billed the client or recorded the transaction.

e. Cassie pays employees $2,000 per five-day work week on Fridays, and June 30 falls on a Wednesday.

f. The company owns a van that cost $18,000 and has a useful life of 6 years. The company purchased the van in early April this year.

g. What type of an account is the account that you credited in "f"? Please show the balance sheet presentation for the van after you have recorded the amortization entry.

2. Please refer to JetForm Corporation's annual report at the end of this study guide for information for answering the following questions. Don't forget to use the **Decision Toolkit** approach for help in the problem-solving.

(SO4) a. Using the consolidated statement of operations and consolidated balance sheet, please identify items that may result in adjusting entries for prepayments.

(SO5) b. Using the consolidated statements of operations and consolidated balance sheets, please identify accounts which may be involved in adjusting entries for accruals.

(SO4) c. Using the consolidated statements of cash flows, what amount is shown for depreciation and amortization for 2000 and 1999?

SOLUTIONS TO SELF-TEST

Matching

1. f
2. j
3. i
4. h
5. c
6. a
7. k
8. d
9. e
10 g

Multiple Choice

1. c The time period assumption says that the economic life of a business can be divided into artificial time periods, the matching principle dictates that expenses be matched with revenues, and the accrued revenues principle is a nonexistent principle.

2. b Revenue can't be reported in 2001 because Abbott did not receive cash. It paid the expenses in 2001 and must report them in that year. Since it recorded no revenue in 2001, it had a net loss of $3,000 (the expenses it paid) in 2001.

3. a It reports revenue in the year when the work is performed (2001, not 2002). Expenses are reported in 2001, when incurred, and net earnings of $7,000 is reported in 2001.

4. d

5. b An accrued revenue arises when money is owed to a company, not when it owes money. "Unrecorded revenue" is an accounting term but is not appropriate in this instance.

6. a The journal entry is:

Insurance Expense	1,500	
Prepaid Insurance		1,500

7. d The journal entry is:

Supplies Expense	700	
Supplies		700

8. c The journal entry is:

Unearned Revenue	2,000	
Service Revenue		2,000

9. b "Accrued expenses principle" is a nonexistent term. The revenue recognition principle states that revenue must be recognized when it is earned, and the time period assumption says that the economic life of a business can be divided into artificial time periods.

10. d The journal entry is:

Accounts Receivable	400	
Rent Revenue		400

11. a The journal entry debits an expense and credits a liability, thereby increasing both accounts. If an expense is not recorded, then net earnings will be overstated (as will shareholders' equity), and if a liability is not recorded, then liabilities will be understated.

12. d The journal entry is:

Salaries Expense	800	
Salaries Payable		800

13. b The trial balance does not have the adjustments updates, the post-closing trial balance has no temporary accounts, and there is no such thing as a reversing trial balance.
14. a The other three types of accounts are all permanent accounts.
15. d Permanent accounts are not closed.
16. b Net earnings and loss are not transferred to the Cash account, permanent accounts are not closed, and revenue and expense accounts are closed first to Income Summary (which is itself closed to Retained Earnings).
17. c
18. a It is neither a journal nor a ledger, and it certainly does have adjustments columns.

Problems

1. a. Supplies Expense   1,200
        Supplies   1,200
        (To record supplies used)
    b. Insurance Expense   600
        Prepaid Insurance   600
        (To record insurance expired)
        $3,600 ÷ 12 months = $300 per month x 2 months
    c. Unearned Rent Revenue   200
        Rent Revenue   200
        (To record rent earned)
        $1,200 ÷ 6 months = $200 per month
    d. Accounts Receivable   900
        Service Revenue   900
        (To record revenue earned)
    e. Salaries Expense   1,200
        Salaries Payable   1,200
        (To record accrued salaries)
        $2,000 ÷ 5 days = $400 per day x 3 days
    f. Amortization Expense   750
        Accumulated
            Amortzation—Van   750
        (To record amortization)
        $18,000 ÷ 6 years = $3,000 per year x 3/12
    g. Accumulated Amortization is a contra asset account, which is offset against, or subtracted from, the asset account. The advantage of this presentation is that the user sees both the original cost of the asset and the total cost that has expired to date.

Van	$18,000
Less: Accumulated Amortzation—Van	750
	$17,250

    The $17,250 is the book value of the asset and has no relationship to the fair market value (what a willing buyer would pay a willing seller) of the asset. Remember that amortization is an allocation concept, not a valuation concept.

2. a. Prepaid expense, Fixed assets and other assets (which need to be amortized) and unearned revenue.
    b. Unbilled receivables, accrued liabilities, net investment income and other income
    c. 2000: $13,941, 1999: $14,838 (in thousands)

NOTES

NOTES

CHAPTER

5

MERCHANDISING OPERATIONS

CHAPTER OVERVIEW

Chapter 5 discusses the differences between service firms and merchandising firms. You will learn about the two types of inventory systems used by merchandisers and how to record purchases and sales of inventory using the perpetual inventory system. You will take a close look at a merchandising firm's financial statements, particularly the statement of earnings, and at factors affecting a firm's profitability.

REVIEW OF SPECIFIC STUDY OBJECTIVES

- **Merchandising companies** buy and sell merchandise as their primary source of revenue. *Merchandising companies that purchase and sell directly to consumers are called* **retailers**. *Merchandising companies that sell to retailers are known as* **wholesalers**.

- The **primary source of revenues** for merchandising companies is the *sale of merchandise*, called sales revenues or sales. **Expenses** are divided into **two categories**: *cost of goods sold* (the total cost of merchandise sold during the period) and *operating expenses*. Net earnings is determined as follows:

Sales Revenue
− Cost of Goods Sold
Gross Profit
− Operating Expenses
Net Earnings

- The **operating cycle of a merchandising company** is *longer than that of a service firm* because of the purchase and sale of merchandise inventory.
- There are **two systems** available to a merchandising company to account for inventory: the *perpetual inventory system* and the *periodic inventory system.*
- With a **perpetual system,** *detailed records of the cost of each inventory purchase and sale are maintained.* These records show at all times the inventory that should be on hand for every item. *Cost of goods sold is determined each time a sale occurs.* The use of calculator systems, bar codes, and optical scanners makes such a system practicable.
- With a **periodic system,** *detailed records are not kept throughout the period. Cost of goods sold is determined only at the end of the accounting period* when a physical count of goods is taken.
- Because the perpetual inventory system is more popular in use, it is illustrated in this chapter.
- A **perpetual system** provides *better inventory control.* Goods can be counted at any time to see if they exist, and shortages can be investigated immediately. The quantity of inventory can be managed so that neither too much, nor too little, is on hand at a given time.

STUDY OBJECTIVE

2

Explain the recording of purchases under a perpetual inventory system.

- **Purchases,** either for cash or on account (credit), are normally *recorded when the goods are received from the seller.* A business document (a cancelled cheque or a cash register receipt for a cash purchase, or a purchase invoice for a credit purchase) will provide written evidence of the purchase.
- A **purchase is recorded by a debit to Merchandise Inventory and a credit to Cash or to Accounts Payable.** The *Merchandise Inventory* account is *used only for purchases of goods which will be resold.* If the company buys an asset, then the debit will be to the individual asset account.
- **Purchased goods might be unsuitable** because they are damaged or defective, are of inferior quality, or do not meet the purchaser's specifications. *A purchase return* occurs when goods are returned to the seller. A *purchase allowance* occurs when the purchaser keeps the merchandise but is granted an allowance (deduction) by the seller. A **purchase return or allowance is recorded by debiting Cash or Accounts Payable and crediting Merchandise Inventory.**
- Either the buyer or the seller must pay **shipping charges for the transportation of the merchandise.** If the **buyer pays,** then the shipping is considered to be *part of the cost of purchasing the inventory.* The cost of the shipping is recorded by a *debit to Merchandise Inventory and a credit to Cash or Accounts Payable.* If the **seller pays,** then the shipping on the outgoing merchandise is considered to be an *operating expense* and is recorded by a *debit to Freight-out or Delivery Expense and a credit to Cash or Accounts Payable.*
- With respect to the **buyer's debit to Merchandise Inventory for shipping charges,** the following is a good rule of thumb to remember: *Any amount which is paid to place an asset in location and condition for use is debited to the asset account.*
- **A seller often offers the buyer of merchandise a cash discount to induce early payment for the goods.** If *credit terms* are expressed as 1/10, n/30 (the purchaser will receive a 1% cash discount if he pays within 10 days; otherwise, the net amount is due in 30 days) or n/60 (the net amount is due in 60 days). Assume that on May 1 a buyer purchased $5,000 of merchandise on account with terms of 2/10, n/30. If he pays by May 11, then the following entry is required:

Accounts Payable	5,000	
Cash		4,900
Merchandise Inventory		100
(To record payment within the discount period)		

If the buyer pays after May 11, then the entry will be:

Accounts Payable	5,000	
Cash		5,000
(To record payment—no discount)		

- It is usually very **advantageous for the buyer to take all cash discounts**. Passing up a 2/10, n/30 discount is the equivalent of paying an annual interest rate of 36.5%! Some companies even borrow money at 8% to 12% to take the discount because that is cheaper than paying 36.5%.

- **Sales revenues are recorded when earned**, in accordance with the revenue recognition principle. As is true for purchases, sales may be for cash or on account (credit) and should be supported by a business document (a cash register tape for cash sales and a sales invoice for credit sales).

> **STUDY OBJECTIVE**
> **3**
> Explain the recording of sales revenues under a perpetual inventory system.

- **Two entries are made for each sale** in the perpetual inventory system. One records the *sale*, the other records the *cost of merchandise sold*. If goods costing $200 are sold for cash of $400, then the following entries are required:

Cash	400	
Sales		400
(To record a cash sale)		

Cost of Goods Sold	200	
Merchandise Inventory		200
(To record the cost of merchandise sold)		

If the goods had been sold on account, then the only thing that would have changed is the debit in the first entry would have been to Accounts Receivable.

- The **Sales account is used only for sales of merchandise inventory**. If an asset is sold, then the credit is to the asset account. *A company may choose to have several Sales accounts, each one dedicated to a type of product. This will help to give management information needed to manage its inventory.* Such a company will report only one Sales figure on the statement of earnings. To report many sales accounts would lengthen the statement of earnings and perhaps give too much detail on operating results to competitors. There are many users of a company's financial statements, and one such group of users is a company's competition.

- If **sold goods are returned to the company**, then *two entries are required*. Assume that the goods sold above are all returned to the company. The required entries are:

Sales Returns and Allowances	400	
Cash		400
(To record return of goods)		

Merchandise Inventory	200	
Cost of Goods Sold		200
(To record cost of goods returned)		

Sales Returns and Allowances is a *contra revenue account* to Sales. If the debit had been to Sales, then the return would have been buried in that account. Management needs to monitor the amount of returned goods so that it may correct an unsatisfactory situation. The goods it is selling may be of poor quality or defective, and management will have to deal with the supplier of the goods. If the company itself is making mistakes in delivery or shipment of goods, then management will have to deal with this internal problem.

- As noted above, **a seller often offers the buyer of merchandise a cash discount to induce early payment for the goods**. Using the previous example, on May 1 a buyer purchased $5,000 of merchandise on account with terms of 2/10, n/30. If the buyer pays by May 11, then the selling company records the following entry:

Cash	4,900	
Sales Discounts	100	
Accounts Receivable		5,000
(To record collection within the discount period)		

If the buyer pays after May 11, then the entry is:

Cash	5,000	
Accounts Receivable		5,000
(To record collection—no discount allowed)		

Sales Discounts is another *contra revenue account* to Sales.

Account Name	Account Type	Normal Balance
Sales	Revenue	Credit
Sales Returns and Allowances	Contra Revenue	Debit
Sales Discounts	Contra Revenue	Debit

STUDY OBJECTIVE

Distinguish between a single-step and a multiple-step statement of earnings.

- A **single-step statement of earnings** works in the following way: All *revenues are totalled*, all *expenses are totalled*, and expenses are then subtracted from revenues to determine net earnings or net loss. (The subtraction gives the name "single-step" to this statement of earnings.) This form is simple and easy to read and understand.

- A **multiple-step statement of earnings** breaks net earnings (or loss) into several components which financial statement users find useful.

  1. *Gross sales revenues are shown.* Any **sales returns and allowances** and **sales discounts are deducted from gross sales**; the resulting *difference is called net sales*.
  2. *Net sales less cost of goods sold* yields **gross profit or gross margin**. This is merchandising profit, the difference between what the company paid for its inventory and what it received when it sold the inventory. Gross profit should be large enough to cover operating expenses and leave something for net earnings.
  3. *Gross profit less operating expenses* yields **earnings from operations**. Operating expenses are often divided into two categories: *selling expenses*, associated with making sales, and *administrative expenses*, related to the general operation of the company. The former include advertising expense and shipping expense, and the latter include expenses such as those related to human resources management and accounting.
  4. *Earnings from operations less non-operating activities* yields **net earnings (or loss)**. Non-operating activities are revenues, expenses, gains, and losses unrelated to a company's main operations. Examples include interest revenue, dividend revenue, interest expense, and loss on the sale of a piece of machinery.

- **Earnings from operating activities** are considered *sustainable and long-term*, while those from **non-operating activities** are considered *nonrecurring and short-term*. It is obviously important for a company to derive the bulk of its earnings from its main line of operations and not from peripheral activities, such as the sale of factories and equipment.

To recap, if there are no non-operating activities:

> Sales Revenue
> − Cost of Goods Sold
> Gross Profit
> − Operating Expenses
> Net Earnings

- A **company's gross profit may be expressed as a percentage**: The *gross profit rate* is calculated by *dividing gross profit by net sales*. This rate is closely monitored. A decline in the rate may result from selling items with lower markup, from having to lower selling prices due to increased competition, or from having to pay higher prices for merchandise without being able to pass those higher costs on to customers.

- The **ratio of operating expenses to sales** is calculated by dividing operating expenses by net sales. If a company's ratio is low, then this suggests that the company is good at controlling its operating costs. It is important to remember, when comparing companies' ratios that a possible problem lies in the fact that one company may classify operating expenses differently from another. This difference in classification, of course, may skew results of comparisons.

STUDY OBJECTIVE

5

Explain the factors affecting profitability.

CHAPTER SELF-TEST

As you work through the exercises and problems, remember to use the **Decision Toolkit** discussed and used in the text:
1. *Decision Checkpoints*: At this point you ask a question.
2. *Info Needed for Decision*: You make a choice regarding the information needed to answer the question.
3. *Tool to Use for Decision*: At this point you review just what the information chosen in step 2 does for the decision-making process.
4. *How to Evaluate Results*: You perform evaluation of information for answering the question.

Note: The notation (SO1) means that the question was drawn from study objective number one.

Matching

Please write the letters of the following terms in the spaces to the left of the definitions.

- a. Contra revenue account
- b. Cost of goods sold
- c. Gross profit
- d. Net sales
- e. Periodic inventory system
- f. Perpetual inventory system
- g. Purchase discount
- h. Sales discount
- i. Sales invoice
- j. Sales

(SO4)   ____   1. Sales revenue less sales returns and allowances and sales discounts.

(SO4)   ____   2. Net sales less cost of goods sold.

(SO1)   ____   3. An inventory system in which two entries are required each time there is a sale of merchandise.

(SO2)   ____   4. A cash discount claimed by a buyer for prompt payment of a balance due.

(SO3)   ____   5. Primary source of revenue for a merchandising company.

(SO1)   ____   6. An inventory system in which cost of goods sold is determined only at the end of an accounting period.

(SO3)   ____   7. A reduction given by a seller for prompt payment of a credit sale.

(SO3,4) ____   8. The total cost of merchandise sold during the period.

(SO3)   ____   9. A document which provides support for credit sales.

(SO3)   ____   10. An account subtracted from Sales on a merchandising company's statement of earnings.

Multiple Choice

Please circle the correct answer.

(SO1)   1. The operating cycle of a merchandising company is ordinarily _____ that of a service firm.
      a. the same as
      b. shorter than
      c. longer than
      d. four times as long as

(SO1)   2. Which of the following statements is correct?
      a. A periodic inventory system gives better control over inventories than a perpetual inventory system does.
      b. A perpetual inventory system gives better control over inventories than a periodic inventory system does.
      c. A periodic inventory system calculates cost of goods sold each time a sale occurs.
      d. A perpetual inventory system calculates cost of goods sold only at the end of the accounting period.

(SO2)   3. Poobah Corporation, which uses a perpetual inventory system, purchased $3,000 of merchandise on account on June 4. What entry is required on June 8, when it returned $500 of the merchandise to the seller?

      a. Accounts Payable   500
          Merchandise Inventory   500
      b. Merchandise Inventory   500
          Accounts Payable   500
      c. Accounts Payable   500
          Purchases Returns   500
      d. Cash   500
          Merchandise Inventory   500

(SO2) 4. Cassie Corporation, which uses a perpetual inventory system, purchased $2,000 of merchandise on account on July 5. Credit terms were 2/10, n/30. It returned $400 of the merchandise on July 9. When the company pays its bill on July 11, the journal entry will require a:
a. debit to Accounts Payable for $2,000.
b. debit to Accounts Payable for $1,600.
c. credit to Cash for $1,600.
d. debit to Merchandise Inventory for $32.

(SO2) 5. Cosmos Corporation, which uses a perpetual inventory system, purchased $2,000 of merchandise on account on July 5. Credit terms were 2/10, n/30. It returned $400 of the merchandise on July 9. When the company pays its bill on July 21, the journal entry will require a:
a. debit to Accounts Payable for $2,000.
b. credit to Accounts Payable for $1,600.
c. credit to Cash for $1,600.
d. debit to Cash for $1,600.

(SO2) 6. Elizabeth Company uses a perpetual inventory system and purchased merchandise on November 30 for which it must pay the shipping charges. When the company pays the shipping charges of $200, the journal entry will require a debit to:
a. Delivery Expense for $200.
b. Cash for $200.
c. Freight-out for $200.
d. Merchandise Inventory for $200.

(SO3) 7. Which of the following statements is correct?
a. A company which uses a perpetual inventory system needs only one journal entry when it sells merchandise.
b. A company which uses a perpetual inventory system needs two journal entries when it sells merchandise.
c. A company which uses a perpetual inventory system debits Merchandise Inventory and credits Cost of Goods Sold when it sells merchandise.
d. None of the above is correct.

(SO3) 8. Cynthia Corporation, which uses a perpetual inventory system, received $500 of returned merchandise, which it had sold a week earlier. When it records the return, the journal entries will require a:
a. debit to Sales Returns and Allowances.
b. debit to Cost of Goods Sold.
c. debit to Accounts Receivable.
d. credit to Merchandise Inventory.

(SO3) 9. Sales Returns and Allowances and Sales Discounts are:
a. revenue accounts.
b. expense accounts.
c. contra revenue accounts.
d. contra expense accounts.

(SO3)   10. A company which uses a perpetual inventory system sold $400 of merchandise on July 23 with credit terms of 1/10, n/30. The purchaser paid the amount due on July 30. Which journal entry will the selling company record on July 30?

a. Cash   400
    Accounts Receivable   400
b. Cash   400
    Sales Discounts   4
    Accounts Receivable   396
c. Accounts Receivable   400
    Sales Discounts   4
    Cash   396
d. Cash   396
    Sales Discounts   4
    Accounts Receivable   400

(SO4)   11. Sales revenues are $10,000, sales returns and allowances are $500, and sales discounts are $1,000. What is the dollar amount of net sales?
a. $11,500
b. $10,500
c. $10,000
d. $8,500

(SO4)   12. Gross profit is $50,000, operating expenses are $15,000, and net sales total $75,000. What is cost of goods sold?
a. $10,000
b. $25,000
c. $35,000
d. $80,000

(SO4)   13. Gross profit is $50,000, operating expenses are $15,000, and net sales total $75,000. What is net earnings?
a. $10,000
b. $25,000
c. $35,000
d. $80,000

(SO4)   14. Net earnings is $15,000, operating expenses are $20,000, and net sales total $75,000. What is gross profit?
a. $60,000
b. $40,000
c. $35,000
d. $15,000

(SO4)   15. Net earnings is $15,000, operating expenses are $20,000, and net sales total $75,000. What is cost of goods sold?
a. $60,000
b. $40,000
c. $35,000
d. $15,000.

(SO5)   16. Net earnings is $15,000, operating expenses are $20,000, and net sales total $75,000. What is the gross profit rate?
   a. 20%
   b. 27%
   c. 47%
   d. 75%

(SO5)   17. Net earnings is $15,000, operating expenses are $20,000, net sales total $75,000, and sales revenues total $95,000. What is the ratio of operating expenses to sales?
   a. 20%
   b. 21%
   c. 27%
   d. 47%

Problems

(SO4)   1. From the appropriate accounts below, please prepare a multiple-step statement of earnings for Buff Corporation for the year ended January 31, 2002.

Cash	$13,000
Utilities expense	15,000
Cost of goods sold	24,000
Insurance expense	2,000
Accounts receivable	12,000
Sales returns and allowances	4,000
Advertising expense	7,000
Merchandise inventory	35,000
Amortization expense	8,000
Sales revenues	98,000
Freight-out	3,000
Sales discounts	5,000
Salaries expense	23,000
Rent expense	10,000

Buff Corporation
Statement of Earnings
For the Year Ended January 31, 2002

2. Please refer to both Cognos' and JetForm's financial statements for information for answering the following questions. Don't forget to use the **Decision Toolkit** approach for help in the problem-solving.

(S04)   a. What is Cognos' operating income in 2000? JetForm's?

(S04)   b. What form of the earnings statement does each firm use?

(S05)   c. In "a" you found the dollar amount of operating income for Cognos. Now please express operating expenses as a percentage of sales in 2000.

(S05)   d. What does the above percentage tell you about management performance?

SOLUTIONS TO SELF-TEST

Matching

1. d
2. c
3. f
4. g
5. j
6. e
7. h
8. b
9. i
10. a

Multiple Choice

1. c
2. b Periodic systems don't show the quantity of goods which should be on hand, making control more difficult. Cost of goods sold is calculated each time a sale occurs under the perpetual system.
3. a Since the sale was on account, the return entry requires a decrease in the liability, and Accounts Payable is debited. Since the company uses a perpetual system, all merchandise dollar amounts are recorded in the Merchandise Inventory account. A decrease because of the returned merchandise requires a credit to Merchandise Inventory. Purchases Returns would have been used if the company had used a periodic system.
4. b The journal entry is:

Accounts Payable	1,600	
Merchandise Inventory		32
Cash		1,568

5. c The journal entry is:

Accounts Payable	1,600	
Cash		1,600

6. d The journal entry is:

Merchandise Inventory	200	
Cash		200

7. b A perpetual inventory system requires two entries when merchandise is sold. One of the entries is a debit to Cost of Goods Sold and a credit to Merchandise Inventory.
8. a
9. c While these accounts have a normal debit balance, they are not expenses, nor are they revenue accounts. They are subtracted from a revenue account, making them contra revenue accounts.
10. d The entry requires a debit to Cash, but not for $400 since the purchaser receives a $4 discount. Accounts Receivable must be credited for $400, the full amount owed. The $4 difference between the amount owed and the amount of cash received is the debit to Sales Discounts.
11. d $10,000 – $500 – $1,000
12. b $75,000 – $50,000
13. c $50,000 – $15,000
14. c $15,000 + $20,000

15. b $15,000 + $20,000 = $35,000 of gross profit;
    $75,000 − $35,000 = $40,000
16. c $15,000 + $20,000 = $35,000 of gross profit;
    $35,000 ÷ $75,000 = 47% (rounded)
17. c $20,000 ÷ $75,000 = 27% (rounded)

Problems

1.

Buff Corporation
Statement of Earnings
For the Year Ended January 31, 2002

Sales revenues		
Sales		$98,000
Less: Sales returns and allowances	$ 4,000	
Sales discounts	5,000	9,000
Net sales		89,000
Cost of goods sold		24,000
Gross profit		65,000
Operating expenses		
Salaries expense	23,000	
Utilities expense	15,000	
Rent expense	10,000	
Amortization expense	8,000	
Advertising expense	7,000	
Freight-out	3,000	
Insurance expense	2,000	
Total operating expenses		68,000
Net loss		($ 3,000)

Since total expenses exceeded revenues, Buff Corporation incurred a net loss for the period.

2. a. Cognos: operating income $74,952; JetForm: operations (loss) ($10,178).
    b. Single step no gross profit is calculated.
    c. Divide operating expenses by sales $291,695 ($238,147 + $53,548) ÷ $385,640 = 75.6%.
    d. This can provide you with information on how well management is controlling operating costs.

NOTES

NOTES

CHAPTER

6

REPORTING AND ANALYSING INVENTORY

CHAPTER OVERVIEW

Chapter 6 discusses in depth the periodic inventory system. You will learn how to record purchases and sales under this system and how to prepare a statement of earnings, focusing on the cost of goods sold section. You will learn about the various ways to assign costs to inventory, and about the financial statement and tax effects of the cost flow methods. Valuing inventory at the lower of cost and market is discussed, as are the inventory turnover ratio and LIFO reserve. Finally, you will see effects of inventory errors on the statement of earnings and the balance sheet.

REVIEW OF SPECIFIC STUDY OBJECTIVES

- A **merchandising firm** has only *one inventory account*, called Merchandise Inventory. A **manufacturing firm** has *three inventory accounts*: finished goods, consisting of goods completed and awaiting sale; work in process, consisting of goods partially completed; and raw materials, consisting of materials waiting to be placed into production.

STUDY OBJECTIVE

1

Explain the recording of purchases and sales of inventory under a periodic inventory system.

- A **periodic inventory system differs from a perpetual inventory system in various ways**, one of which is the time at which cost of goods sold is calculated. With a **periodic system**, *cost of goods sold is calculated only at the end of an accounting period*, while with a **perpetual system**, *cost of goods sold is calculated each time inventory is sold*.

- With a **periodic system**, a *physical count of inventory must be taken at the end of the accounting period* to determine the cost of merchandise on hand and the cost of goods sold during the period. **Purchases of inventory are recorded in a Purchases account**, not in Merchandise Inventory, and there are *separate accounts for purchase returns and allowances, purchase discounts, and freight costs on purchases.*

- Consider the following data. On April 4 Orion Company purchased $5,000 of inventory on account with credit terms of 2/10, n/30. It paid shipping costs of $200 on April 5, and on April 7 it returned $500 of merchandise. It paid the amount due on April 13. The journal entries for these transactions are as follows:

April 4	Purchases	5,000	
	Accounts Payable		5,000
April 5	Freight-in	200	
	Cash		200
April 7	Accounts Payable	500	
	Purchase Returns and Allowances		500
April 13	Accounts Payable	4,500	
	Purchase Discounts		90
	Cash		4,410

Please note the following:
a. **Purchases** is a *temporary account* (which must be closed) with a *normal debit balance*.
b. **Purchase Returns and Allowances and Purchase Discounts** are *temporary accounts* with a *normal credit balance*.
c. Discounts do not apply to Freight-in charges. **Freight-in is part of cost of goods purchased** and is a *temporary account* with a *normal debit balance*.

- **Sales of merchandise are recorded in the same way as they are recorded in a perpetual system**. Sales has a normal credit balance, while the contra revenue accounts, Sales Returns and Allowances and Sales Discounts, have a normal debit balance.

STUDY OBJECTIVE

2

Explain how to determine cost of goods sold under a periodic inventory system.

- To **determine cost of goods sold** under a periodic system, it is necessary to *record merchandise purchases, determine the cost of goods purchased*, and *determine the cost of goods on hand at the beginning and end of the accounting period*. The cost of the ending inventory must be determined by a physical count and by application of the cost to the items counted in the inventory.

- To determine cost of goods sold, it is necessary first to determine the **cost of goods purchased**:

	Gross purchases	
Less:	Purchase returns and allowances	
	Purchase discounts	
	Net purchases	
Add:	Freight-in	
	Cost of goods purchased	

- Determining inventory quantities involves **two steps**: *taking a physical count of goods on hand* and *determining ownership of goods*.

- A **physical count** involves *counting, weighing, or measuring each kind of inventory on hand* at the end of the accounting period. It can be a time-consuming and formidable task. The quantity of each kind of inventory is **listed on inventory summary sheets** and should be verified by a second employee or supervisor.
- **Determining ownership of goods** can be complex because of situations such as the following: Inventory in a warehouse does not belong to the owner of the warehouse, and a company's inventory may not be physically present at the time of the physical count.
- If **goods are in transit** at the time of the physical count, then *ownership is determined by who has legal title to the goods*, and legal title is determined by the terms of the sale. When terms are **FOB (free on board) shipping point**, *ownership passes to the buyer when the goods arrive at the public carrier*. If goods are being shipped from Edmonton, Alberta to Vancouver, British Columbia, and terms are FOB shipping point, the buyer in Vancouver has legal title to and ownership of the inventory when the seller in Edmonton delivers the goods to the public carrier in Edmonton. When terms are **FOB destination**, *ownership of the goods remains with the seller until the goods reach the buyer*. In our example, if the goods are shipped FOB destination, the seller in Edmonton has title to the goods until they reach the buyer in Vancouver.
- **Consigned goods** pose another problem. Charlie takes goods that he wishes to sell to Barb's place of business. Barb agrees to try to sell them for Charlie, for a commission, of course. Charlie is at all times the owner of the goods until they sell. Even though the goods are physically at Barb's place of business, Barb never has title to the goods. So, at the time of the physical count of the inventory, Charlie must remember to *count those consigned goods as part of his inventory*.
- The format for calculating **cost of goods sold** is the following:

Beginning inventory
Add: Cost of goods purchased
Cost of goods available for sale
Less: Ending inventory
Cost of goods sold

If this is the skeleton for calculating cost of goods sold, then remember that cost of goods purchased must be determined:

Gross purchases
Less: Purchase returns and allowances
Purchase discounts
Net purchases
Add: Freight-in
Cost of goods purchased

- The **statement of earnings is the same whether a perpetual or a periodic inventory system is used**, but the *cost of goods sold section contains more detail*.
- The **balance sheet is exactly the same**: Merchandise Inventory appears in the current assets section.
- Sometimes the **number of columns on the statement of earnings** confuses students, but it will be easier if you remember the following: *Each column to the left gives information about a number to the right*. The Sales revenues section of a statement of earnings looks like this:

Sales			$50,000
Less:	Sales returns and allowances	$4,000	
	Sales discounts	6,000	10,000
Net sales			$40,000

If a user looks at the $10,000 and wonders what comprises the number, then his eye can move one column to the left and see that sales returns and allowances total $4,000 while sales discounts total $6,000.

STUDY OBJECTIVE 3
Describe the steps in determining inventory quantities.

STUDY OBJECTIVE 4
Identify the unique features of the statement of earnings for a merchandising company under a periodic inventory system.

Remember that your goal is to produce a readable and understandable document. If you make sure that you've labelled everything correctly and have added and subtracted correctly, then you have gone a long way toward producing such a document.

STUDY OBJECTIVE

5

Explain the basis of accounting for inventories and apply the inventory cost flow methods under a periodic inventory system.

• **Cost of goods available for sale must be allocated** to two items: *cost of goods sold* and *ending inventory.* Once ending inventory has been determined, it is a simple matter to subtract that number from cost of goods available for sale to determine cost of goods sold. (The format for cost of goods sold is a powerful tool. Given numbers can be plugged into the formula so that you can solve for an unknown.)

• There are **four ways of assigning cost to ending inventory**. The first is called *specific identification* and is used for high-cost, low-volume items such as cars or antiques. Each item has a cost sheet or ticket attached to it, and valuing ending inventory consists of adding up the sheets or tickets of the items in stock. This is not an appropriate method for a hardware store which has many small items in stock or for a retailer with millions of items in the store.

• The other ways of assigning cost are called assumed **cost flow assumptions**, and there are three: *first-in, first-out (FIFO), average cost* and *last-in, first-out (LIFO).*

• **First-in, first-out** assumes that *the earliest ("first") goods purchased are the first sold.* FIFO parallels the actual physical flow of goods. With few exceptions, retailers want to sell the oldest inventory first because of shelf-life or style issues. *Ending inventory consists of the most recent purchases.*

• **Average cost** removes the effects of rising or falling prices. An *average unit cost is calculated by dividing the cost of goods available for sale by the total units available for sale.* That unit cost is then applied to the units in ending inventory and the units sold. It is a *weighted average cost* that is calculated.

• **Last-in, first-out** assumes that the *most recent ("last") goods purchased are the first sold.* This is usually opposite the physical flow of goods, but there is no accounting requirement that the cost flow assumption approximate the physical flow of goods. *Ending inventory consists of the oldest purchases.*

• Using the following data, let's calculate ending inventory and cost of goods sold under each of the assumed cost flow assumptions.

Date	Units	Unit Cost	Total Cost
Feb. 2	300	$4.00	$ 1,200
Mar. 9	400	5.00	2,000
May 8	600	6.00	3,600
Jun. 3	500	7.00	3,500
	1,800		$10,300

A physical count shows that there are 550 units in ending inventory. The February 2 units are the beginning inventory, and $10,300 is the cost of goods available for sale. Please note that this is a time of rising prices.

FIFO: The most recent purchases are assumed to be in ending inventory; so, to get to 550, begin counting with the June 3 purchase.

June 3	500	x	$7.00	=	$3,500
May 8	50	x	6.00	=	300
	550				$3,800 ending inventory

Cost of goods available for sale	$10,300
Less: Ending inventory	3,800
Cost of goods sold	$ 6,500

Average cost: To calculate an average unit cost, divide cost of goods available for sale of $10,300 by the total units available for sale, 1,800. The average unit cost is $5.72 (rounded). This unit cost is applied to the 550 units in ending inventory: 550 x $5.72 = $3,146.

Cost of goods available for sale	$10,300
Less: ending inventory	3,146
Cost of goods sold	$ 7,154

LIFO: The oldest purchases are assumed to be in ending inventory; so, to get to 550, begin counting with the February 2 beginning inventory.

Feb. 2	300	x	$4.00	=	$1,200	
Mar. 9	250	x	5.00	=	1,250	
	550				$2,450	ending inventory

Cost of goods available for sale	$10,300
Less: ending inventory	2,450
Cost of goods sold	$ 7,850

Summarizing these results:

	FIFO	Average Cost	LIFO
Cost of goods available	$10,300	$10,300	$10,300
Less: ending inventory	3,800	3,146	2,450
Cost of goods sold	$ 6,500	$ 7,154	$ 7,850

Please note that the results of average cost are between those of FIFO and LIFO. Average cost removes the effects of rising or falling prices. The company did not pay $5.72 for any units purchased, this is simply a weighted average unit cost.

- **All three methods are acceptable**, according to GAAP and *a company may use more than one method at the same time*. It may have two classes of inventories and use LIFO for one and FIFO for the other. It should be noted that LIFO is not commonly used in Canada as it is not allowed for income tax purposes.

- You can see the **statement of earnings effects** of the three methods with the above summarization. Remember that the example shows a period of **rising prices**.

    FIFO: lowest cost of goods sold, highest net earnings.
    Average cost: in the middle for both items.
    LIFO: highest cost of goods sold, lowest net earnings.
- The **balance sheet effects** of the three methods can also be seen with the summarization. Remember that *results would have been opposite had this been a period of falling prices*.
    FIFO: highest inventory valuation (because most recent purchases are in ending inventory).
    Average cost: in the middle.
    LIFO: lowest inventory valuation (because oldest purchases are in ending inventory). LIFO can produce a severe understatement of inventory, if inventories contain items purchased in one or more prior accounting periods.
- While a **company must be consistent in its use of the inventory methods**, a *company is allowed to change methods if it will result in better financial reporting*. The change and its effects on net earnings must be disclosed in the notes to the financial statements.

- **At times companies have in inventory, items for which they paid one price but would currently pay a lower price if they were to purchase those same inventory items**.
- This situation **requires a departure from the cost principle**, and the inventory will be *valued at the lower of cost and market (LCM)*. Market is not defined under GAAP but the most commonly used definition in Canada is net realizable value.
- **LCM is an example of the accounting concept of conservatism**, which means *the best choice among accounting alternatives is the method which is least likely to overstate assets and net earnings*. (Conservatism does *not* mean that items should be intentionally understated.)

STUDY OBJECTIVE 6

Explain the financial statement and tax effects of each of the inventory cost flow assumptions.

STUDY OBJECTIVE 7

Explain the lower of cost and market basis of accounting for inventories.

STUDY OBJECTIVE

8

Calculate and interpret the inventory turnover ratio.

- **Managing inventory levels** so that neither too much nor too little is on hand can be complex and is critical to a company's success.
- The **inventory turnover ratio** can help in managing inventory levels. It is *calculated by dividing cost of goods sold by average inventory*. (Average inventory is calculated by adding together the beginning and the ending inventories of a period and dividing the sum by 2.) If a company's cost of goods sold is $50,000 and its average inventory is $16,000, then its inventory turnover ratio is 3.13 (rounded). This means that the company sells its entire inventory about 3 times every accounting period.
- **Days in inventory** is *calculated as 365 days divided by the inventory turnover ratio*. Using the same example above, $365 \div 3.13 = 116.6$ days. This means that it takes the company about 116 days to sell its inventory.
- **Both the inventory turnover ratio and days in inventory must be compared with something to be meaningful.** They may be compared with the same company's numbers from prior periods or with numbers of other companies in the same industry.

STUDY OBJECTIVE

9

Apply the inventory cost flow methods to perpetual inventory records. (Appendix 6A)

- The **cost flow methods you've learned to use with a periodic system of inventory can also be applied to a perpetual system.**
- For **FIFO** and **LIFO**, it is *important to keep each purchase of inventory in a separate layer.* Consider the following data:

Purchases
Oct. 10	100 units @ $2.00	$ 200
Nov. 11	200 units @ $3.00	$ 600
Dec. 20	150 units @ $3.50	$ 525
		$1325

Sales
Dec. 15	250 units @ $7.00	$1,750

The physical inventory account on December 31 shows 200 units on hand.
Solution: under a perpetual inventory system the cost of goods sold (450 - 200 = 250 units) under each cost flow method is as follows:

FIFO yields the following:

Date	Purchases	Sales	Balance
Oct. 10	(100 units @ $2.00) $200		(100 units @ $2.00) $200
Nov. 11	(200 units @ $3.00) $600		(100 units @ $2.00) / (200 units @ $3.00) } $800
Dec. 15		100 units @ $2.00 / 150 units @ $3.00 } $650	(50 units @ $3.00) $150
Dec. 20	(150 units @ $3.50) $525		(50 units @ $3.00) / (150 units @ $3.50) } $675

Ending inventory $675. Cost of goods sold $1,325–$675=$650
Please note that FIFO always yields the same results regardless of whether a periodic or a perpetual inventory system is used.

LIFO yields the following:

Date	Purchases	Sales	Balance
Oct. 10	(100 units @ $2.00) $200		(100 units @ $2.00) $200
Nov. 11	(200 units @ $3.00) $600		(100 units @ $2.00) / (200 units @ $3.00) } $800
Dec. 15		200 units @ $3.00 / 50 units @ $2.00 } $700	(50 units @ $2.00) $100
Dec. 20	(150 units @ $3.50) $525		(50 units @ $2.00) / (150 units @ $3.50) } $625

Ending inventory $625. Cost of goods sold $1,325–$625=$700

- The **average cost method** when applied to a perpetual inventory system is called the *moving average method*. **A new average cost is calculated after each purchase.**

Moving average yields the following:

Date	Purchases	Sales	Balance
Oct. 10	(100 units @ $2.00) $200		(100 units @ $2.00) $200
Nov. 11	(200 units @ $3.00) $600		(300 units @ $2.67) $800
Dec. 15		(250 units @ $2.67) $667	(50 units @ $2.67) $133
Dec. 20	(150 units @ $3.50) $525		(200 units @ $3.29) $658

Ending inventory $658. Cost of goods sold $1,325–$658=$667

- **Inventory errors affect the determination of cost of goods sold and net earnings over two periods** because the ending inventory of one period becomes the beginning inventory of the next period.

- An **error in beginning inventory** will have a *reverse effect on net earnings of the same accounting period* (if beginning inventory is understated, then net earnings will be overstated). An **error in ending inventory** will have the *same effect on net earnings of the same accounting period* (if ending inventory is understated, then net earnings will be understated, too).

- An **error in ending inventory of the current period** will have a *reverse effect on net earnings of the next accounting period*. Even though there is an error, **total net earnings will be correct over the two periods because the errors offset each other**.

- An **error in beginning inventory** *does not result in a corresponding error in the ending inventory for that same period*.

- On the **balance sheet**, if *ending inventory is overstated, then both assets and shareholders' equity will be overstated. If ending inventory is understated, then both assets and shareholders' equity will be understated*.

STUDY OBJECTIVE

10

Indicate the effects of inventory errors on the financial statements. (Appendix 6B)

CHAPTER SELF-TEST

As you work the exercises and problems, remember to use the **Decision Toolkit** discussed and used in the text:

1. *Decision Checkpoints*: At this point you ask a question.
2. *Info Needed for Decision*: You make a choice regarding the information needed to answer the question.
3. *Tool to Use for Decision*: At this point you review just what the information chosen in step 2 does for the decision-making process.
4. *How to Evaluate Results*: You perform evaluation of information for answering the question.

Note: The notation (SO1) means that the question was drawn from study objective number one.

Completion

Please write in the word or words which will complete the sentence.

(SO1) 1. A company using a periodic inventory system will debit _____ when it purchases inventory.

(SO2) 2. Net purchases is calculated by deducting purchase returns and allowances and purchase discounts from _____ purchases.

(SO3) 3. If merchandise is shipped FOB shipping point, then the goods belong to the _____ while they are in transit.

(SO4) 4. If cost of goods sold is $100,000, gross profit is $60,000, and operating expenses are $40,000, then net earnings must be _____.

(SO5) 5. _____ _____ is an appropriate method for costing inventory which is low-volume and high-cost.

(SO6) 6. In a period of rising prices, _____ will produce the lowest income tax bill.

(SO6) 7. If a company changes its inventory methods, then it must _____ the change and its effects on net earnings.

(SO7) 8. In the phrase "lower of cost and market," "market" is usually defined as _____ _____ _____.

(SO8)   9. If the inventory turnover ratio is 4.5 times, then the days in inventory calculation yields _____ days.

(SO9)   10. The average cost method is called _____ _____ _____ in a perpetual inventory system.

Multiple Choice

Please circle the correct answer.

(SO1)   1. Which of the following is the correct journal entry to record a return of purchased merchandise for a company, which uses a periodic inventory system?
a.   Debit Purchase Returns and Allowances; credit Accounts Payable
b.   Debit Merchandise Inventory; credit Accounts Payable
c.   Debit Accounts Payable; credit Merchandise Inventory
d.   Debit Accounts Payable; credit Purchase Returns and Allowances

(SO1)   2. When a company using a periodic inventory system pays shipping costs on merchandise it has purchased, it debits:
a.   Merchandise Inventory.
b.   Purchases.
c.   Freight-in.
d.   Delivery expense.

(SO1)   3. A company purchased merchandise for $3,000 with credit terms of 2/10, n/30. When it pays the amount due within the discount period, the journal entry will include a debit to:
a.   Accounts Payable for $3,000.
b.   Accounts Payable for $2,940.
c.   Purchase Discounts for $60.
d.   Cash for $2,940.

(SO2)   4. Gross purchases are $17,000, purchase returns and allowances are $3,000, purchase discounts are $2,000, and freight-in is $1,000. Net purchases total:
a. $17,000.
b. $16,000.
c. $12,000.
d. $11,000.

(SO2)   5. Gross purchases are $20,000, purchase returns and allowances are $4,000, purchase discounts are $3,000, and cost of goods purchased are $15,000. Freight-in is:
a. $1,000.
b. $2,000.
c. $3,000.
d. $4,000.

(SO3)   6. If goods are shipped FOB destination, then which of the following parties includes in its inventory the goods while they are in transit?
a.   Shipping company
b.   Buyer
c.   Seller
d.   Both the buyer and the seller include the goods in their inventory.

(SO3) 7. Ceil gives goods on consignment to Jerry who agrees to try to sell them for a 25% commission. At the end of the accounting period, which of the following parties includes in its inventory the consigned goods?
    a. Ceil
    b. Jerry
    c. Both Ceil and Jerry
    d. Neither Ceil nor Jerry

(SO3) 8. Beginning inventory is $30,000, ending inventory is $25,000, and cost of goods purchased is $45,000. What is cost of goods sold?
    a. $10,000
    b. $40,000
    c. $45,000
    d. $50,000

(SO3) 9. Beginning inventory is $50,000, cost of goods purchased is $70,000, and cost of goods sold is $90,000. What is ending inventory?
    a. $ 30,000
    b. $ 50,000
    c. $ 70,000
    d. $110,000

(SO4) 10. Net sales are $120,000, cost of goods sold is $50,000, and operating expenses are $30,000. What is gross profit?
    a. $120,000
    b. $ 90,000
    c. $ 70,000
    d. $ 40,000

(SO4) 11. Net sales are $120,000, cost of goods sold is $50,000, and operating expenses are $30,000. What is net earnings?
    a. $120,000
    b. $ 90,000
    c. $ 70,000
    d. $ 40,000

(SO5) 12. Which of the following inventory costing methods often parallels the physical flow of goods?
    a. LIFO
    b. FIFO
    c. Average cost
    d. Specific identification

Please use the following data for 13, 14, and 15:

Date	Units	Unit Cost	Total Cost
Feb. 5	200	$2.00	$ 400
Mar. 6	500	4.00	2,000
Apr. 9	400	6.00	2,400
Jun. 7	300	7.00	2,100
	1,400		$6,900

On June 30 there are 350 units in ending inventory. Assume a periodic inventory system.

(SO5)   13. What is the value of ending inventory using first-in, first-out (FIFO)?
     a. $1,000
     b. $1,726
     c. $2,400
     d. $5,177

(SO5)   14. What is the cost of goods sold using average cost?
     a. $1,000
     b. $1,726
     c. $2,400
     d. $5,177

(SO5)   15. What is the value of ending inventory using last-in, first-out (LIFO)?
     a. $1,000
     b. $1,726
     c. $2,400
     d. $5,177

(SO6)   16. In a period of rising prices, which of the following methods will give the highest ending inventory?
     a.   Specific identification
     b.   Average cost
     c.   LIFO
     d.   FIFO

(SO6)   17. In a period of falling prices, which of the following methods will give the highest net earnings?
     a.   Specific identification
     b.   Average cost
     c.   LIFO
     d.   FIFO

(SO7)   18. Using lower of cost and market is an example of the accounting concept of:
     a.   revenue recognition.
     b.   conservatism.
     c.   matching.
     d.   full disclosure.

(SO8)   19. Net sales are $80,000, cost of goods sold is $30,000, and average inventory is $20,000. The inventory turnover ratio is:
     a.   4.00 times.
     b.   2.67 times.
     c.   1.50 times.
     d.   0.25 times.

(SO10)   20. If beginning inventory is overstated, then the current year's:
     a.   cost of goods sold is overstated.
     b.   cost of goods sold is understated.
     c.   ending inventory is overstated.
     d.   ending inventory is understated.

Problems

1. Below are data for Hattie Corporation for the year ended December 31, 2002. Please use these data to answer the questions.

Sales	$250,000
Purchase discounts	8,000
Sales discounts	40,000
Operating expenses	65,000
Sales returns and allowances	10,000
Freight-in	30,000
Purchase returns and allowances	15,000
Inventory, January 1, 2002	38,000
Inventory, December 31, 2002	32,000
Purchases	102,000

(SO1)   a. What are net sales?

(SO2,3)   b. What is cost of goods purchased?

(SO2,3)   c. What is cost of goods sold?

(SO4)   d. What is gross profit?

(SO4)   e. What is net earnings?

2. Please refer to both Cognos' and JetForm's financial statements for information for answering the following questions. Don't forget to use the **Decision Toolkit** approach for help in the problem-solving.

(SO1)   a. What type of company is Cognos Corporation?

(SO5, SO7)   b. Where in the notes to the Cogno's financial statements is there information pertaining to inventories?

(SO8)   c. For both Cognos and JetForm, in 2000 how many days did items remain in inventory?

SOLUTIONS TO SELF-TEST

Completion

1. Purchases
2. gross
3. buyer
4. $20,000 ($60,000 – 40,000)
5. Specific identification
6. Average cost (LIFO is not permitted for income tax use in Canada).
7. disclose
8. net replacement value
9. 81.1 (365 ÷ 4.5)
10. moving average method

Multiple Choice

1. d Merchandise Inventory is used in a perpetual system. When merchandise is returned, the liability is reduced by debiting, not crediting, Accounts Payable.
2. c Merchandise Inventory is used in a perpetual system. Purchases, used in a periodic system, is debited only for the actual cost of the purchased merchandise. Delivery Expense is used when goods are shipped to another company or individual.
3. a The journal entry is:

Accounts Payable	3,000	
Purchase Discounts		60
Cash		2,940

4. c $17,000 – $3,000 – $2,000
5. b $20,000 – $4,000 – $3,000 + x = $15,000
6. c When goods are shipped FOB destination, the seller retains title to the goods until they reach the buyer's place of business. Since the seller has title, he pays the shipping costs.
7. a Consigned goods are always the property of the person who has put them out on consignment. They are Ceil's; Jerry never has title to the goods.
8. d $30,000 + $45,000 – $25,000
9. a $50,000 + $70,000 – $90,000
10. c $120,000 – $50,000
11. d $120,000 – $50,000 – $30,000
12. b LIFO is opposite the physical flow of the goods, and average cost and specific identification do not parallel the physical flow.
13. c

June 7	300	×	$7.00	=	$2,100
Apr. 9	50	×	6.00	=	300
	350				$2,400 ending inventory

14. d $6,900 ÷ 1,400 = $4.93 (rounded)/unit X 1,050 units
15. a

Feb. 5	200	×	$2.00	=	$ 400
Mar. 6	150	×	4.00	=	600
	350				$1,000 ending inventory

16. d LIFO gives the lowest ending inventory, and average cost results will be between those of FIFO and LIFO.
17. c The method with the lowest cost of goods sold will yield the highest net earnings: This method is LIFO.

18. b Revenue recognition says that revenue is recognized when it is earned, matching dictates that expenses be matched with revenues, and full disclosure says that circumstances and events that make a difference to financial statement users should be disclosed.
19. c $30,000 ÷ $20,000
20. a An error in beginning inventory does not have an effect on ending inventory of the same year.

Problems

1. a.

Sales	$250,000
Sales ret. and allow.	− 10,000
Sales discounts	− 40,000
Net sales	$200,000

b.

Purchases	$102,000
Purch. ret. and allow.	− 15,000
Purchase discounts	− 8,000
Freight-in	+ 30,000
Cost of goods purch.	$109,000

c.

Inventory, Jan. 1	$ 38,000
Cost of goods purch.	+109,000
Inventory, Dec. 31	− 32,000
Cost of goods sold	$115,000

d.

Net sales	$200,000
Cost of goods sold	− 115,000
Gross profit	$ 85,000

e.

Gross profit	$ 85,000
Operating expenses	− 65,000
Net earnings	$ 20,000

2 a. In the significant accounting policies (note 1), the company describes its nature of operations. Cognos is in the high tech industry developing software and providing consulting services.

b. In note 1, Cognos describes its inventories.

c. To calculate how many days items remain in inventory, you must calculate the inventory turnover ratio by dividing average inventory into cost of goods sold.
Cognos:
Average inventory = ($806 + $807) ÷ 2 = $806.5
($5235 + $13,758) ÷ 806.5 = 23.55 times
Then to determine how many days items remain in inventory you divide the inventory turnover ratio into 365.
365 ÷ 23.55 = 15.5 days.

JetForm:
Average inventory ($1139 + $1084) ÷ 2 = 1111.5
($12,053 + $12,373) ÷ 1111.5 = 21.98 times
365 ÷ 21.98 = 16.6 days

NOTES

_____

_____

_____

_____

_____

_____

_____

_____

_____

_____

_____

_____

_____

_____

_____

_____

_____

_____

_____

_____

NOTES

NOTES

CHAPTER

7

INTERNAL CONTROL AND CASH

CHAPTER OVERVIEW

Chapter 7 discusses the principles of internal control, particularly with respect to cash. You will learn about the limitations as well as the strengths of internal control. You will learn how to prepare a bank reconciliation and how to report cash on the balance sheet. You will learn the basic principles of cash management and tools for help in managing and monitoring cash. Finally, you will learn about the establishment and operation of a petty cash fund.

REVIEW OF SPECIFIC STUDY OBJECTIVES

- **Internal control** consists of all the related *methods and measures adopted within a business to*:
  1. **safeguard its assets** *from theft, robbery, and unauthorized use; and*
  2. **enhance the accuracy and reliability of its accounting records** *by preventing and detecting errors (unintentional mistakes) and irregularities (intentional mistakes and misrepresentations) in the accounting process.*

- There are **six principles of internal control**:
  1. *Establishment of responsibility.* Control is most effective when only one person is responsible for a given task. This area includes authorization and approval of transactions.
  2. *Segregation of duties.*
     a. The responsibility for **related activities** should be assigned to different individuals: This should decrease the potential for errors and irregularities. *Related purchasing activities* include ordering merchandise, receiving goods, and paying (or authorizing payment) for merchandise. *Related sales activities* include making a sale, shipping (or delivering) the goods, and billing the customer.
     b. **Record-keeping and custody of assets** should be assigned to different individuals. In a corporation the controller is responsible for record-keeping functions, while the treasurer has physical custody of assets.
  3. *Documentation procedures.* Wherever possible, **documents should be prenumbered,** and **all documents should be accounted for** (this includes voided documents). Source documents should be forwarded promptly to the accounting department to ensure accurate and timely recording of a transaction.
  4. *Physical, mechanical, and electronic controls.* Their use is essential. Physical controls (such as safes and locked computer rooms) relate to the safeguarding of assets, while mechanical and electronic controls (such as time clocks, television monitors, and computer passwords) safeguard assets and enhance the accuracy and reliability of the accounting records.
  5. *Independent internal verification.* This involves the **review, comparison, and reconciliation of data prepared by employees.** Verification should be made periodically or on a surprise basis; verification should be done by an employee who is independent of the personnel responsible for the information; and discrepancies and exceptions should be reported to a management level that can take appropriate corrective action. Such verification is often performed by **internal auditors** who are *employees of the company, and who evaluate on a continuous basis the effectiveness of the company's system of internal control.*
  6. *Other controls.* These include **bonding of employees who handle cash, and rotating employees' duties and requiring employees to take vacations**. The former involves acquiring of insurance protection against misappropriation of assets by dishonest employees. The latter helps to deter employees from attempting theft because the employees know that they cannot permanently conceal their theft.
- **Internal controls** generally *provide reasonable assurance that assets are safeguarded and that the accounting records are accurate and reliable.* In constructing the system, a company tries to have the best system at the least cost. It attempts to have the benefits of the system outweigh the costs. There are, however, **limitations of any internal control system**. One involves the *human element.* A dishonest or incompetent employee can render the system ineffective, and two or more employees may collude to circumvent the system. Performing a thorough background check when considering whether to hire a person is crucial. The *size of the company* is also a factor. A large company has the resources, both human and financial, to put into place a sophisticated system of internal control. A small company may be very limited in both areas and must do the best it can with what it has.
- **Cash** consists of *coins, currency (paper money), cheques, money orders, and money on hand or on deposit in a bank or similar depository.* If a bank will accept an item at face value for deposit, then it is cash. Because cash is readily convertible into other assets, easily concealed and transported, and highly desired, internal control over cash is absolutely necessary.

STUDY OBJECTIVE

2

Explain the applications of internal control to cash receipts.

- A company must have effective **internal control over cash receipts**. While different size companies may apply them differently, all six internal control principles are important:
  1. *Establishment of responsibility.* Only designated personnel should be authorized to handle cash receipts.
  2. *Segregation of duties.* Custody of and record-keeping for cash should be separated.
  3. *Documentation procedures.* A company must use remittance advices, cash register tapes, and deposit slips.

4. *Physical, mechanical, and electronic controls.* A company must store cash in secure areas, limit access to storage areas, and use cash registers.
5. *Independent internal verification.* Supervisors should count receipts daily, and the treasurer should compare total receipts to bank deposits daily.
6. *Other controls.* Cash-handling personnel should be bonded and required to take vacations, and all cash should be deposited on a daily basis.

- A **major internal control over cash disbursements** is to *make payments by cheque,* except for very small amounts which may be disbursed via a petty cash fund. Again, all six internal control principles apply:

STUDY OBJECTIVE

3

Explain the applications of internal control to cash disbursements.

  1. *Establishment of responsibility.* Only authorized personnel should sign cheques.
  2. *Segregation of duties.* Again, custody and record-keeping should be separated: Those who make payments should not record the transactions.
  3. *Documentation procedures.* Cheques should be prenumbered and used in sequence, and they should be issued only if an invoice has been approved.
  4. *Physical, mechanical, and electronic controls.* Blank cheques should be secured, and cheque amounts should be printed with indelible ink.
  5. *Independent internal verification.* Cheques and invoices should be compared, and a monthly bank reconciliation should be prepared.
  6. *Other controls.* Invoices should be stamped "Paid."
- **Electronic funds transfers (EFT)** are *disbursement systems which use wire, telephone, telegraph, or computer to transfer cash from one location to another.* Use of EFT is widespread and growing rapidly.

- The **use of a bank can increase good internal control over cash**. A company may *use a bank as a depository and clearinghouse for cheques received and written.* Use of a bank minimizes the amount of currency that must be kept on hand, and a double record of all transactions is kept.

STUDY OBJECTIVE

4

Prepare a bank reconciliation.

- A **company receives monthly bank statements** and must reconcile the ending balance on the statement with the ending balance in the general ledger account "Cash." The two numbers are often not the same because of *time lags (the bank has recorded something that the company has not, or vice versa)* and *errors made by either the bank or the company.*
- It is **customary to reconcile the balance per books and balance per bank to their adjusted (correct or true) cash balances**. The reconciliation should be prepared by someone who has no other responsibilities for cash.
- The following are **adjustments made to the column called "Balance per bank statement"**:
  1. *Deposits in transit* (deposits which the company has recorded but the bank has not) are always *added* to the balance per bank column.
  2. *Outstanding cheques* (cheques recorded by the company which have not yet been paid by the bank) are always *subtracted* from the balance per bank column.
  3. *Errors* may either be added to or subtracted from the column depending on the nature of the error.
- The following are **adjustments made to the column called "Balance per books"**:
  1. *NSF cheques* (bounced cheques) are subtracted from the balance per books column.
  2. *Bank service charges* are *subtracted* from the balance per books column.
  3. *Note and interest collections* are *added* to the balance per books column.
  4. *Errors* may either be added to or subtracted from the column depending on the nature of the error.
- The **key question to ask when preparing a bank reconciliation** is *"Who knows about the transaction and has already recorded it, and who doesn't yet know about it?"* For example, with respect to bank service charges, the bank knows about them and has already subtracted them from the company account, reflecting this on the bank statement, but the company does not know the exact amount of the charges until it receives the statement.

- After the bank reconciliation has been prepared, **each reconciling item in the balance per books column must be recorded by the company in a journal entry**. (Bank personnel record any adjustments in the balance per bank statement column.) It is important to note that an *NSF cheque is debited to Accounts Receivable*, signaling the intention of the company to try to collect on the bounced cheque. *After the entries are journalized and posted, the balance in the Cash account should equal the total shown on the bank reconciliation.*

STUDY OBJECTIVE 5

Explain the reporting of cash.

- **Cash is reported on the balance sheet and on the statement of cash flows.** On the balance sheet a company usually shows only one Cash account, which can be a combination of cash on hand, cash in banks, and petty cash. *Cash is listed first in the current assets section because it is the most liquid of assets.*
- Companies often label the first current asset **"Cash and cash equivalents."** A **cash equivalent** is a *short-term, highly liquid investment which is readily convertible to cash and so near its maturity that its market value is relatively insensitive to changes in interest rates.* Examples include Treasury bills, commercial paper, and money market funds.
- If **cash is restricted for a special purpose**, then it should be *reported separately* as *"restricted cash."* If it is to be used within the next year, then it is reported as a current asset; if it is to be used at a time beyond one year, then it is reported as a noncurrent asset.

STUDY OBJECTIVE 6

Discuss the basic principles of cash management.

- A **company's objective in the management of cash** is to *have sufficient cash to meet payments as they come due but to minimize the amount of non-revenue-generating cash on hand.* Many companies have employees whose sole job responsibility is to manage cash.
- **Management of cash is the job of a company's treasurer and is critical to a company's success.** There are **five principles of cash management**:
  1. *Increase the speed of collection on receivables.* A company wants to receive cash as speedily as possible so that it can have the use of this money.
  2. *Keep inventory levels low.* There are many so-called "carrying costs" of inventory which a company wants to minimize as much as possible.
  3. *Delay payment of liabilities.* A company wants to pay its bills on time but not too early. It certainly wants to take advantage of all cash discounts offered.
  4. *Plan the timing of major expenditures.* A company tries to make major expenditures when it has excess cash, usually during its off-season.
  5. *Invest idle cash.* Cash which does not earn a return does a company little good. Invested cash should be highly liquid (easy to sell) and risk-free (there is no concern that the party will default on its promise to pay principal and interest).

STUDY OBJECTIVE 7

Identify the primary elements of a cash budget.

- A **cash budget is an important tool in effective cash management**. It helps a company *plan its cash needs* by showing its anticipated cash flows. The cash budget *has three sections: cash receipts, cash disbursements, and financing.*
- The **cash receipts section** shows all anticipated cash receipts: from cash sales and collections of accounts receivable; from interest and dividends; and proceeds from planned sales of investments, capital assets, and the company's share capital.
- The **cash disbursements section** shows expected payments for direct materials, direct labour, manufacturing overhead, selling and administrative expenses, income taxes, dividends, investments, and capital assets.
- The **financing section** shows expected borrowings and the repayment of principal and interest.
- The **accuracy of the cash budget** *depends on the accuracy of assumptions made by the company.* Any significant error in the budget will affect all subsequent cash budgets because the ending balance on one budget is the beginning balance on the next budget.

- There are **several ratios which help a company measure the adequacy of cash.**
- The **ratio of cash to daily cash expenses** *calculates the number of days of cash expenses that the cash on hand can cover.* It is calculated by *dividing cash and cash equivalents by average daily cash expenses.* Daily cash expenses are calculated by subtracting amortization (a noncash expense) from total expenses and dividing by 365 days. This ratio *shows the number of days the company can operate without an extra infusion of cash.*
- **Free cash flow analysis** *helps investors and management understand a company's solvency and overall financial strength.* Free cash flow is calculated by *subtracting capital expenditures and cash dividends from cash provided by operations.* **Free cash flow is the amount of discretionary cash flow a company has for purchasing additional investments, paying its debts, or adding to its liquidity.** A company with substantial free cash flow can take advantage of opportunities that another company cannot. It is more likely to survive in rough economic times.

STUDY OBJECTIVE

Identify and interpret measures that evaluate the adequacy of cash.

- A **petty cash fund** is used for *small disbursements,* disbursements for which it would not be economical to write a company cheque.
- To **establish a petty cash fund,** a *custodian must be selected,* and the *size of the fund must be determined.* If the company sets up the fund for $200, then it writes a cheque to the custodian for that amount and records a journal entry *debiting Petty Cash and crediting Cash* for $200.
- **Operation of the fund** should *follow established procedures which clearly set out acceptable disbursements.* If an employee needs money from the fund for postage, then he should fill out a voucher (or receipt) stating the purpose of the disbursement, the date, and the amount. Both the employee and the petty cash custodian should sign the voucher.
- **At all times the total of the cash in the petty cash drawer and the vouchers should equal the total of the petty cash fund.** Periodic surprise counts of the drawer are a good idea to determine whether the fund is being maintained correctly. Mutilation of the paid vouchers so that they cannot be resubmitted is also a good idea.
- The **fund should be replenished** when it is running *low on funds, and at the end of every accounting period* (so that all expenses will be recorded before financial statements are prepared). Once again, a cheque is made payable to the custodian for the required amount, and a journal entry is written *debiting various expenses and crediting Cash* (not Petty Cash). If the total of the receipts does not equal the total cash required, the difference is either debited or credited to *Cash Over and Short,* a temporary account. If this account has an overall debit balance, then it is reported as a miscellaneous expense on the statement of earnings; if it has an overall credit balance, then it is reported as a miscellaneous revenue on the statement of earnings.
- Consider the following example. A company has a balance in the Petty Cash account of $300. At the end of the period, there are receipts in the petty cash drawer totalling $225, and there is cash in the drawer of $73. To bring the drawer up to $300, a cheque must be written for $227 ($300 – $73). When the journal entry is written, various expense accounts will be debited for $225 (the amount of the receipts), Cash will be credited for $227, and the difference of $2 will be debited to Cash Over and Short.

STUDY OBJECTIVE

Explain the operation of a petty cash fund.

CHAPTER SELF-TEST

As you work through the exercises and problems, remember to use the **Decision Toolkit** discussed and used in the text:

1. *Decision Checkpoints*: At this point you ask a question.
2. *Info Needed for Decision*: You make a choice regarding the information needed to answer the question.
3. *Tool to Use for Decision*: At this point you review just what the information chosen in step 2 does for the decision-making process.
4. *How to Evaluate Results*: You perform evaluation of information for answering the question.

Note: The notation (SO1) means that the question was drawn from study objective number one.

Completion

Please write in the word or words which will complete the sentence.

(SO1)   1. Internal control consists of measures to _____ assets and _____ the accuracy and reliability of accounting records.

(SO1)   2. A good system of internal control can be circumvented by a dishonest or incompetent _____.

(SO1)   3. If a _____ will accept an item at face value for deposit, then it is considered to be _____.

(SO3)   4. A company should generally make payments by _____ rather then by cash.

(SO3)   5. A previously deposited cheque which "bounces" because the company which issued it does not have the money to cover the cheque is called _____.

(SO4)   6. In its journal entries relating to a bank reconciliation, a company will debit _____ _____ for bank service charges.

(SO5)   7. _____ and _____ are examples of cash equivalents.

(SO6)   8. Two basic principles of cash management are to increase the speed of collection on _____ and to delay payment of _____.

(SO7)   9. The _____ section of a cash budget shows expected borrowings and repayment of principal and interest.

(SO8)   10. A company with substantial _____ _____ _____ can take advantage of profitable investments even in tough times.

Multiple Choice

Please circle the correct answer.

(SO1)   1. Which of the following statements is correct?
   a. Control is most effective when two or three people are given responsibility for the same task.
   b. The person who has custody of assets should not perform the record-keeping for the assets.
   c. The person who has custody of assets should also perform the record-keeping for the assets.
   d. It is a waste of company resources to have an employee perform independent internal verification.

(SO1)   2. Which of the following statements is incorrect?
- a.   Related purchasing activities should be assigned to different individuals.
- b.   Safeguarding of assets is enhanced by the use of physical controls.
- c.   Independent internal verification should be done by an employee independent of the personnel responsible for the information.
- d.   The use of prenumbered documents is not an important internal control principle.

(SO1)   3. Which of the following is not considered cash?
- a.   Coins
- b.   Money orders
- c.   Short-term investment in stock
- d.   Chequing account

(SO1)   4. A company has the following items: cash on hand, $1,000; cash in a chequing account, $3,000; cash in a savings account, $5,000; postage stamps, $50; and Treasury bills, $10,000. How much should the company report as cash on the balance sheet?
- a. $ 9,000
- b. $ 9,050
- c. $19,000
- d. $19,050

(SO3)   5. Effective internal control over cash disbursements includes:
- a.   the use of prenumbered cheques.
- b.   the storage of blank cheques in a secure place.
- c.   the separation of authorization of cheques and the actual writing of the cheques.
- d.   All of the above are part of effective internal control over cash disbursements.

(SO4)   6. Which of the following is added to the balance per books side of a bank reconciliation?
- a.   An outstanding cheque for $300
- b.   A note of $500 collected by the bank
- c.   A deposit in transit of $150
- d.   A bank service charge for $50 for cheque printing

(SO4)   7. Cooper Corporation showed a balance in its Cash account of $1,250 when it received its monthly bank statement. It found the following reconciling items: deposits in transit, $256; outstanding cheques, $375; NSF cheque in the amount of $102; bank service charges of $27; and note and interest collection by the bank for $850. What is the adjusted cash balance Cooper will show on its bank reconciliation?
- a. $1,131
- b. $1,852
- c. $1,971
- d. $1,981

(SO5)   8. On which two financial statements is Cash reported?
- a.   Balance sheet and statement of cash flows
- b.   Balance sheet and statement of earnings
- c.   Balance sheet and statement of retained earnings
- d.   Statement of earnings and statement of cash flows

(SO5)   9. If cash is restricted as to its use and will be used within the next year, then it should be:
- a.   included in the Cash and Cash Equivalents line on the balance sheet.
- b.   reported as a current liability on the balance sheet.
- c.   reported as a noncurrent asset on the balance sheet.
- d.   reported as a current asset separate from Cash and Cash Equivalents on the balance sheet.

(SO6) 10. Keeping inventory levels low and planning the timing of major expenditures are two basic principles of:
  a. internal control.
  b. cash management.
  c. inventory management.
  d. share capital management.

(SO6) 11. With respect to cash management, most companies try to:
  a. keep as much spare cash on hand as possible in case of emergency.
  b. keep a lot of cash in a non-interest-bearing chequing account because that type of account has the lowest fees.
  c. invest idle cash, even if only overnight.
  d. invest idle cash in illiquid investments because that is where money earns the greatest return.

(SO7) 12. Expected incoming dividends and interest will be listed in the _____ section of a cash budget.
  a. cash receipts
  b. cash disbursements
  c. cash investments
  d. financing

(SO7) 13. Expected payments for direct materials will be listed in the _____ section of a cash budget.
  a. cash receipts
  b. cash disbursements
  c. cash investments
  d. financing

(SO8) 14. Which of the following measures the amount of discretionary cash a company has for purchasing additional investments, paying its debts, or adding to its liquidity?
  a. Free cash flow
  b. Ratio of cash to daily expenses
  c. Cash current debt coverage ratio
  d. Cash total debt coverage ratio

(SO8) 15. Which of the following has cash and cash equivalents in the numerator?
  a. Free cash flow
  b. Ratio of cash to daily expenses
  c. Cash current debt coverage ratio
  d. Cash total debt coverage ratio

(SO9) 16. The journal entry to establish a petty cash fund involves a:
  a. debit to Cash and a credit to Petty Cash.
  b. debit to Accounts Receivable and a credit to Cash.
  c. debit to Petty Cash and a credit to Cash.
  d. debit to Petty Cash Expense and a credit to Cash.

(SO9) 17. The Petty Cash account has a balance of $500. The total of the receipts in the petty cash drawer is $392, and the cash in the drawer totals $105. When the fund is replenished, the journal entry will include a:
  a. debit to Cash for $395.
  b. credit to Petty Cash for $395.
  c. credit to Cash Over and Short for $3.
  d. debit to Cash Over and Short for $3.

Problems

1. Please use the following data for J By J Corporation to prepare a bank reconciliation as of June 30, 2002. Remember to prepare any required journal entries.

Balance per bank, June 30	$2,417
Balance per books, June 30	2,151
Outstanding cheques	559
Deposits in transit	802
NSF cheque	46
Bank service charges	35
Note collection	500
Interest on note	90

J By J Corporation
Bank Reconciliation
June 30, 2002

2. Please refer to both Cognos' and JetForm's financial statements at the end of this study guide for information for answering the following questions. Don't forget to use the **Decision Toolkit** approach for help in the problem-solving.

(SO5)   a. What is the name of the first current asset on each company's balance sheet? Please explain the two components.

(SO5)   b. On a percentage basis, for each company how much did Cash and Cash Equivalents increase or decrease from 1999 to 2000?

(SO8)   c. Does Cognos have any discretionary cash available in 2000 and 1999?

(SO8)   d. Please evaluate the results of your computations in "c."

SOLUTIONS TO SELF-TEST

Completion

1. safeguard, enhance
2. employee
3. bank, cash
4. cheque
5. NSF (not sufficient funds)
6. Miscellaneous Expense
7. Treasury bills or short-term notes or money market funds
8. receivables, liabilities
9. financing
10. free cash flow

Multiple Choice

1. b Only one person should have responsibility for a task, and custody and record-keeping should always be separated. Internal verification is a critical function, certainly not a waste of resources.
2. d The use of prenumbered documents is very important.
3. c The short-term investment is just that and not cash.
4. a $1,000 + $3,000 + $5,000. Postage stamps are office supplies or are expensed when purchased; Treasury bills are investments.
5. d
6. b The outstanding cheque and the deposit in transit are dealt with on the balance per bank side, and the service charge is subtracted from the balance per books side.
7. c $1,250 − $102 − $27 + $850
8. a Cash does not appear on the statement of earnings and the statement of retained earnings.
9. d To be included in Cash and Cash Equivalents, cash must be unrestricted. It certainly is not a liability and is not noncurrent since it will be used within the next year.
10. b
11. c Keeping spare cash on hand or in a non-interest-bearing account is not taking advantage of cash's interest-earning ability. It is unwise to invest in illiquid investments because they cannot be converted into cash when the need arises.
12. a.
13. b
14. a The ratio of cash to daily expenses addresses whether the company has adequate cash to meet its daily needs, and the cash current debt coverage ratio helps to determine whether the company can meet its near-term obligations. The cash total debt coverage ratio helps to determine whether the company can meet its long-term obligations.
15. b Free cash flow has no numerator or denominator, and the debt coverage ratios have as their numerator net cash provided by operations.
16. c Accounts Receivable is not involved, and there typically is no "Petty Cash Expense" account.
17. d The journal entry is:

Various expense accounts	392	
Cash Over and Short	3	
Cash		395

Problems

1.

J By J
Bank Reconciliation
June 30, 2002

Balance per bank statement		$2,417
Add: Deposits in transit		802
		3,219
Less: Outstanding cheques		559
Adjusted cash balance per bank		$2,660
Cash balance per books		$2,151
Add: Note collection	$500	
Interest on note	90	590
		2,741
Less: NSF cheque	46	
Bank service charges	35	81
Adjusted cash balance per books		$2,660

Journal entries are recorded only for the "cash balance per books" side of the bank reconciliation. Bank personnel record journal entries for the "balance per bank" side.

June 30	Cash	590	
	Notes Receivable		500
	Interest Revenue		90
	(To record collection of note and interest)		
	Accounts Receivable	46	
	Miscellaneous Expense	35	
	Cash		81
	(To record NSF cheque and bank service charges)		

2.
a. The first current asset is cash and cash equivalents. Cash represents all coins, currency and amounts in bank accounts. Cash equivalents are short term highly liquid investments.
b. Cognos: The amount has increased by 41% (132,435 – 93,617 ÷ 93,617)
   JetForm: The amount has decreased by 10.9%.
c. To determine this you have to calculate the free cash flow which involves subtracting capital expenditures and cash dividends from net cash provided by operating activities.
   Discretionary cash available:
   1999: $63,471   2000: ($83,218 – $28,096 – 0 = $55,122).
d. In both years there was substantial free cash flow.

NOTES

NOTES

CHAPTER

8

REPORTING AND ANALYSING RECEIVABLES

CHAPTER OVERVIEW

In this chapter you learn how to recognize and value accounts receivable, including how to record both estimated and actual bad debts. You will learn about notes receivable, including how to determine the maturity date, how to calculate interest, and how to write journal entries for both the honouring and dishonouring of notes. Finally, you will learn about the issues involved in managing receivables.

REVIEW OF SPECIFIC STUDY OBJECTIVES

- The term **"receivables" refers to amounts due from individuals and companies**: They are *claims that are expected to be collected in cash*. Receivables are often one of the largest assets for a company and are one of the most liquid assets.

- **Accounts receivable** are *amounts owed by customers on account*, and result from the sale of goods and services.

- **Notes receivable** represent *claims for which formal instruments of credit are issued as evidence of the debt*. Unlike accounts receivable, notes receivable involve receipt of interest from the debtor. Notes and accounts receivable that result from sales transactions are called *trade receivables*.

STUDY OBJECTIVE

1

Identify the different types of receivables.

- **Other receivables include nontrade receivables** such as *interest receivable, loans to company officers, advances to employees, recoverable sales, and income taxes.* They are generally classified and reported separately from accounts and notes receivable on the balance sheet.

STUDY OBJECTIVE

2

Explain how accounts receivable are recognized in the accounts.

- For a **service organization**, accounts receivable are *recorded when service is provided on account.*
- For a **merchandiser**, accounts receivable are *recorded at the point of sale of merchandise on account.*
- Receivables are **reduced as a result of sales discounts and sales returns**.

STUDY OBJECTIVE

3

Describe the method used to account for bad debts.

- **Receivables are reported on the balance sheet as a current asset.**
- The amount at which receivables are reported can be problematic. If a credit customer cannot pay their bill, then the credit loss is debited to **Bad Debts Expense**, a statement of earnings account. The following entry is written when a *specific customer's account is uncollectible*:

> Bad Debts Expense
>   Accounts Receivable
> (To write off an uncollectible account)

If we wait to record this entry until it is known with certainty that a credit customer is unable to pay their bill, *bad debts expense will show only actual losses.* Because revenues might be recorded in one period while the (bad debts) expense might be recorded in the next period, **waiting until the loss occurs has the potential for violating the matching principle**. This is known as the direct write-off method. *Unless bad debt losses are insignificant, the direct write-off method is not acceptable for financial reporting purposes.*

- Instead, **the allowance method is used to record estimated uncollectibles**. A feature of this method is that *uncollectible accounts receivable are estimated and matched against sales in the same accounting period in which the sales occurred.*
- The adjusting **journal entry to record estimated uncollectibles** is as follows:

> Bad Debts Expense
>   Allowance for Doubtful Accounts
> (To record estimate of uncollectible accounts)

Bad Debts Expense appears on the *statement of earnings as an operating expense (usually as a selling expense).* **Allowance for Doubtful Accounts** appears on the *balance sheet as a contra asset account.* When it is subtracted from accounts receivable, the *difference is the net (cash) realizable value of the accounts receivable.*

The number in this journal entry is purely an estimate: At this point the company does not know which customer will not pay its bill. Failure to write the entry would violate the matching principle. Recording this entry keeps the matching principle in operation.

- Later, when it is known with certainty that a specific customer is unable to pay their bill, their account is written off. The **journal entry to record the write-off of an uncollectible account** is as follows:

> Allowance for Doubtful Accounts
>   Accounts Receivable
> (To write off an uncollectible account)

Bad Debts Expense is not used in this entry because it was used in the adjusting journal entry (in order to match revenues of the period to their related expense). *The number in this entry is an actual, not an estimated, number*; at this point the company knows which customer is not paying its bill and the exact dollar amount of the bill.

Proper authorization of a write-off is critical. The entry to record a cash collection on an account requires a debit to Cash and a credit to Accounts Receivable. If an employee wished to steal money from customers paying on their accounts and to hide it from the company, then the employee could use the write-off entry. In each case, the cash collection and the write-off, the credit is to Accounts Receivable, thereby closing out that account balance. The write-off entry would allow the employee to steal the cash and to close out the customer's account balance.

Net realizable value is the same after a write-off as it was before a write-off because both accounts receivable and the allowance account are reduced by the same amount.

- **Two journal entries are required to record the recovery of an amount previously written off:** The first reinstates the customer's account, and the second records the cash collection.

> Accounts Receivable
>   Allowance for Doubtful Accounts
> (To reverse write-off of an account)
>
> Cash
>   Accounts Receivable
> (To record collection on account)

The first entry is simply a reversal of the original write-off entry. While the net effect of the two entries is a debit to Cash and a credit to the allowance account, it is important to reinstate the receivable and then show its collection for an information trail on the customer.

- **One way to estimate the amount used in the adjusting entry for uncollectible accounts** is the *percentage of receivables basis* which provides an estimate of the net realizable value of the receivables as well as a reasonable matching of expense to revenue. The company prepares an *aging schedule* in which customer balances are classified by the length of time they have been unpaid. A percentage is applied to each class of unpaid receivables: The longer the period unpaid, the higher the percentage. Consider the following example. Edison Inc. aged its receivables and calculated that *estimated bad debts totalled $2,500*. At the time the *Allowance for Doubtful Accounts had a credit balance of $300*. The required adjusting entry is:

Bad Debts Expense	2,200	
Allowance for Doubtful Accounts		2,200
(To record estimate of uncollectible accounts)		

The Allowance account must have $2,500 in it *after* the adjusting entry is written. Since there is already a balance of $300, $2,200 must be added to the account to bring it up to that balance.

If the *Allowance account had had a $400 debit balance* in it before adjustment, then the adjusting entry would have been:

Bad Debts Expense	2,900	
Allowance for Doubtful Accounts		2,900
(To record estimate of uncollectible accounts)		

Remember that the Allowance account must have $2,500 in it *after* the adjusting entry is written. If there is a debit balance of $400, then the account must be credited for $2,900 in order to have an overall credit balance of $2,500.

STUDY OBJECTIVE

Explain how notes receivable are recognized and valued in the accounts.

- A **promissory note** is a *written promise to pay a specified amount of money on demand or at a definite time*. The **maker** of a note is the *party making the promise to pay;* the **payee** is the *party to whom payment is to be made.*
- **Notes receivable give the holder a stronger legal claim** to assets than do accounts receivable; both types of receivables can easily be sold to another party. The majority of notes arise from lending transactions.
- The **formula for calculating interest** is as follows:

$$\text{Interest} = \text{Principal} \times \text{Rate} \times \text{Time}$$

The principal is the face value of the note, the rate is the annual interest rate, and the time is a fraction (in terms of one year). The *interest on a $12,000, 90-day note with an interest rate of 10% is $300*, calculated as follows:

$$\$300 = \$12,000 \times 10\% \times 3/12 \text{ months}$$

When the maturity date is stated in days (e.g., 90 days), the time factor is 90 days divided by 365 days ($296 = $12,000 × 10% × 90/365 days). This can also be stated in months as we have done above, e.g., 3 months divided by 12 months for adjusting entry (accrual of interest) purposes. The difference between interest calculated using the actual number of days ($296), versus months ($300), will not be material.

- A **note receivable** is *recorded at its face value*, and *no interest revenue is recorded when the note is accepted*. Interest is a rental charge for the use of money, and only a very immaterial amount of time has elapsed on the day the note is accepted. *If a note is exchanged for cash*, then the entry is a debit to Notes Receivable and a credit to Cash. *If a note is accepted in settlement of an open account*, then the entry is a debit to Notes Receivable and a credit to Accounts Receivable.
- **Short-term notes receivable** are *reported at their net realizable value*. The notes receivable allowance account is Allowance for Doubtful Notes. **Long-term notes receivable** pose additional estimation problems; determining the proper allowance is more difficult than it is for short-term notes.

STUDY OBJECTIVE

Describe the entries to record the disposition of notes receivable.

- A **note may be held until its maturity date**, at which time both principal and interest are due. Occasionally a **maker defaults on a note**. In some cases a **note may be sold by the holder before its maturity date**.
- A **note is honoured** if it is *paid in full at the maturity date*. Consider again the note mentioned above: $12,000, 90-day note with an interest rate of 10%, with total interest due of $300. On the maturity date, the holder records the following journal entry:

Cash	12,300	
Notes Receivable		12,000
Interest Revenue		300
(To record collection of note)		

If the note had been issued on December 1 and the holder had a December 31 year-end, then the holder would have accrued interest on December 31 with the following entry:

Interest Receivable	100	
Interest Revenue		100
(To record accrued interest: $12,000 × 10% × 1/12)		

On the maturity date, March 1, the following entry would be recorded:

Cash	12,300	
Notes Receivable		12,000
Interest Receivable		100
Interest Revenue		200

- A **note is dishonoured** if it *is not paid in full at maturity*. If the $12,000, 10%, 90-day note had not been paid on March 1, then the following journal entry would have been required:

Accounts Receivable	12,300	
Notes Receivable		12,000
Interest Revenue		300

While the note no longer has legal validity on the due date, the holder of the note records the entire amount as a receivable, signaling his intention to try to collect from the maker of the note. If the holder later determines that the account is not collectible, then he will write off the account by debiting the Allowance account and crediting Accounts Receivable.

- **Short-term receivables** are a *current asset presented below short-term investments on the balance sheet*. They are presented at their net realizable value. Notes receivable are listed before accounts receivable because they are more liquid (near to cash).

- **Bad Debts Expense** appears *on the statement of earnings as an operating expense (in the selling expense section)*. **Interest Revenue** is also a *statement of earnings item, shown as an Other Revenues and Gains item*.

- A **company must disclose any particular problem with receivables, such as significant risk of uncollectible accounts**.

STUDY OBJECTIVE

6

Explain the statement presentation of receivables.

- **Managing receivables** involves *five steps*:
  1. Determine to whom to extend credit.
  2. Establish a payment period.
  3. Monitor collections.
  4. Evaluate the receivables balance.
  5. Accelerate cash receipts from receivables when necessary.

- **Determining who receives credit** is a *critical issue for a company*. If a credit policy is too generous, then the company may extend credit to risky customers. If the policy is too tight, then it may lose sales. If a **company requires references from new customers**, then it must check out the references before it extends credit and periodically after it extends credit to monitor the financial health of customers.

- When a company **establishes a payment period**, it must make sure to communicate the policy to customers. The payment period should be consistent with the period offered by competitors.

- In order to **monitor collections**, a company may *calculate a credit risk ratio*, calculated by *dividing the Allowance for Doubtful Accounts by Accounts Receivable*. Changes in the ratio should be monitored and investigated carefully because they indicate that the company's credit risk is increasing or decreasing. An *aging schedule* helps in the following ways: It helps to establish the allowance for bad debts; it aids estimation of the timing of future cash inflows; and it provides information about the collection experience of the company, identifying problem accounts. A company should disclose in the notes to the financial statements a **concentration of credit risk**, which is a *threat of nonpayment from a single customer or class of customers that could adversely affect the company's financial health*.

STUDY OBJECTIVE

7

Describe the principles of sound accounts receivable management.

- To help **evaluate its receivables balance, a company calculates the receivables turnover ratio**, calculated by *dividing net credit sales by average net receivables*. (Average receivables are calculated by adding together the beginning and ending balances of receivables and dividing the sum by two.) If net credit sales total $25,000 and average receivables total $5,000, then the receivables turnover ratio is 5 times, meaning that the company collects its receivables 5 times during the accounting period.

- This ratio *measures the number of times receivables are collected during the period*. A decreasing ratio should be of concern to a company, particularly if its competitors' ratios are holding steady or increasing.

STUDY OBJECTIVE

8

Identify ratios used to analyse a company's receivables.

- To calculate the **average collection period**, the company *divides the receivables turnover ratio into 365 days.* Using the numbers above, the average collection period is 73 days (365 ÷ 5). *A general rule is that the collection period should not greatly exceed the credit term period.*

- A company can borrow money from a bank by **using its accounts receivable as collateral**.
- A **company frequently sells its receivables to another company to shorten the operating cycle.** There are *three reasons for the sale of receivables*: They may be a very large asset that a company wishes to convert to cash; they may be the only reasonable source of cash; and billing and collection are time-consuming and costly for companies.
- A company may sell its receivables to a **factor**, which is a *finance company or bank which buys receivables from businesses for a fee and then collects the payments directly from the customers.*
- A **retailer may allow its customers to use credit cards to charge purchases**, and its acceptance of a national credit card is *another form of selling the receivable* by the retailer. Use of such credit cards translates to more sales with zero bad debts for the retailer.
- **Sales resulting from the use of credit cards are considered cash sales by the retailer.** Issuing banks charge the retailer a fee. If a jewellery store sells $5,000 of jewellery to customers using bank credit cards and its bank charges a fee of 4%, then the jewellery store records the following entry after depositing the credit card slips:

Cash	4,800	
Service Charge Expense	200	
Sales		5,000
(To record credit card sales)		

CHAPTER SELF-TEST

As you work through the exercises and problems, remember to use the **Decision Toolkit** discussed and used in the text:

1. *Decision Checkpoints*: At this point you ask a question.
2. *Info Needed for Decision*: You make a choice regarding the information needed to answer the question.
3. *Tool to Use for Decision*: At this point you review just what the information chosen in step 2 does for the decision-making process.
4. *How to Evaluate Results*: You perform evaluation of information for answering the question.

Note: The notation (SO1) means that the question was drawn from study objective number one.

Matching

Please write the letters of the following terms in the spaces to the left of the definitions.

a. Allowance method
b. Average collection period
c. Net realizable value
d. Credit risk ratio
e. Aging the accounts receivable
f. Factor
g. Maker
h. Nontrade receivables

      i.   Payee
      j.   Receivables turnover ratio
      k. Trade receivables

(SO3)   _____   1. Amount expected to be received in cash.

(SO4)   _____   2. The party in a promissory note who has issued the promise to pay.

(SO3)   _____   3. Classifying customer accounts by the length of time they have been unpaid.

(SO8)   _____   4. A measure of the liquidity of receivables, calculated by dividing net credit sales by average net receivables.

(SO9)   _____   5. A finance company or bank which buys receivables from businesses for a fee.

(SO1)   _____   6. Receivables which do not result from sales transactions.

(SO3)   _____   7. A method of accounting for bad debts that involves estimating uncollectible accounts at the end of each period.

(SO7)   _____   8. A ratio calculated by dividing Allowance for Doubtful Accounts by Accounts Receivable.

(SO4)   _____   9. The party to whom payment of a promissory note is to be made.

(SO8)   _____ 10.The average amount of time that a receivable is outstanding.

Multiple Choice

Please circle the correct answer.

(SO1)   1. Accounts and notes receivable which result from sales transactions are called:
       a.   other receivables.
       b.   nontrade receivables.
       c.   trade receivables.
       d.   noncurrent receivables.

(SO1)   2. Interest receivable and loans to company officers are included in:
       a.   nontrade receivables.
       b.   trade receivables.
       c.   notes receivable.
       d.   accounts receivable.

(SO2)   3. For a service organization, a receivable is recorded when:
       a.   the customer pays the bill.
       b.   when service is provided on account.
       c.   thirty days after service is provided.
       d.   when the bill is sent to the customer one week after service is provided.

(SO3)   4. The entry to record estimated uncollectibles is:
   a. Bad Debts Expense
         Accounts Receivable
   b. Allowance for Doubtful Accounts
         Accounts Receivable
   c. Accounts Receivable
         Allowance for Doubtful Accounts
   d. Bad Debts Expense
         Allowance for Doubtful Accounts

(SO3)   5. The entry to record the write-off of an uncollectible account is:
   a. Bad Debts Expense
         Accounts Receivable
   b. Allowance for Doubtful Accounts
         Accounts Receivable
   c. Accounts Receivable
         Allowance for Doubtful Accounts
   d. Bad Debts Expense
         Allowance for Doubtful Accounts

(SO3)   6. Before a write-off of an uncollectible account, Accounts Receivable had a $10,000 balance, and the Allowance for Doubtful Accounts had a $500 balance. After a write-off of $100, the net realizable value is:
   a. $10,000.
   b. $9,500.
   c. $9,400.
   d. $9,300.

(SO3)   7. The Allowance for Doubtful Accounts has a $400 credit balance. An aging schedule shows that total estimated bad debts is $3,600. The adjusting entry will require a debit and a credit for:
   a. $4,000.
   b. $3,600.
   c. $3,200.
   d.   some other amount.

(SO3)   8. The Allowance for Doubtful Accounts has a $400 debit balance. An aging schedule shows that total estimated bad debts is $3,600. The adjusting entry will require a debit and a credit for:
   a. $4,000.
   b. $3,600.
   c. $3,200.
   d.   some other amount.

(SO4)   9. A company issues a 4 month, 9% note for $30,000. The total interest on the note is:
   a. $90.
   b. $900.
   c. $2,700.
   d. $3,000.

(SO5)   10. The journal entry written on the maturity date by the holder of a 3-month, 12%, $15,000 note will include a:
   a.   debit to Cash for $15,000.
   b.   credit to Notes Receivable for $15,450.
   c.   debit to Interest Revenue for $450.
   d.   debit to Cash for $15,450.

(SO5) 11. A company holds a 4 month, 10%, $21,000 note which was not paid in full on the maturity date. The journal entry on the maturity date will include a:
    a. debit to Accounts Receivable for $21,700.
    b. credit to Notes Receivable for $21,700.
    c. debit to Cash for $21,700.
    d. debit to Notes Receivable for $21,000.

(SO6) 12. Which of the following is the correct sequence for receivables on the balance sheet?
    a. Notes receivable, other receivables, accounts receivable
    b. Accounts receivable, notes receivable, other receivables
    c. Notes receivable, accounts receivable, other receivables
    d. Accounts receivable, other receivables, notes receivable

(SO7) 13. Net credit sales are $100,000, accounts receivable are $80,000, and the allowance for doubtful accounts totals $2,000. The credit risk ratio is:
    a. 2.0%
    b. 2.5%.
    c. 40 to 1.
    d. 50 to 1.

(SO7) 14. A threat of nonpayment from a single customer or class of customers that could adversely affect the financial health of a company is called:
    a. accounts receivable concentration risk.
    b. notes receivable concentration risk.
    c. credit risk.
    d. a concentration of credit risk.

(SO8) 15. Net credit sales are $800,000, average net receivables total $150,000, average inventory totals $200,000,and the allowance for doubtful accounts totals $8,000. The receivables turnover ratio is:
    a. 100 times.
    b. 5.33 times.
    c. 4.00 times.
    d. 1.33 times.

(SO8) 16. Please use the information from number 15. The average collection period is:
    a. 100 days.
    b. 75.0 days.
    c. 68.5 days.
    d. 5.33 days.

(SO9) 17. Kerrison Corporation sold $6,000 of merchandise to customers who charged their purchases with a bank credit card. Kerrison's bank charges it a 4% fee. The journal entry to record the credit card sales will include a:
    a. debit to Cash for $5,760.
    b. credit to Sales for $5,760.
    c. debit to Cash for $6,000.
    d. credit to Service Charge Expense for $240.

Problems

1. Please record journal entries for the following items for Morrison Corp. (all are SO3):

   a. At the end of the accounting period on June 30, Morrison prepares an aging schedule of accounts receivable which shows total estimated bad debts of $5,200. On this date the Allowance for Doubtful Accounts has a debit balance of $300, and Accounts Receivable has a balance of $85,000.

   b. On July 5, Morrison receives word that Sperry Ltd. has declared bankruptcy, and Morrison writes off their account receivable of $800.

   c. On September 12, Sperry Ltd. notifies Morrison that it can pay its $800 debt and includes a cheque for the entire amount.

Date	Account Titles	Debit	Credit

   d. What is the net realizable value of accounts receivable after the entry in "a" is written? What is the net realizable value after the write-off in "b"?

2. Please refer to Cognos Corporation financial statements at the end of this study guide for information for answering the following questions. Don't forget to use the **Decision Toolkit** approach for help in the problem-solving.

(S07)   a. What is concentration of credit risk? What is Cognos's evaluation of the possibility of this affecting it?

(S01)   b. What is the percentage increase or decrease in accounts receivable from 1999 to 2000?

(S08)   c. Did Cognos collect its receivables in a timely fashion in 2000? Assume all sales are on credit

SOLUTIONS TO SELF-TEST

Matching

1. c
2. g
3. e
4. j
5. f
6. h
7. a
8. d
9. i
10. b

Multiple Choice

1. c Other and nontrade receivables are basically the same thing and arise from such items as interest and loans to company officers. Accounts receivable are always current assets.
2. a Trade receivables arise from sales transactions, notes receivable are written promises and usually include interest, and accounts receivable are amounts owed by customers on account.
3. b A receivable is recorded before the customer pays the bill. The receivable should be recorded when the service is performed, not at some other specific date.
4. d The answer in "a" is the write-off of a debt under the direct write-off method. The answer in "b" is the write-off of a debt under the allowance method. The answer in "c" is the reinstatement of a written-off account under the allowance method.
5. b
6. b The net realizable value is $9,500 ($10,000 – $500) before the write-off and $9,500 ($9,900 – $400) after.
7. c $3,600 is the amount which must be in the Allowance account after adjustment. Since it already has a credit balance of $400, only $3,200 is needed to raise the balance to $3,600.
8. a $3,600 is the amount which must be in the Allowance account after adjustment. Since it has a debit balance of $400, $4,000 is needed to raise the balance to $3,600.
9. b $30,000 × 9% × 4/12 months
10. d The journal entry is:

Cash	15,450	
Notes Receivable		15,000
Interest Revenue		450
($15,000 × 12% × 3/12 = $450)		

11. a The journal entry is:

Accounts Receivable	21,700	
Notes Receivable		21,000
Interest Revenue		700
($21,000 × 10% × 4/12 = $700)		

12. c
13. b Allowance ÷ Accts. Rec. = $2,000 ÷ $80,000 = 2.5%
14. d

15. b Net cr. sales ÷ Av. net rec. = $800,000 ÷ $150,000 = 5.33 times
16. c 365 days ÷ rec. turnover ratio = 365 ÷ 5.33 = 68.5 days
17. a The journal entry is:

Cash	5,760	
Service Charge Expense		240
Sales		6,000

Problems

1.

a. June 30	Bad Debts Expense	5,500	
	Allowance for Doubtful Accounts		5,500
	(To record the estimate of uncollectible accounts: $300 + $5,200)		
b. July 5	Allowance for Doubtful Accounts	800	
	Accounts Receivable—Sperry		800
	(To write off the Sperry account)		
c. Sep. 12	Accounts Receivable—Sperry	800	
	Allowance for Doubtful Accounts		800
	(To reinstate Sperry account)		
	Cash	800	
	Accounts Receivable—Sperry		800
	(To record collection on Sperry account)		

d.

	Before Write-Off	After Write-off
Accounts Receivable	$85,000	$84,200
− Allowance	5,200	4,400
Net Realizable Value	$79,800	$79,800

The net realizable value does not change because both accounts are reduced by the same amount.

2.
a. The concentration of credit risk is the threat of non-payment from a single customer that could adversely affect the financial health of the company. In Note 8 the Cognos indicates that it does not have a concentration of credit risk for trade receivables as they have a large customer base and geographic dispersion.
b. The trade receivables increased from 1999 to 2000 by 40% $107,823 − $76,876 = 30,947 ÷ 76,876.
c. To answer this question, you must determine the receivables turnover ratio calculated by dividing net credit sales by average net receivables, and the average collection period, calculated by dividing 365 days by the receivables turnover ratio. To calculate the average receivables, the 1999 and 2000 receivable balances are added together and divided by 2.
Average receivables: ($76,876 + $107,823) ÷ 2 = 92,350;
$385,640 ÷ 92,350 = 4.2
Average collection period: 365 ÷ 4.2 = 86.9
If Cognos has a 30 day collection period, this represents a poor collection record.

<u>NOTES</u>

CHAPTER

9

REPORTING AND ANALYSING LONG-LIVED ASSETS

CHAPTER OVERVIEW

In this chapter you will learn how to account for long-lived assets with physical substance—tangible capital assets, such as buildings and machinery. You will learn about the amounts at which they are recorded in the accounting records and how to allocate their cost to expense using periodic amortization. You will learn how to dispose of tangible capital assets and methods used by companies for evaluating their use. You will also learn about intangible capital assets, long-lived assets which have no physical substance. Finally, you will learn how all these capital assets are reported on the balance sheet.

REVIEW OF SPECIFIC STUDY OBJECTIVES

Tangible capital assets are *resources that have physical substance, are used in the operations of a business, and are not intended for sale to customers*. Other names for these assets are property, plant, and equipment; plant and equipment; and fixed assets. Of the following four classes of these assets, land is the only which does usually retains its value:

1. Land
2. Land improvements, such as driveways and parking lots
3. Buildings, such as offices and factories
4. Equipment, such as office furniture, cash registers, and delivery equipment.

- **Tangible capital assets are recorded at cost**, which consists of *all expenditures necessary to acquire the asset and make it ready for its intended use.*
- **Revenue (or operating) expenditures** are *costs expensed immediately, not included in the cost of a tangible capital asset.*
- **Capital expenditures** are those *costs included in a tangible capital asset account, not expensed immediately.*
- **Cost** is *measured by the cash paid in a cash transaction or by the cash equivalent price paid when noncash assets are used in payment.* The **cash equivalent price** is *equal to the fair market value of the asset given up or the fair market value of the asset received,* if the fair market value of the asset given up is not determinable.
- The **cost of land** includes *the cash purchase price, closing costs, real estate brokers' commissions, and accrued property taxes and other liens assumed by the purchaser.* All costs incurred in making land ready for its intended use increase the Land account: Clearing, draining, filling, grading, and razing old buildings are included.
- The **cost of land improvements** includes *all expenditures necessary to make the improvements ready for their intended use.* For example, building a parking lot includes paving, fencing, and lighting.
- The **cost of buildings** includes *all expenditures relating to the purchase or construction of a building.* If a **building is purchased**, then the costs include the purchase price, closing costs, and brokers' commissions, as well as remodeling costs. If a **building is constructed**, then costs include the contract price, architects' fees, building permits, excavation costs, and interest costs incurred to finance the project (the inclusion of the latter is limited to the construction period).
- The **cost of equipment** includes *the cash purchase price, provincial sales taxes* (if applicable), *freight charges, and insurance during shipping (if paid by the purchaser), as well as assembling, installation of, and testing of the unit.* Fees, which occur, and recur, after the equipment is operational, such as vehicle licences and accident insurance, are debited to an expense account or treated as a prepaid asset.
- **Companies often lease assets.** In a lease, a **lessor** agrees to allow another party, the **lessee**, to use the asset for an agreed period of time at an agreed price. Some **advantages of leasing** include *reduced risk of obsolescence, low down payment, shared tax advantages, and non-reporting of assets and liabilities.* In an **operating lease**, the lessee uses the asset but does not record an asset or a liability. Under a **capital lease**, the lessee uses the asset and does record an asset and a liability.

- **Amortization** is the *process of allocating to expense the cost of a capital asset over its useful (service) life in a rational and systematic manner.* It provides a matching of revenues and expenses.
- **Amortization is a process of cost allocation**, not a process of asset valuation. Thus, the *book value (cost less accumulated amortization) may differ significantly from the fair market value of the asset.*
- **Land improvements, building, and equipment are amortizable assets**, but *land is not.* In fact, land very often does the opposite and appreciates in value.
- **Amortizable assets lose their utility** because of *wear and tear* and *obsolescence,* the process by which an asset becomes out of date before it physically wears out.
- **Amortization in no way provides cash for the eventual replacement of the asset.**
- **Three factors** affect the calculation of amortization: *cost, useful life* (an estimate of the

productive, or service life of the asset, expressed in terms of time, units of activity, or units of output), and *salvage value* (an estimate of the asset's value at the end of its useful life).

- The **straight-line, declining-balance, and units-of-activity methods** of amortization are *all acceptable under generally accepted accounting principles*. Management of a company chooses the method that it feels best measures the asset's contribution to revenue and then applies that method consistently. The *straight-line method is the most widely used because it is simple to apply and understand*.
- The journal entry to record amortization is:

Amortization Expense
    Accumulated Amortization

Amortization Expense appears on the statement of earnings, and the Accumulated Amortization account is a contra-asset account, subtracted from the asset's cost to give its book value.

- Under the **straight-line method**, amortization is considered to be a *function of time*, and the same dollar amount of amortization is taken each full year. *Amortizable cost*, which is the asset's cost less its salvage value, *is divided by the useful life* to give the annual amortization expense. A straight-line rate can also be calculated (100% ÷ useful life) and multiplied by the amortizable cost to give the dollar amount of expense.

Consider the following example. A company purchased on January 2 for $18,000 a truck with a useful life of 6 years and a salvage value of $3,000. The amortizable cost is $15,000 ($18,000 – $3,000), and annual amortization is $2,500 (15,000 ÷ 6 years). The straight-line rate is 16.67% (100% ÷ 6 years); multiplying $15,000 by 16.67% also yields $2,500 per year. After 6 years, the total accumulated amortization is $15,000, and the book value of the asset is $3,000 ($18,000 – $15,000). Note that the book value equals the salvage value after all amortization is taken. If this asset had been purchased on July 1, then amortization for the year ended December 31 would have been $1,250 ($2,500 x 6/12).

- The **declining-balance method** is called an *accelerated method because it results in more amortization in the early years of an asset's life than does the straight-line method*. The amortization expense is lower than under straight-line in the later years of the asset's life. A common way to apply this method is to use a rate that is double the straight-line rate, thus producing double-declining-balance. Just as is true for straight line, amortization under this method is a function of time.
- Under the **units-of-activity method**, *useful life is expressed in terms of the total units of production or the use expected from the asset*. Units of output, machine hours, miles driven, and hours flown can all be used. This method is excellent for machinery, vehicles, and airplanes.
- Under all three methods *total* amortization is the same. The only thing which differs is the timing at which the expense is taken.
- Calculations for declining-balance and units-of-activity are shown in Study Objective 9.
- A **company must disclose in the notes to the financial statements** its *choice of amortization method*.

- **Amortization must be revised** if *wear and tear or obsolescence indicates that annual amortization is inadequate or excessive*.
- The **change in amortization** is *made in current and future years but not in prior periods*. This means that prior years' financial statements do not have to be restated. Continual restatement would undermine confidence in the financial statements.
- **Significant changes** in estimates must be *disclosed in the financial statements or notes to the statements*.

STUDY OBJECTIVE

Calculate periodic amortization using the straight-line method, and contrast its expense pattern with those of other methods.

STUDY OBJECTIVE

Describe the procedure for revising periodic amortization.

- There are **two possibilities** on _how to treat money spent on assets during their useful lives._ **Ordinary repairs** are expenditures that maintain the operating efficiency and expected productive life of the asset: They maintain the asset in its current operating condition. These costs are _revenue (or operating) expenditures_ and are debited to an expense account. **Additions and improvements** increase the operating efficiency, productive capacity, or expected useful life of the asset. Usually material in amount, they improve the asset. These costs are _capital expenditures_ and are debited to the asset account.

- An **impairment** is a _permanent decline in the market value of an asset_, resulting from obsolescence or market conditions. When this occurs, the asset is _written down to its new market value during the year in which the decline in value occurs_. The CICA frowns on **earnings management**, which is the practice of delaying recording losses on impairments until a year when the impact on a firm's earnings is minimized. A recent standard requires immediate recognition of a write-down.

- Regardless of the method of disposal, **amortization must be brought up to date, if necessary**. Then, when the disposal journal entry is written, the _asset account is credited for its cost_, and the related _Accumulated Amortization account is debited._

- If the **disposal is a sale**, then the _book value of the asset is compared with the proceeds of the sale._ If the proceeds exceed the book value, then there is a **gain on the sale**. If the proceeds are less than the book value, then there is a **loss on the sale**.

  Consider the following example. A company sells a piece of machinery that cost it $10,000 and which has accumulated amortization of $6,000 for $5,000. The journal entry to record the sale is as follows:

Cash	5,000	
Accumulated Amortization	6,000	
Machinery		10,000
Gain on Disposal		1,000
(To record sale of machinery at a gain)		

  The book value of the asset is $4,000 ($10,000 – $6,000). Since the company received $5,000 for the asset, it sold the asset for a $1,000 gain. Gain on Disposal appears in the Other Revenues and Gains section of the statement of earnings.

  If the company had sold the asset for $2,000, then it would have incurred a loss of $2,000 ($4,000 book value – $2,000 cash proceeds). The journal entry is as follows:

Cash	2,000	
Accumulated Amortization	6,000	
Loss on Disposal	2,000	
Machinery		10,000
(To record sale of machinery at a loss)		

  Loss on Disposal appears in the _Other Expenses and Losses_ section of the statement of earnings.

- If the **disposal is a retirement**, then it is _recorded as a special case of a sale in which no cash is received_. The asset is credited for its cost, Accumulated Amortization is debited for the proper amount, and a loss is debited for the book value of the asset on the date of retirement. If the asset sold in the two journal entries above is simply retired, then the journal entry is as follows:

Accumulated Amortization	6,000	
Loss on Disposal	4,000	
Machinery		10,000
(To record retirement of machinery)		

- The following are **three measures** used to analyse tangible capital assets.
- **Average useful life** is *calculated by dividing the average cost of capital assets by amortization expense.* This is a good tool to use when the notes to a company's financial statements simply say that capital assets are amortized over a wide-ranging period, for example, from 10 to 40 years. A company using **aggressive accounting policies** uses long useful lives to produce smaller amortization expense. A company using **conservative accounting policies** uses shorter useful lives, thereby increasing amortization expense and reducing net earnings.
- The **average age of capital assets** is *calculated by dividing Accumulated Amortization by Amortization Expense.* Comparing the average age gives an indication of the potential effectiveness of a company's capital assets relative to other companies in the same industry.
- The **asset turnover ratio**, *calculated by dividing net sales by average total assets*, indicates how efficiently a company is able to generate sales with a given amount of assets. It shows *how many dollars of sales are generated by each dollar invested in assets.* The higher the ratio, the more efficiently the company is operating. If the ratio is 1.25 times, then this means that for each dollar invested in assets, the company generates sales of $1.25. Asset turnover ratios vary considerably among industries.

STUDY OBJECTIVE

6

Describe methods for evaluating the use of tangible capital assets.

- **Intangible assets** are *rights, privileges, and competitive advantages that result from ownership of long-lived assets that do not possess physical substance.* Examples include patents, copyrights, goodwill, franchises, licences, trademarks, and trade names. Intangibles may arise from government grants, purchase of another business, and private monopolistic arrangements.
- **Intangible assets are recorded at cost**, and the *cost is amortized* in a rational and systematic manner over the useful life of the intangible. The straight-line method is used. The **journal entry to record amortization** includes a *debit to amortization expense and a credit to the asset account* directly: No contra account is used for the credit. The **amortization period** is the *shortest of the useful life of the intangible, the legal life of the intangible, or 40 years.* Since the legal life of a patent is 20 years, 40 years is never an issue for a patent. If a company purchases a patent with a legal life of 10 years but estimates that the useful life is only 4 years, then the amortization period will be 4 years.
- A **patent** is an *exclusive right issued by the Canadian Intellectual Property Office of Industry Canada that enables the recipient to manufacture, sell, or otherwise control an invention for a period of 20 years from the date of grant.* The **initial cost** of a patent is the *cash or cash equivalent price paid to acquire the patent.* If the owner of a patent successfully defends the patent in a lawsuit, then the costs of the lawsuit are debited to the Patent account and amortized over the remaining life of the patent.
- **Research and development costs** are *expenditures that may lead to patents, copyrights, new processes, and new products.* These costs are not intangible assets and are **usually recorded as an expense when incurred**. Development costs can be capitalized in certain circumstances when future benefits are assured.
- A **copyright** is *granted by the federal government, giving the owner the exclusive right to reproduce and sell an artistic or published work.* The **legal life** of a copyright is the life of the creator plus 50 years, and the **cost** is the *cost of acquiring and defending it.*
- A **trademark or trade name** is a *word, phrase, jingle, or symbol that distinguishes and identifies a particular enterprise or product.* Trademarks and trade names have tremendous value to companies and are vigorously defended. The **legal life** of these intangibles is 15 years, and they may be renewed every 15 years as long as they are in use. If they are **purchased**, then the cost is the purchase price. If they are **developed**, then the *cost includes lawyer's fees, registration fees, design costs, successful legal defence costs, and other such expenditures.*
- A **franchise** is a *contractual agreement under which the franchisor grants the franchisee the right to sell certain products, to render specific services, or to use certain trademarks or trade names, usually within a designated geographic area.* Another type of franchise is granted by a

STUDY OBJECTIVE

7

Identify the basic issues related to reporting intangible capital assets.

governmental body and permits an enterprise to use public property in performing its services. This operating right is called a **licence**. Both franchises and licences may be granted for a definite period of time, an indefinite period, or in perpetuity. **Initial costs associated with the acquisition** are *debited to the asset account*; after that, annual recurring costs are recorded as operating expenses.

- **Goodwill** is *recorded only when there is an exchange transaction that involves the purchase of an entire business*. In other words, goodwill arises only when one business purchases another. It is the **excess of cost over the fair market value of the net assets (assets minus liabilities) acquired**. Factors giving rise to goodwill include excellent management, employees, customer relations, products, and location. When company A purchases company B, it records the purchased assets and liabilities at their fair market values.

STUDY OBJECTIVE

8

Indicate how capital assets are reported on the balance sheet.

- **Capital assets—both tangible and intangible**—are shown at their book value in the section entitled **Capital Assets**. Sometimes tangible capital assets are reported as *Property, Plant, and Equipment* and intangible capital assets as *Intangible Assets*.
- There should be **disclosure in the financial statements or in the notes to the statements** of the *balances of the major classes of assets and accumulated amortization by major classes or in total. Amortization methods used should be disclosed, as should the amount of expense for the period.*

STUDY OBJECTIVE

9

Calculate periodic amortization using the declining-balance method and the units-of-activity method.

- Under the **declining-balance method**, amortization expense is calculated by *multiplying the book value of the asset by a rate*. **Salvage value is initially ignored in the calculations**. Double-declining-balance is one of the forms of this method: The rate is the straight-line rate multiplied by 2. If an asset has a useful life of 4 years, then the straight-line rate is 25% (100% ÷ 4 years). Double that rate is 50%.

Assume that the asset with a 4-year useful life originally cost $50,000 and has a salvage value of $5,000. Amortization expense for the 4 years will be:

Year	Book Value		Rate		Amrt. Exp.
1	$50,000	x	50%	=	$25,000
2	$25,000	x	50%	=	$12,500
3	$12,500	x	50%	=	$ 6,250
4	$ 6,250	x	50%	=	$ 1,250
					$45,000

Note that in year 4 only $1,250 of amortization was taken, even though the book value of $6,250 multiplied by 50% yields $3,125. Remember that book value must equal salvage value at the end of the 4 years, and $3,125 would have violated that. In the final year, only amortization which will make the total amortization $45,000 is taken.

Amortization under this method is a function of time. Therefore, an asset purchased during the year must have its amortization prorated. If the asset above had been purchased on April 1, then amortization for year 1 would have been $18,750 ($50,000 x 50% x 9/12). Book value for year 2 would have been $31,250 ($50,000 – $18,750).

- Under the **units-of-activity method**, a *rate per unit is calculated and applied to actual units during the accounting period*.

A company purchased an asset with a cost of $30,000, a salvage value of $5,000, an estimated useful life of 5 years, and estimated units of output of 50,000. In year 1 the asset produced 12,000 units. Amortization is calculated as follows:

$30,000 – $5,000 = $25,000 amortizable cost
$25,000 ÷ 50,000 units = $ 0.50 per unit
$ 0.50 per unit x 12,000 actual units = $6,000

Note that the useful life in years is not used in the calculation. Note, too, that this method starts with the amortizable cost, just as straight-line amortization does. Declining-balance, however, ignores salvage value in the initial calculation. Since the units-of-activity method is a function of usage and not of time, it is not necessary to prorate amortization if the asset is purchased at a time other than the beginning of the accounting period.

• Remember that **all three methods produce the same total amount of amortization over the life of an asset**. It is the timing of the expense which differs among the methods.

CHAPTER SELF-TEST

As you work through the exercises and problems, remember to use the **Decision Toolkit** discussed and used in the text:
1. *Decision Checkpoints*: At this point you ask a question.
2. *Info Needed for Decision*: You make a choice regarding the information needed to answer the question.
3. *Tool to Use for Decision*: At this point you review just what the information chosen in step 2 does for the decision-making process.
4. *How to Evaluate Results*: You perform evaluation of information for answering the question.

Note: The notation (SO1) means that the question was drawn from study objective number one.

Completion

Please write in the word or words which will complete the sentence.

(SO1) 1. Costs related to capital assets that are not expensed immediately but are included in a capital asset account are considered _____ expenditures.

(SO2) 2. Amortization is a process of _____ allocation, not a process of _____ valuation.

(SO3) 3. The cost of an asset less its salvage value is called _____ cost.

(SO4) 4. Ordinary repairs are _____ expenditures.

(SO5) 5. If the proceeds from the sale of a capital asset exceed the book value of the asset, then a _____ on disposal occurs.

(SO6) 6. The average age of capital assets is calculated by dividing _____ _____ by _____ _____.

(SO7) 7. The maximum amortization period for an intangible asset is _____.

(SO7) 8. A _____ protects artistic or published work.

(SO9) 9. If the useful life of an asset is 8 years, then the straight-line rate is _____.

(SO9) 10. Under the declining-balance method of amortization, the _____ _____ is ignored in determining the amount to which the rate is applied.

Multiple Choice

Please circle the correct answer.

(SO1)   1. Massey Corporation purchased a piece of land for $50,000. It paid legal fees of $5,000 and brokers' commissions of $4,000. An old building on the land was torn down at a cost of $2,000, and proceeds from the scrap were $500. The total to be debited to the Land account is:
   a. $61,000.
   b. $60,500.
   c. $59,000.
   d. $50,000.

(SO1)   2. Newcome Corporation installed a new parking lot for its employees at a cost of $10,000. The $10,000 should be debited to:
   a. Repairs and Maintenance Expense.
   b. Land.
   c. Land Improvements.
   d. Parking Lot.

(SO1)   3. Oliver Co. Ltd. purchased a piece of equipment for $20,000. It paid shipping charges of $500 and insurance during transit of $200. Installation and testing of the new equipment cost $1,000. The total to be debited to the Equipment account is:
   a. $20,000.
   b. $20,500.
   c. $20,700.
   d. $21,700.

(SO2)   4. Which of the following is not an amortizable asset?
   a. Land
   b. Building
   c. Driveway
   d. Equipment

(SO2)   5. Which of the following is a way to express the useful life of an amortizable asset?
   a. Five years
   b. Ten thousand machine hours
   c. Thirty thousand units
   d. All of the above are expressions of useful life

(SO3)   6. At the beginning of the year, Powers Corp. purchased a piece of machinery for $50,000. It has a salvage value of $5,000, an estimated useful life of 9 years, and estimated units of output of 90,000 units. Actual units produced during the first year were 11,000. Amortization expense for the first year under the straight-line method is:
   a. $5,556.
   b. $5,500.
   c. $5,300.
   d. $5,000.

(SO3)   7. Which of the following statements is correct?
   a. Straight-line amortization is an accelerated method of amortization.
   b. The total amount of amortization for an asset is the same, regardless of the method used.
   c. The total amount of amortization for an asset differs depending on the method used.
   d. In the later years of an asset's useful life, straight-line amortization gives lower expense than does declining-balance.

(SO4)   8. Which of the following statements is correct?
  a. Once amortization expense is set, it may never be changed for an asset.
  b. When a change in estimate for amortization is required, the change is made to prior periods.
  c. When a change in estimate for amortization is required, the change is made in current and future years but not to prior periods.
  d. When a change in estimate for amortization is required, the change is made to prior periods and in current and future years.

(SO4)   9. A permanent decline in the market value of an asset is called:
  a. an impairment.
  b. a write-down.
  c. earnings management.
  d. a capital expenditure.

(SO5)   10. A company sold for $3,000 a capital asset, which had a cost of $10,000 and accumulated amortization of $7,500. The company had a:
  a. loss of $500.
  b. gain of $500.
  c. gain of $3,000.
  d. loss of $7,000.

(SO5)   11. A company sold for $2,000 a capital asset which had a cost of $10,000 and accumulated amortization of $7,500. The company had a:
  a. loss of $500.
  b. gain of $500.
  c. gain of $2,000.
  d. loss of $8,000.

(SO5)   12. Quick Corporation retired a piece of equipment, which had cost $8,000 and had accumulated amortization of $7,000. The journal entry to record the retirement will include a:
  a. debit to Gain on Disposal for $1,000.
  b. credit to Gain on Disposal for $1,000.
  c. credit to Loss on Disposal for $1,000.
  d. debit to Loss on Disposal for $1,000.

(SO6)   13. The average cost of a company's capital assets is $200,000, amortization expense is $10,000, and accumulated amortization is $60,000. The average useful life of the company's capital assets is:
  a. 3.33 years.
  b. 6 years.
  c. 20 years.
  d. None of the above is correct.

(SO6)   14. A company's average total assets is $200,000, amortization expense is $10,000, and accumulated amortization is $60,000. Net sales total $250,000. The asset turnover ratio is:
  a. 0.8 times.
  b. 1.25 times.
  c. 3.33 times.
  d. 4.17 times.

(SO7)   15. Which of the following gives the recipient to manufacture, sell, or otherwise control an invention for a period of 20 years?
    a.   Patent
    b.   Copyright
    c.   Trademark
    d.   Licence

(SO7)   16. A company successfully defended its copyright on a piece of literature at a cost of $75,000. The journal entry to record that cost includes a debit to:
    a.   Legal Fees Expense for $75,000.
    b.   Capital Assets for $75,000.
    c.   Copyright for $75,000.
    d.   Research and Development Expense for $75,000.

(SO7)   17. At the beginning of the year Righter Company purchased for $10,000 a patent with a legal life of 8 years. Righter estimates that the useful life of the patent will be 4 years. Amortization expense on the patent for the year is:
    a. $2,500.
    b. $1,250.
    c. $588.
    d. $250.

(SO8)   18. With respect to capital assets, which of the following must be disclosed in the financial statements or notes to the financial statements?
    a.   The balances of major classes of assets
    b.   Accumulated amortization by major classes of assets
    c.   Amortization methods used
    d.   All of the above must be disclosed

(SO9)   19. On January 3, 2002, Powers Corp. purchased a piece of machinery for $50,000. It has a salvage value of $5,000, an estimated useful life of 9 years, and estimated units of output of 90,000 units. Actual units produced during the first year were 11,000. Amortization expense for 2002 under the units-of-activity method is:
    a. $5,556.
    b. $5,500.
    c. $5,300.
    d. $5,000.

(SO9)   20. On January 4, 2002, Sacks Corporation purchased a piece of equipment for $20,000. It has a salvage value of $4,000 and an estimated useful life of 8 years. Amortization expense for 2002 under the double-declining-balance method is:
    a. $5,000.
    b. $4,000.
    c. $2,000.
    d.   None of the above is the correct amount.

Problems

1. Townsend Corporation owns a piece of machinery it had purchased 3 years ago for $40,000. The machinery has an estimated salvage value of $5,000 and an estimated useful life of 10 years. At the end of 2000, the Accumulated Amortization account had a balance of $10,500. On April 1, 2002, the corporation sold the machinery for $27,000.

REQUIRED: Please record the following journal entries:
   a. The amortization entry on December 31, 2001.
   b. The entry or entries to record the sale on April 1, 2002.

Date	Account Titles	Debit	Credit

c. If Townsend had simply retired the machinery on April 1, then what would the journal entry or entries have been?

Date	Account Titles	Debit	Credit

2. Please refer to Cognos' and JetForm's financial statements at the end of this study guide for information for answering the following questions. Don't forget to use the **Decision Toolkit** approach for help in the problem-solving.

(S08)   a. What line items concerning fixed assets, depreciation and amortization can be found on JetForm's statement of earnings, statement of cash flows, and balance sheet?

(S07,8)   b. In JetForm's annual report, what does Note 1 disclose about fixed assets and intangible assets?

(S08)   c. Is there any more information in JetForm's notes concerning fixed assets and intangible assets?

(S06)   d. In 2000 how successful was Cognos at generating sales from its assets?

SOLUTIONS TO SELF-TEST

Completion

1. capital
2. cost, asset
3. amortizable
4. revenue
5. gain
6. accumulated amortization, amortization expense
7. 40 years
8. copyright
9. 12.5% (100% ÷ 8 years)
10. salvage value

Multiple Choice

1. b $50,000 + $5,000 + $4,000 + $2,000 – $500
2. c Using an expense account is incorrect because the parking lot will benefit future periods, and land does not have a limited useful life, as does a parking lot. Typically a company will not call an account "Parking Lot" but will use "Land Improvements."
3. d $20,000 + $500 + $200 + $1,000
4. a The other three are amortizable.
5. d
6. d ($50,000 - $5,000) ÷ 9 years = $5,000
7. b Straight-line gives an even amount of amortization for each year of an asset's useful life. In the later year of an asset's useful life, straight-line gives higher expense than does declining-balance.
8. c Amortization methods may be changed. A change in estimate never affects prior periods, only current and future periods.
9. a Earnings management involves timing the recognition of gains and losses to achieve certain results. A capital expenditure is money spent on an asset after its purchase. A write-down is what is done when there is an impairment.
10. b Book value is $2,500 ($10,000 – $7,500). Since the proceeds exceed the book value by $500, there is a gain.
11. a Book value is $2,500 ($10,000 – $7,500). Since the book value exceeds the proceeds by $500, there is a loss.
12. d Since the book value is $1,000 ($8,000 – $7,000), there is a Loss on Disposal, and losses are always debited.
13. c Average useful life = average cost of capital assets ÷ amortization expense; $200,000 ÷ $10,000 = 20 years.
14. b Asset turnover ratio = net sales ÷ average total assets; $250,000 ÷ $200,000 = 1.25 times.
15. a A copyright protects literary and artistic works. A trademark is a word, phrase, jingle, or symbol that distinguishes or identifies an enterprise or product. A licence is an operating right.
16. c The money spent for a successful legal defence of an intangible is debited to the asset account. Use of an expense account is inappropriate.
17. a $10,000 ÷ 4 years. The shorter period is used.
18. d
19. b $50,000 – $5,000 = $45,000 ÷ 90,000 units = $0.50/unit
$0.50/unit x 11,000 actual units = $5,500

20. a The double-declining-balance rate is 25% [(100% ÷ 8 years) x 2], and $20,000 x 25% = $5,000.

Problems

1. a. and b.

Dec. 31, 2001	Amortization Expense	3,500	
	Accumulated Amortization		3,500
	(To record annual amortization)		
	$40,000 – $5,000 = $35,000 ÷ 10 years = $3,500		

Apr. 1, 2002	Amortization Expense	875	
	Accumulated Amortization		875
	(To bring amortization up to date)		
	$3,500 annual amortization x 3/12 = $875		

Apr. 1, 2002	Cash	27,000	
	Accumulated Amortization	14,875	
	Machinery		40,000
	Gain on Disposal		1,875
	(To record disposal at a gain)		
	Accumulated Amortization = $10,500 + $3,500 + $875 = $14,875		
	Book value = $40,000 – $14,875 = $25,125		
	Gain = $27,000 – $25,125 = $1,875		

c.

Apr. 1, 2002	Amortization Expense	875	
	Accumulated Amortization		875
	(To bring amortization up to date)		
	$3,500 annual amortization x 3/12 = $875		

Apr. 1, 2002	Loss on Disposal	25,125	
	Accumulated Amortization	14,875	
	Machinery		40,000
	(To record retirement of asset)		
	Accumulated Amortization = $10,500 + $3,500 + $875 = $14,875		
	Book value = $40,000 – $14,875 = $25,125		
	The loss on disposal equals the book value of the machinery.		

2.

   a. Consolidated Statements of Earnings: Depreciation and Amortization, Consolidated Statement of Cash Flows: Depreciation and Amortization, Purchase of Fixed Assets Consolidated Balance Sheet: Fixed Assets.

   b. Note one describes how the fixed assets are recorded and what depreciation and amortization methods are used. It also refers to the periodic management review to determine if there is an impairment in fixed assets.

   c. Notes 3 and 4 provide more detail on the nature of the fixed and intangible assets. The amount of accumulated depreciation and amortization is given for each type of asset.

   d. To answer this question, you must compute the asset turnover ratio, calculated by dividing net sales by average total assets. Average total assets is calculated by adding the asset balance for 1999 and 2000 and dividing by 2.

   Average total assets ($289,129 + $379,886) ÷ 2 = $334,507

   Net Sales $385,640 ÷ 334,507 = 1.15

   This means for every dollar of assets $1.15 of revenue is generated.

NOTES

_____

_____

_____

_____

_____

_____

_____

_____

_____

_____

_____

_____

_____

_____

_____

_____

_____

_____

_____

NOTES

CHAPTER

10

REPORTING AND ANALYSING LIABILITIES

CHAPTER OVERVIEW

Chapter 10 discusses the two basic types of liabilities, current and long-term. In the former category you will learn about notes payable, sales taxes payable, payroll taxes payable, unearned revenues, and current maturities of long-term debt. In the latter category you will learn about bonds: their issuance, payment of interest and amortization of discount or premium, and their redemption. For both categories you will learn about financial statement presentation and analysis. Finally, you will learn about contingent liabilities and lease liabilities.

REVIEW OF SPECIFIC STUDY OBJECTIVES

- A **current liability** is a *debt that can reasonably be expected to be paid from existing current assets or through the creation of other current liabilities within 1 year or the operating cycle*, whichever is longer. A debt that does not meet both criteria is a long-term liability.
- **Current liabilities** include *notes payable, accounts payable, unearned revenues, and accrued liabilities such as taxes, salaries and wages, and interest.* All material current liabilities should be reported on the balance sheet.

STUDY OBJECTIVE

1

Explain what is a current liability and identify the major types of current liabilities.

STUDY OBJECTIVE

2

Describe the accounting
for notes payable.

- **Notes payable** are *obligations in the form of written notes*. They give written documentation of a liability and usually require the borrower to pay interest. If a note is due for payment within 1 year of the balance sheet, then it is classified as a current liability.
- Consider the **following example**. Robinson Co. Ltd. borrows $20,000 and issues a 3-month, 12% note on May 1. The *entry on May* 1 is:

Cash	20,000	
Notes Payable		20,000
(To record issuance of note)		

If Robinson prepares financial statements on June 30, necessitating adjusting entries, then the *adjusting entry* for accrued interest is:

Interest Expense	400	
Interest Payable		400
(To record accrued interest:		
$20,000 x 12% x 2/12)		

On the *maturity date*, August 1, the following entry is recorded:

Notes Payable	20,000	
Interest Payable	400	
Interest Expense	200	
Cash		20,600
(To record payment of note		
plus interest)		

Total interest on the note is $600, and the maturity value is $20,600. The Interest Payable of $400 must be taken off the books since it is no longer payable, and the Interest Expense is the third month's interest ($20,000 x 12% x 1/12).

- There are usually **sales taxes (GST, PST, and/or HST) on items sold**. The retailer serves as a collection agent for the taxing authority, usually the provincial and federal government, and must periodically remit to the government the sales taxes collected. *When an item is sold, the amount of the sale and the amount of each sales tax are usually rung up separately on the cash register.* If $500 of merchandise is sold, and the GST percentage is 7%, and the PST percentage is 8%, then the following entry records the sale:

STUDY OBJECTIVE

3

Explain the accounting for
other current liabilities.

Cash	575	
Sales		500
GST Payable		35
PST Payable		40
(To record sales and sales taxes)		

When these two sales taxes are remitted to the government, the entry is:

GST Payable	35	
PST Payable	40	
Cash		75
(To remit sales taxes to		
tax agencies)		

- If **sales taxes are not rung up separately**, then the *retailer must calculate the dollar amount of sales taxes on the daily sales*. In the above example, if the cash register tape shows $575 of sales, and the sales tax percentage is 7% and 8%, then $575 represents 1.15 times the sales total. To calculate sales, divide $575 by 1.15. This yields $500 of sales. If that amount is deducted from $575, total sales taxes of $75 can then be determined. The sales of $500 can then be multiplied by each respective percentage (7% and 8%) to yield the GST ($500 x 7%) and PST ($500 x 8%) Payable.

- **Every employer incurs liabilities relating to employees' salaries and wages.** Amounts withheld from employees' paycheques, called *withholding taxes*, must be remitted to the appropriate authorities. Withheld amounts include *federal and provincial income taxes, CPP, EI, and other amounts specified by employees such as charitable contributions, union dues, and health insurance.*

- **Every employer also incurs liabilities to pay various payroll taxes levied upon the employer.** An *employer must also contribute CPP (1 x employee's CPP withholdings) and EI (1.4 x employee's EI withholdings).*

- **Payroll and payroll tax liability accounts** are *classified as current liabilities because they must be paid in the very near term.* Employers who do not calculate correctly or remit promptly these amounts face stiff fines and penalties.

- **Corporate income taxes payable** must be estimated and remitted *monthly.*

- **Unearned revenues** arise when *cash is received before goods are delivered or services are performed.* When the cash is received, Cash is debited and Unearned Revenue is credited. When the goods are delivered or services are performed, then Unearned Revenue is debited and Revenue is credited. Unearned revenues are common in the magazine and newspaper industries, in the sports and entertainment industries, and in the travel industry.

- Companies often have **long-term debt of which a portion is due in the current period**. If a company has a 10-year mortgage, then the portion due in the current period must be classified as current. These items are often *identified on the balance sheet as "long-term debt due within 1 year."* No adjusting entry is required: The proper classification is recognized when the balance sheet is prepared.

- **Current liabilities** are the *first category under Liabilities on the balance sheet.* Each of the principal types is listed separately, and important data relating to them are disclosed in the notes to the financial statements.

- A **common method of presenting current liabilities** is to *list them in order of magnitude, with the largest obligations first.*

- **Liquidity ratios** *measure the short-term ability of a company to pay its maturing obligations.* The **current ratio** (current assets divided by current liabilities) and **working capital** (current assets minus current liabilities) are two such measures of liquidity. A **third measure** is the *acid-test, or quick, ratio, calculated by dividing current liabilities into the sum of cash, short-term investments, and net receivables.* These assets are very liquid, and this ratio **measures immediate liquidity.** Because the current ratio denominator includes inventories and prepaid expenses, the current ratio will always be higher than the acid-test ratio.

- **Many companies keep few liquid assets on hand** because they cost too much to hold, and thus, they must rely on other sources of liquidity. A **bank line of credit** is a *prearranged agreement between a company and a lender that permits a company to borrow up to an agreed-upon amount.*

- **Long-term liabilities** are *obligations that are expected to be paid after 1 year.* They are often in the form of *bonds* or *long-term notes.*

- **Bonds** are a *form of interest-bearing note payable issued by corporations, universities, and governmental agencies.* Bonds are used when a corporation or other entity must borrow so much money that one lender does not want to lend the entire amount. Bonds are sold in small denominations (usually $1,000 or multiples of $1,000) and attract many investors.

- **Bonds offer advantages over common shares**: *Shareholder control is not affected* because bondholders do not have voting rights. *Tax savings result* because bond interest is tax-deductible. *Earnings per share (a ratio) may be higher* because no new shares are issued.

- **Disadvantages of bonds** include the fact that *interest payments must be made in good times or bad and principal must be repaid at maturity.*

STUDY OBJECTIVE 4

Identify the requirements for the financial statement presentation and analysis of current liabilities.

STUDY OBJECTIVE 5

Explain why bonds are issued and identify the types of bonds.

- The following are **types of bonds**:
  a) *Secured bonds* have specific assets of the issuer pledged as collateral for the bonds.
  b) *Unsecured bonds* are issued against the general credit of the borrower. These are also called *debenture bonds*.
  c) *Term bonds* are due for payment at a single specified future date.
  d) *Serial bonds* mature in instalments.
  e) *Convertible bonds* may be converted into common shares at the bondholder's option.
  f) *Redeemable (callable) bonds* are subject to retirement at a stated dollar amount prior to maturity at the option of the issuer.
  g) *Retractable bonds* are subject to retirement at a stated dollar amount prior to maturity at the option of the bondholder.

- The **board of directors and shareholders usually must approve issuance of bonds**. The board stipulates the total number of bonds to be authorized, the total face value, and the contractual interest rate.

- The **face value** is the *amount of principal due at the maturity date*. The **contractual interest rate** is the *rate used to determine the amount of cash interest the borrower pays and the investor receives*. The *bond indenture* is the *contract setting out terms of the bond issue*. **Bond certificates** are the *securities themselves* and provide information such as the name of the issuer, the face value, the contractual interest rate, and the maturity date. Bonds are sold through an investment company which underwrites the issue.

- The **current market value (present value)** of a bond is a *function of three factors: the dollar amounts to be received, the length of time until the amounts are received*, and *the market rate of interest*. The **market interest rate** is the *rate investors demand for lending funds to the corporation*. The process of finding the present value (the value at the present time) is referred to as discounting the future amount. The **current market value** of a bond is *equal to the present value of all the future cash payments promised by the bond*, the future cash payments being periodic interest payments and the repayment of principal.

STUDY OBJECTIVE

6

Prepare the entries for the issuance of bonds and interest expense.

- **Bonds may be issued** *at face value, at a discount (below face value), or at a premium (above face value)*.

- **Bond prices** are *quoted as a percentage of the face value of the bond*, such as 97 or 101. If a $1,000 bond sells at 97, then the issuing corporation receives 97% of the face value, or $970. If the bond sells at 101, then the corporation receives $1,010.

- When a **bond sells at face value (the contractual rate of interest equals the market interest rate)**, the journal entry to record the issuance is a *debit to Cash and a credit to Bonds Payable*. When **bond interest is paid**, the *debit is to Bond Interest Expense, and the credit is to Cash*. If **interest is accrued**, then the *debit is to Bond Interest Payable, and the credit is to Bond Interest Payable*. Bonds Payable is reported as a long-term liability, and Bond Interest Payable is a current liability.

- When a bond is issued, if the **contractual rate of interest exceeds the market rate of interest**, then the bond is *issued at a premium*. If the **contractual rate of interest is lower than the market rate of interest**, then the bond is *issued at a discount*.

- Consider the **following example**. A corporation issued $500,000, 5-year, 10% bonds at 96 on January 1, 2002, with interest payable each July and January 1. The **journal entry on January 1, 2002**, is as follows:

Cash ($500,000 x 96%)	480,000	
Discount on Bonds Payable	20,000	
Bonds Payable		500,000
(To record issuance of bonds)		

Note that Bonds Payable is always credited for the face amount of the bonds. **Discount on Bonds Payable** is a *contra account*, deducted from Bonds Payable (a credit and a debit are subtracted one from the other). Right after issuance, the balance sheet presentation of the bond is:

Long-term liabilities:
Bonds payable $500,000
Less: Discount on bonds payable   20,000
                                                 $480,000

The **$480,000 is the carrying (or book) value of the bonds**.

The **discount** is an *additional cost of borrowing and should be recorded as bond interest expense over the life of the bonds*. This is accomplished by *amortizing the bond discount using the straight-line method*. On **July 1, 2002, the following entry is written**:

Bond Interest Expense   27,000
   Cash   25,000
   Discount on Bonds Payable   2,000
   (To record payment of interest and
    amortization of discount)

Cash is calculated as follows: $500,000 × 10% × 6/12
Discount is calculated as follows: $20,000 ÷ 10 interest payment periods (the bond is a 5-year bond which pays interest twice a year).
Bond Interest Expense is simply the sum of the two credits.

On **December 31, 2002, the following entry is written**:

Bond Interest Expense   27,000
   Bond Interest Payable   25,000
   Discount on Bonds Payable   2,000
   (To accrue interest and discount
    amortization)

These **same two entries will be written over the next 4 years**, eventually reducing the balance in the Discount account to zero. On the maturity date, the carrying value of the bonds will be $500,000, their face value, which is correct because that is the amount, which must be paid back on that date.

- Consider the **following example**. A corporation issued $500,000, 5-year, 10% bonds at 102 on January 1, 2002, with interest payable each July and January 1. The **journal entry on January 1, 2002**, is as follows:

Cash ($500,000 × 102%)   510,000
   Premium on Bonds Payable   10,000
   Bonds Payable   500,000
   (To record issuance of bonds)

Note again that Bonds Payable is always credited for the face amount of the bonds. **Premium on Bonds Payable** is an *adjunct account*, added to Bonds Payable (two credits are added together). Right after issuance, the balance sheet presentation of the bond is:

Long-term liabilities:
Bonds payable $500,000
Add: Premium on bonds payable   10,000
                                                 $510,000

The **$510,000 is the carrying (or book) value of the bonds**.

The **premium** is a _reduction in the cost of borrowing and reduces bond interest expense over the life of the bonds_. Just as discount is amortized, so, too, is premium amortized using the straight-line method. On **July 1, 2002, the following entry is written**:

Bond Interest Expense	24,000	
Premium on Bonds Payable	1,000	
Cash		25,000
(To record payment of interest and		
amortization of premium)		

Cash is calculated as follows: $500,000 x 10% x 6/12
    Premium is calculated as follows: $10,000 ÷ 10 interest payment periods (the bond is a 5-year bond which pays interest twice a year).
    Bond Interest Expense is simply the difference between the cash and the premium.

On **December 31, 2002, the following entry is written**:

Bond Interest Expense	24,000	
Premium on Bonds Payable	1,000	
Bond Interest Payable		25,000
(To accrue interest and premium		
amortization)		

These **same two entries will be written over the next 4 years**, eventually reducing the balance in the Premium account to zero. Once again, on the maturity date the carrying value of the bonds will be $500,000, their face value, which is correct because that is the amount which must be paid back on that date.

STUDY OBJECTIVE

7

Describe the entries when bonds are redeemed.

- **At maturity, the book value of bonds equals the face value**, and the journal entry to redeem the bonds involves a debit to Bonds Payable and a credit to Cash.
- If **bonds are redeemed before maturity**, then _the carrying value must be eliminated, cash paid must be recorded_, and _a gain or loss on redemption must be recognized_. If $500,000 of bonds with a carrying value of $496,000 are purchased by the corporation at 101, then the following entry is required:

Bonds Payable	500,000	
Loss on Redemption	9,000	
Discount on Bonds Payable		4,000
Cash		505,000
(To record redemption of bonds)		

Discount is calculated as follows: $500,000 – $496,000

Cash is calculated as follows: $500,000 x 101

Loss is calculated as follows: $505,000 – $496,000

The loss on redemption is reported separately in the statement of earnings. The same is true for a gain on redemption.

STUDY OBJECTIVE

8

Identify the requirements for the financial statement presentation and analysis of long-term liabilities.

- **Long-term liabilities** are _reported in a separate section of the balance sheet_, immediately following Current Liabilities.
- **Solvency ratios** _measure the ability of a company to survive over a long period of time_. One solvency ratio is **debt to total assets**, calculated by _dividing total liabilities by total assets_. Another is the **times interest earned ratio**, calculated by _dividing earnings before interest expense and income tax by interest expense_. This ratio calculates how many times the company has earned

its interest payments in an accounting period, thus providing an indication of a company's ability to meet interest payments as they come due. The cash interest coverage ratio is the same as the times interest earned ratio, except expressed on a cash-basis. It is calculated by dividing earnings before interest, tax, and amortization (EBITDA) expenses by interest expense.

- **Contingent liabilities** are *events with uncertain outcomes*. A classic example of a contingency is a lawsuit, and other contingencies are product warranties and environmental problems. If it is probable that the contingency will occur and the company can *reasonably estimate* the expected loss, then the **company must accrue the loss** by debiting a loss or expense account and crediting a liability account. If *both conditions are not met*, then the **company must disclose the loss in the notes to the financial statements.**

- There are **two types of leases**: *capital and operating*. With an **operating lease**, the lessee simply has rent expense while it uses the lessor's asset. With a **capital lease**, the *lease transfers substantially all the benefits and risks of ownership to the lessee, so that the lease is in effect a purchase of the property*. The lessee capitalizes the fair value of the leased asset by recording it and a related liability on its balance sheet. There are strict criteria for determining if a lease is a capital lease, and lessees, who often do not want to report a lease on their balance sheet, try to structure the lease so that it is an operating lease. This *procedure of keeping liabilities off the balance sheet* is called **off-balance sheet financing**. Such off-balance sheet financing must be considered by a person who is analysing a company.

CHAPTER SELF-TEST

As you work through the exercises and problems, remember to use the **Decision Toolkit** discussed and used in the text:

1. *Decision Checkpoints*: At this point you ask a question.
2. *Info Needed for Decision*: You make a choice regarding the information needed to answer the question.
3. *Tool to Use for Decision*: At this point you review just what the information chosen in step 2 does for the decision-making process.
4. *How to Evaluate Results*: You perform evaluation of information for answering the question.

Note: The notation (SO1) means that the question was drawn from study objective number one.

Matching

Please write the letters of the following terms in the spaces to the left of the definitions.

a. Acid-test (quick) ratio
b. Capital lease
c. Contingencies
d. Contractual interest rate
e. Discount (on a bond)
f. Face value
g. Market interest rate
h. Off-balance sheet financing
i. Operating lease
j. Premium (on a bond)
k. Times interest earned ratio

(SO4)   _____   1. A measure of a company's immediate short-term liquidity.

(SO8)   _____   2. A measure of a company's long-term solvency.

(SO8)   _____   3. Intentional effort by a company to structure its financing arrangements so as to avoid showing liabilities on its books.

(SO6)   _____   4. Occurs when the contractual interest rate of a bond is lower than the market interest rate.

(SO5)   _____   5. Rate used to determine the amount of interest the borrower pays and the investor receives.

(SO8)   _____   6. A type of lease which the lessee accounts for as a rental.

(SO8)   _____   7. Events with uncertain outcomes.

(SO4)   _____   8. The rate investors demand for loaning funds to the corporation.

(SO5)   _____   9. Amount of principal due at a bond's maturity date.

(SO8)   _____   10. A type of lease whose characteristics make it similar to a debt-financed purchase and is consequently accounted for in that fashion.

Multiple Choice

Please circle the correct answer.

(SO1)   1. Which of the following is a criterion for the classification of a liability as current?
   a. It is a debt which can be paid from existing current assets.
   b. It is a debt which can be paid through the creation of other current liabilities.
   c. It must be paid within 1 year or the operating cycle, whichever is longer.
   d. All of the above are criteria for the classification of a liability as current.

(SO2)   2. A corporation issued a $50,000, 9%, 4-month note on July 1. If the corporation's year end is September 30, then the adjusting entry for interest on that date is:

a. Interest Expense	1,125	
Notes Payable		1,125
b. Interest Expense	1,125	
Interest Payable		1,125
c. Interest Expense	1,500	
Notes Payable		1,500
d. Interest Expense	1,500	
Interest Payable		1,500

(SO2)   3. When the corporation in number 2 pays the amount due on the maturity date, the journal entry will include a:
   a. debit to Notes Payable for $51,500.
   b. credit to Cash for $50,000.
   c. debit to Interest Expense for $1,500.
   d. debit to Interest Payable for $1,125.

(SO3)   4. A company's cash register tape shows $1,284 for the day: This number includes the 7%
GST. The dollar amount of sales is:
a. $1,284.
b. $1,200.
c. $1,194 (rounded).
d. $84.00.

(SO3)   5. On November 1, 2002, a company issued a note payable of $50,000, of which $10,000 is
repaid each year. What is the proper classification of this note on the December 31, 2002,
balance sheet?
a. $10,000 current liability; $40,000 long-term liability
b. $50,000 current liability
c. $50,000 long-term liability
d. $10,000 long-term liability; $40,000 current liability

(SO4)   6. Which is a very common way to present current liabilities on the balance sheet?
a. Notes payable are always listed first.
b. Current maturities of long-term debt are always listed first.
c. By order of magnitude
d. By order of maturity date

(SO4)   7. Dividing cash, short-term investments, and net receivables by current liabilities yields
the:
a. debt to total assets ratio.
b. times interest earned ratio.
c. acid-test ratio.
d. current ratio.

(SO5)   8. Bonds which are issued against the general credit of the borrower are called:
a. unsecured bonds.
b. secured bonds.
c. term bonds.
d. redeemable bonds.

(SO5)   9. A corporation issues $1,000,000 of 8%, 5-year bonds. The 8% rate of interest is called the
_____ rate.
a. yield
b. effective
c. market
d. contractual

(SO5)   10. The current market value of a bond is equal to the:
a. present value of the principal only.
b. present value of the principal and the interest payments.
c. present value of interest payments only.
d. face value of the principal only.

(SO6)   11. When the contractual rate of interest exceeds the market rate of interest, the bond sells at:
a. face value.
b. a discount.
c. a premium.
d. some amount other than those listed above.

(SO6)   12. Bonds with a face value of $800,000 and a contractual rate of interest of 8% sold at 98 on January 1. Interest is payable on July 1 and January 1, and the bonds mature in 10 years. On July 1 the dollar amount of discount to be amortized is:
a. $ 800.
b. $1,600.
c. $2,000.
d. $2,400.

(SO6)   13. When calculating the carrying or book value of bonds payable:
a. premium is subtracted from and discount is added to bonds payable.
b. discount is subtracted from and premium is added to bonds payable.
c. both discount and premium are subtracted from bonds payable.
d. both discount and premium are added to bonds payable.

(SO6)   14. Bonds with a face value of $600,000 and a contractual rate of interest of 8% sold at 102 on January 1. Interest is payable on July 1 and January 1, and the bonds mature in 10 years. On July 1 the journal entry to pay interest and record amortization will include a:
a. credit to Cash for $23,400.
b. debit to Premium on Bonds Payable for $1,200.
c. credit to Premium on Bonds Payable for $600.
d. debit to Bond Interest Expense for $23,400.

(SO7)   15. Bonds payable with a face value of $200,000 and a carrying value of $196,000 are redeemed prior to maturity at 102. There is a:
a. loss on redemption of $4,000.
b. gain on redemption of $4,000.
c. loss on redemption of $8,000.
d. gain on redemption of $8,000.

(SO7)   16. A gain or loss on the early redemption of bonds payable is classified as a(n):
a. operating expense on the statement of earnings.
b. extraordinary item on the statement of earnings.
c. other expense or loss or other revenue or gain on the statement of earnings.
d. long-term liability on the balance sheet.

(SO8)   17. A company's total debt is $250,000 while its total assets are $500,000. Earnings before interest expense and income tax is $300,000, and interest expense is $30,000. The company's times interest earned ratio is:
a. 10 times.
b. 2 times.
c. 50%.
d. 10%.

(SO8)   18. Rouse Corporation is being sued by a customer. At the balance sheet date, Rouse's lawyers feel that it is probable that the company will lose the lawsuit and that a reasonable estimate of the loss is $50,000. On the balance sheet date Rouse should:
a. not disclose the lawsuit because a jury has not yet ruled.
b. disclose the lawsuit in the notes to the financial statements.
c. accrue the loss by debiting an expense and crediting a liability.
d. ask for a second opinion from an outside law firm.

(SO8)   19. Some companies finance assets without the liability showing on the balance sheet. This
procedure is called:
a. fraud
b. capital leasing
c. off-balance sheet financing
d. capitalizing

(SO8)   20. The ability of a company to survive over a long period of time is measured by:
a. liquidity ratios
b. solvency ratios
c. profitability ratios
d. cash management ratios

Problems

1. Please record for Jansen Corporation journal entries concerning the following current and
long-term liabilities:
a. On May 1 the corporation issued a 6-month, 12% note in the amount of $20,000. Please
record the adjusting entry for interest on June 30.
b. On June 1 the corporation received $12,000 in advance from a customer who is renting
a small building from Jansen for 12 months. Please record the adjusting entry on June
30.
c. On July 1 the corporation sold $400,000 of 10%, 5-year bonds at 101. The bonds pay
interest every January 1 and July 1.
d. On November 1 the corporation paid the amount due on the $20,000 note payable.
e. On December 31, the company recorded the adjusting entry concerning the transaction
in "b."
f. On December 31, the corporation recorded the adjusting entry for interest and amortization of the bond issued in "c."

Date	Account Titles	Debit	Credit

2. Please refer to both Cognos' and JetForm's financial statements at the end of this study guide for information for answering the following questions. Don't forget to use the **Decision Toolkit** approach for help in the problem-solving.

(SO1)   a. What are Cognos' combined long-term debt and long-term liabilites in 2000, and how much did it increase or decrease from 1999?

(SO1)   b. For Cognos, in 2000 what percentage of total liabilities are current liabilities? For JetForm?

(SO4)   c. In 2000 can JetForm meet its current obligations? (Do not calculate the current ratio: Use a test of immediate liquidity.)

Solutions to Self-Test

Matching

1. a
2. k
3. h
4. e
5. d
6. i
7. c
8. g
9. f
10. b

Multiple Choice

1. d
2. b $\$50,000 \times 9\% \times 3/12$
3. d The journal entry is:

Notes Payable	50,000	
Interest Payable	1,125	
Interest Expense	375	
Cash		51,500

4. b $\$1,284 \div 107\% = \$1,200$

5. a The $10,000 is a current maturity of long-term debt.
6. c
7. c Debt to total assets is total debt divided by total assets. Times interest earned is earnings before interest expense and income taxes divided by interest expense. The current ratio is current assets divided by current liabilities.
8. a Secured bonds are secured by some sort of collateral, term bonds are due at a specific future date, and callable bonds may be repurchased by the issuing corporation before the maturity date.
9. d Yield, effective, and market rates are different terms for the same thing.
10. b Bonds involve two streams of cash flows: principal and interest.
11. c If the rates are the same, then the bond sells at par value. If the contractual rate is lower than the market rate, then the bond sells at a discount.
12. a The journal entry is:

Bond Interest Expense	32,800	
Discount on Bonds Payable		800
Cash		32,000

   Discount amortized = $16,000 ÷ 20 interest payment periods
13. b Premium is added to bonds payable; discount is subtracted from bonds payable.
14. d The journal entry is:

Bond Interest Expense	23,400	
Premium on Bonds Payable	600	
Cash		24,000

   Premium = $12,000 ÷ 20 interest payment periods
   Cash = $600,000 × 8% × 6/12
   Bond Interest Expense = $24,000 − $600
15. c The company had to pay $204,000 for bonds with a carrying value of $196,000. The difference between these two numbers is a loss on redemption.
16. c
17. a The ratio is calculated by dividing earnings before interest expense and income tax by interest expense. In this case, $300,000 ÷ $30,000 = 10 times.
18. c It is simply disclosed in the notes if both conditions (reasonable estimate and probable) are not met. Only if the possibility of loss is remote does the company do nothing.
19. c This procedure is allowed under certain circumstances, capital leases are recorded as liabilities. Off-balance sheet financing should be considered by financial statement analysts.
20. b Liquidity ratios measure short-term viability and profitability ratios measure managements ability to generate profits from assets available.

Problems

1.

a. June 30	Interest Expense	400	
	Interest Payable		400
	(To record interest on note:		
	$20,000 × 12% × 2/12)		
b. June 30	Unearned Revenue	1,000	
	Rent Revenue		1,000
	(To record revenue earned:		
	$12,000 × 1/12)		
c. July 1	Cash	404,000	
	Bonds Payable		400,000
	Premium on Bonds Payable		4,000
	(To record sale of bonds at premium)		

d. Nov. 1	Notes Payable	20,000	
	Interest Payable	400	
	Interest Expense	800	
	Cash		21,200
	(To record payment on note)		

e. Dec. 31	Unearned Revenue	6,000	
	Rent Revenue		6,000
	(To record revenue earned:		
	$12,000 \times 6/12$)		

f. Dec. 31	Bond Interest Expense	19,600	
	Premium on Bonds Payable	400	
	Bond Interest Payable		20,000
	(To accrue bond interest and amortization)		
	Premium = $4,000 \div 10$ interest payment periods		
	Bond Int. Payable = $400,000 \times 10\% \times 6/12$		
	Bond Int. Expense = $20,000 - $400		

2.

  a. Cognos' combined long-term debt and long-term liabilites in 2000 are $2,699. This repre-sents a $5,610 reduction from 1999.
  b. Current liabilities divided by total liabilities
     Cognos: $146,733 \div $164,582 = 89\%$
     JetForm: $43,696 \div $45,034 = 97\%$
  c. To determine this calcuate the quick (acid-test) ratio by dividing cash and cash equivalents and accounts receivable by current liabilities. $63,508 \div 43,696 = 1.45$. This means that JetForm has $1.45 of liquid assets to cover current liabilities.

NOTES

_____

_____

_____

_____

_____

_____

_____

_____

_____

_____

_____

_____

_____

_____

_____

_____

_____

_____

_____

_____

_____

_____

_____

_____

NOTES

11

REPORTING AND ANALYSING SHAREHOLDERS' EQUITY

CHAPTER OVERVIEW

In this chapter you will learn about advantages and disadvantages of the corporate form of business organization. You will learn about the issuance and repurchase of shares and about the mechanics of cash and dividends. After reviewing retained earnings, you will learn how to prepare a comprehensive shareholders' equity section of the balance sheet. Finally, you will learn how to measure corporate performance using various ratios.

REVIEW OF SPECIFIC STUDY OBJECTIVES

- A **corporation** is created by law and thus is a *legal entity* with most of the rights and privileges of a person.
- **Corporations** may be *classified in two ways: by purpose*, such as for-profit or not-for-profit (charitable or medical organizations), and by *ownership* (publicly held, which may have thousands of shareholders, and privately held, which have few shareholders and do not offer shares for sale to the public).

- The following are **characteristics of a corporation**:
    1. **Separate legal existence**, which means that a *corporation acts under its own name and has most of the same rights as does a person*. It may buy, own, or sell property, borrow money, enter into contracts, and sue or be sued, and it pays its own taxes.
    2. **Limited liability of shareholders**, which means that the *liability of shareholders is generally limited to the amount of their investment*. Shareholders' personal assets are not at risk unless fraud has occurred.
    3. **Transferable ownership rights**, which means that a *shareholder may buy or sell shares without approval of the corporation or other shareholders*.
    4. **Ability to acquire capital**, resulting from the *issuance of its shares*.
    5. **Continuous life**, which means that the *life of the corporation is not affected by the withdrawal, death, or incapacity of a shareholder, employee, or officer*.
    6. **Management which is separate from the owners**, meaning that *shareholders manage the company indirectly through the board of directors*. While professional managers may be hired, some view the separation of ownership and management in a negative fashion.
    7. **Government regulation**, both *by federal and provincial governments*, which can be burdensome from both time and money standpoints.
    8. **Additional taxes**, resulting from the fact that the *corporation pays taxes on its income and shareholders pay taxes on dividends received from the corporation*.

- Characteristics 1 through 5 are usually viewed as advantages; characteristics 6 through 8 are usually viewed as disadvantages. The advantages can sometimes be disadvantages, and vice versa. For example, taxation in the corporate form of organization can sometimes be an advantage, if a corporation is eligible for certain tax incentives.

- A **corporation** is *incorporated under The Canadian Business Corporation Act or provincial acts*. Corporations which operate interprovincially must obtain licences from each province where the corporation does business. After incorporating its charter, the corporation establishes by-laws for conducting its affairs.

- A **corporation may sell ownership rights** in the form of share capital. If it has only one class of shares, then that class is **common shares**. *Each common shareholder has the following rights*:
    1. The **right to participate in management** by electing the board of directors and voting on matters requiring shareholder approval.
    2. The **right to share in corporate earnings** through receipt of dividends.
    3. The **right to maintain the same percentage ownership when new shares are issued** (called the preemptive right, eliminated by many corporations because they view it as unnecessary and cumbersome).
    4. The **right to share in distribution of assets upon liquidation of the corporation**.

- A **share certificate** is a *printed or engraved form which is proof of share ownership*. Share purchases or sales are often "book transactions," and owners rarely hold the share certificates. Instead, brokerage firms store the certificates for the shareholders.

- **Authorized share capital** is just that: *Shares that the company may sell as authorized by the corporation act which grants the corporate charter*. If a company wishes to sell more than the authorized amount, then it must amend its charter. A corporate charter may also specify an unlimited amount of authorized share capital. No formal journal entry is required for authorized shares, but the number of shares authorized must be disclosed in the shareholders' equity section of the balance sheet.

- A **corporation may sell its share capital** *either directly to investors or indirectly through an investment banking firm*. Shares are traded on stock exchanges, such as the Toronto Stock Exchange.

- **Par value shares** are *share capital that has been assigned a value per share in the corporate charter*. Par value is an **arbitrary amount which has absolutely nothing to do with the fair market value of the share**. Share capital with a par value of a nickel may sell for $100 per share on a given trading day. Par value is usually set at a low amount because provinces often tax a corporation based on its par value. **Par value has legal significance**: It *represents* *the legal capital per share that must be retained in the business for the protection of corporate creditors.* Federally incorporated companies are prohibited from issuing par value shares because of the arbitrariness of the amount.

- **No-par value shares** are *share capital that has not been assigned a value in the corporate charter.* Most companies in Canada now issue no-par value share capital. With no-par value shares the *entire proceeds of the sale* of such shares are considered to be *legal capital per share.*
- In many provinces the board of directors is allowed to assign a **stated value** to no-par value shares It then *becomes the legal capital per share.* The board may change the stated value at any time.
- A **critical point to remember** is that *legal capital per share always establishes the credit to the Common Shares account* when share capital is issued.

- Remember that **shareholders' equity in a corporation** consists of *two parts*:
  1. *Share (contributed) capital,* the amount contributed to the corporation by shareholders in exchange for shares of ownership; and
  2. *Retained earnings (earned capital),* held for future use in the business.
- **The issuance of no par value common shares** *affects only the Common Shares (share capital) account.* The entire proceeds is considered to be legal capital of the no-par value shares. If 100 no par value common shares are sold for $5 per share, then the journal entry is:

STUDY OBJECTIVE

Record the issuance of common shares.

Cash	500	
Common Shares		500
(To record sale of 100 no par value common shares for $5 per share)		

If another 100 no par value common shares are sold for $7 per share, then the journal entry is:

Cash	700	
Common Shares		500
(To record sale of 100 no par value common shares for $7 per share)		

Note in each case the Common Shares account is credited with the entire proceeds of the role.

- **Preferred shares** have contractual provisions that give it *preference or priority over common shares in certain areas,* usually in relation to dividends and to assets in the event of liquidation. Preferred shares usually have no voting rights. If a corporation issues 500 no par value preferred shares for $30 per share, then the journal entry is:

STUDY OBJECTIVE

Differentiate preferred shares from common shares.

Cash	15,000	
Preferred Shares		15,000
(To record sale of 500 shares at $30 per share)		

- **Preferred shares** are *listed before common shares on the balance sheet* because of its preferences in the areas of dividends and liquidation.
- **Preferred shares have priority over common shares in the matter of dividends.** This does not guarantee that preferred shares will always receive the dividend. The dividend amount is a stated amount per share; e.g. $5 preferred shares.
- If preferred shares are **cumulative**, then *any dividend that has not been declared and paid is not forever lost.* When the corporation has money again for dividends, it must first pay the prior year's or years' dividends before the current year's dividends are paid. Preferred dividends not declared in a given period are called *dividends in arrears* and *should be disclosed in the notes* to the financial statements. Dividends in arrears are *not a liability*: No obligation exists until the board of directors declares the dividend. If a corporation must pay its preferred shareholders $10,000 a year in dividends and has not paid dividends in the past

two years, and if it has $50,000 for dividend distribution in the current year, then the distribution will be:

Preferred dividends in arrears	$20,000
Preferred dividends—current year	10,000
Common dividends	20,000
Total dividends distributed	$50,000

The common shareholders simply receive the difference between the total of $50,000 and the $30,000 which must be distributed to the preferred shareholders.

- If preferred shares are **noncumulative**, then *any dividend not declared and paid is forever lost.* Since this is very unattractive to investors, most companies do not issue noncumulative preferred shares.

- **Preferred shareholders** also have a *preference in the event of liquidation of the corporation.* Creditors must be paid first, then preferred shareholders, then common shareholders. The preference may be for the legal capital value of the shares or for a specified liquidating value.

- Convertible preferred shares allow the shareholder to exchange preferred shares into common shares at a specified ratio.

- **Redeemable (callable) preferred shares** offer an option for the corporation to repurchase its shares from the shareholder in the future. **Retractable preferred shares** offer the option to the shareholder to resell its shares to the corporation in the future.

- A company may require its own shares on the open market. These shares must be cancelled and restored to the status of authorized but unissued shares.

STUDY OBJECTIVE

Prepare the entries for
cash dividends and stock
dividends.

- A **dividend** is a *distribution by a corporation to its shareholders on a pro rata basis.* Dividends may be in the form of cash, property, script (promissory note to pay cash), or shares.

- To pay a **cash dividend**, a corporation must have *retained earnings, adequate cash, and dividends declared by the board of directors.* While many companies pay a quarterly dividend, there are companies, called growth companies, which pay no dividends but reinvest earnings in the company so that it can grow.

- There are **three dates of importance for all dividends**: *date of declaration, date of record,* and *date of payment.* Journal entries are required on the first and third dates. For a **cash dividend**, the journal entry on the *date of declaration* will be as follows if a corporation declares a $0.25 per share cash dividend on 100,000 shares:

Cash Dividends (or Retained Earnings)	25,000	
Dividends Payable		25,000
(To declare a cash dividend of $0.25		
per share on 100,000 shares)		

Dividends Payable is a current liability. It will normally be paid within the next month.

On the **date of record**, *ownership of the outstanding shares is determined for dividend purposes.* No journal entry is required.

On the **date of payment**, the following entry is required:

Dividends Payable	25,000	
Cash		25,000
(To record payment of cash dividend)		

Declaration and payment of a cash dividend reduce both shareholders' equity and total assets.

A **stock dividend** is a *pro rata distribution of the corporation's own shares to shareholders.* A stock dividend results in *a decrease in retained earnings and an increase in share capital. Total shareholders' equity will remain the same* because dollar amounts are simply transferred from retained earnings to share capital accounts. A stock dividend is interesting because an investor really receives nothing extra on the day he receives the shares: His ownership percentage has not changed. In the future, however, if the share price rises, he will have more shares on which there may be price appreciation.

Corporations issue stock dividends for various reasons:
1. To *satisfy shareholders' dividend expectations without spending cash.*
2. To *increase the marketability of the shares by reducing the price per share.*
3. To *emphasize that a portion of equity has been permanently reinvested in the business and is unavailable for cash dividends.*

Consider the **following example of a stock dividend**. A corporation has outstanding 500,000 common shares on the day on which the board of directors declares a 10% stock dividend. The fair market value of the shares is $30 per share. Fifty thousand new shares (500,000 x 10%) will be issued. The journal entry on the **date of declaration** is:

Stock Dividends (or Retained Earnings)   1,500,000
    Common Stock Dividends Distributable   1,500,000
        The calculation is as follows: 50,000 shares x $30 = $1,500,000

Common Stock Dividends Distributable is a *shareholders' equity account*. If a balance sheet is prepared after the dividend declaration, then the account will appear directly under the Common Shares account in the share capital section.

On the **date of payment**, the journal entry is:

Common Stock Dividends
Distributable   1,500,000
    Common Shares   1,500,000
(To record distribution of stock dividend)

Like a stock dividend, a **stock split** involves the *issuance of additional shares to shareholders according to their percentage ownership.* Unlike a stock dividend, however, a stock split *results in a reduction in the legal capital per share and is usually much larger than a stock dividend.* The **purpose of a stock split** is to *increase the marketability of the shares by lowering the market value per share.* A corporation has 200,000 common shares outstanding; the market price of the shares is $100 per share. The corporation declares a 2-for-1 stock split. The number of shares will double to 400,000 the market price will be reduced by half, to $50 per share. Note that the Common Shares account has $1,000,000 in it both before and after the split. A stock split *has no effect on total share capital, retained earnings, and total shareholders' equity,* and no journal entry is required to record it.

- **Retained earnings** are *net earnings that are retained in the business and part of the shareholders' claim on the total assets of the corporation.* Just as net earnings is credited to the Retained Earnings account, so net loss is debited to the account, even if an overall debit balance in the account results. A *debit balance in Retained Earnings* is called a **deficit** and is reported as a deduction in the shareholders' equity section of the balance sheet.

- The **balance in retained earnings** is generally *available for dividend declarations.* There may be **retained earnings restrictions** which *make a portion of the balance currently unavailable for dividends.* Restrictions result from legal, contractual, or voluntary causes and are *usually disclosed in the notes* to the financial statements.

- **Share capital and retained earnings are reported**, and the *specific sources of share capital are identified.* Share capital consists of preferred and common shares. Additional share capital includes the excess of amounts paid in over par or stated value, if any.

STUDY OBJECTIVE 5

Identify the items that affect retained earnings.

STUDY OBJECTIVE 6

Prepare a comprehensive shareholders' equity section.

STUDY OBJECTIVE

7

Evaluate a corporation's dividend and earnings performance from a shareholder's perspective.

- To **measure a corporation's dividend record**, an investor can _calculate the payout ratio and the dividend yield._

- The **payout ratio** _measures the percentage of earnings distributed in the form of cash dividends to common shareholders._ It is calculated by _dividing total cash dividends to common shareholders by net earnings._ The **dividend yield** _reports the rate of return an investor earned from dividends during the year._ It is calculated by _dividing dividends declared per share by the share price at the end of the year._ A company with a high growth rate typically has a low payout ratio and dividend yield because it reinvests earnings in the business.

- To **measure a corporation's earnings performance**, an investor _can calculate earnings per share and the price-earnings ratio._

- **Earnings per share** _measures the net earnings earned on each common share._ It is calculated by _dividing net earnings available to common shareholders (net earnings minus preferred share dividends) by the average number of common shares outstanding during the year._ Comparisons of earnings per share across companies are not meaningful because of the wide variations in numbers of shares outstanding and the market price per share.

- The **price-earnings ratio** _measures the ratio of the market price of each common share to the earnings per share._ It is calculated by _dividing the market price per share by earnings per share._ The price-earnings (P-E) ratio reflects the investors' assessment of a company's future earnings and helps to make meaningful comparisons of earnings across firms.

- The **return on shareholders' equity ratio** _shows how many dollars were earned for each dollar invested by common shareholders._ It is calculated by _dividing net earnings available to common shareholders (net earnings minus preferred share dividends) by average common shareholders' equity._

CHAPTER SELF-TEST

As you work the exercises and problems, remember to use the **Decision Toolkit** discussed and used in the text:

1. *Decision Checkpoints:* At this point you ask a question.
2. *Info Needed for Decision*: You make a choice regarding the information needed to answer the question.
3. *Tool to Use for Decision*: At this point you review just what the information chosen in step 2 does for the decision-making process.
4. *How to Evaluate Results*: You perform evaluation of information for answering the question.

Note: The notation (SO1) means that the question was drawn from study objective number one.

Completion

Please write in the word or words which will complete the sentence.

(SO1) 1. A _____ _____ corporation may have thousands of shareholders, and its shares are traded on a securities market.

(SO1) 2. The number of shares which a corporation is permitted to sell, as listed in the corporate charter, is called _____ shares.

(SO2) 3. The issuance of no par value common shares affects only _____ _____ accounts.

(SO2) 4. Preferred shares that have rights to unpaid dividends are called _____ preferred shares.

(SO3) 5. _____ shareholders have the right to receive dividends before _____ shareholders do.

(SO4) 6. For dividend purposes, a corporation determines ownership of outstanding shares on the date of _____.

(SO4) 7. A _____ occurs when new shares are issued as a ratio of the outstanding shares.

(SO5) 8. A debit balance in the Retained Earnings account is called a _____.

(SO6) 9. There are two classifications within shareholders' equity: _____ _____ and _____ _____.

(SO7) 10. If the dividend paid per share is $1.00 and the share price at the end of the year is $80.00, then the dividend yield is _____.

Multiple Choice

Please circle the correct answer.

(SO1) 1. Which of the following is considered to be a disadvantage of the corporate form of business organization?
   a. Limited liability of shareholders
   b. Separate legal existence
   c. Continuous life
   d. Provincial and federal government regulation

(SO1)   2. Share capital which has not been assigned a value per share in the corporate charter is called:
a. legal capital shares.
b. par value shares.
c. no par value shares.
d. stated value shares.

(SO1)   3. The amount per share which must be retained in the business for the protection of corporate creditors is called:
a. legal capital.
b. par value.
c. market value.
d. stated value.

(SO2)   4. If 3,000 no par value common shares are sold for $6 per share, then the journal entry includes a:
a. credit to Additional Contributed Capital for $18,000.
b. credit to Cash for $18,000.
c. credit to Retained Earnings for $18,000.
d. credit to Common Shares for $18,000.

(SO2)   5. If the Common Shares account has a balance of $23,000, and Retained Earnings has a balance of $40,000, then total shareholders' equity is:
a. $63,000.
b. $60,000.
c. $57,000.
d. $17,000.

(SO3)   6. A corporation has cumulative preferred shares on which it must pay dividends of $20,000 per year. The dividends are in arrears for two years. If the corporation has in the current year $90,000 available for dividends, then the common shareholders will receive:
a. $20,000.
b. $30,000.
c. $40,000.
d. $60,000.

(SO3)   7. Which of the following statements is incorrect?
a. Dividends cannot be paid to common shareholders while any dividend on preferred shares is in arrears.
b. Dividends in arrears on preferred are not considered a liability.
c. Dividends may be paid on common shares while dividends are in arrears on preferred shares.
d. When preferred shares are noncumulative, any dividend passed in a year is lost forever.

(SO4)   8. On December 1, a corporation has declared a $1.00 cash dividend per share on its 500,000 common shares. The journal entry on the date of payment of the dividend, December 20, includes a debit to:
a. Dividends Payable for $500,000.
b. Cash Dividends for $500,000.
c. Cash for $500,000.
d. Common Shares Dividends Distributable for $500,000.

(SO4)   9. A corporation is authorized to sell 1,000,000 common shares. Today there are 500,000 shares outstanding, and the board of directors declares a 10% stock dividend. How many new shares will ultimately be issued as a result of the stock dividend?
   a. 100,000
   b. 50,000
   c. None. The corporation will pay the dividend in cash.
   d. None of the above is correct.

(SO4)   10. The board of directors of a corporation declares a 5% stock dividend while there are 20,000 no par value common shares outstanding. On this day, the fair market value of each share is $40. The journal entry to declare the stock dividend includes a:
   a. debit to Retained Earnings for $1,000.
   b. debit to Cash for $40,000.
   c. credit to Common Stock Dividends Distributable for $40,000.
   d. credit to Common Shares for $40,000.

(SO4)   11. A corporation has outstanding 100,000 common shares with a fair market value of $80 per share. If the board of directors declares a 2-for-1 stock split, then:
   a. the number of shares doubles and the fair market value decreases to $40.
   b. the number of shares and fair market value remain the same.
   c. the number of shares halves and the fair market value doubles.
   d. the number of shares and fair market value both halve.

(SO5)   12. If a corporation has incurred a net loss, then the loss is:
   a. debited to Retained Earnings in a closing entry.
   b. credited to Retained Earnings in a closing entry.
   c. debited to a share capital in a closing entry.
   d. credited to a share capital in a closing entry.

(SO5)   13. A retained earnings restriction:
   a. makes a portion of the balance of retained earnings unavailable for dividends.
   b. may arise from legal, contractual, or voluntary causes.
   c. generally is disclosed in the notes to the financial statements.
   d. All of the above are correct.

(SO6)   14. A corporation shows the following account balances:

Retained Earnings	$10,000
Common Shares Dividends Distributable	20,000
Common Shares	255,000

What is total shareholders' equity?
   a. $245,000
   b. $255,000
   c. $275,000
   d. $285,000

(SO7)   15. Consider the following data for a corporation:

Net earnings	$800,000
Preferred dividends	$ 50,000
Market price per share	$25
Average common shares outstanding	500,000

What is earnings per share?
a. $1.50
b. $1.60
c. $0.625
d. $0.667

(SO7)   16. Using the data in number 17, what is the price-earnings ratio?
a. 1.5 times
b. 1.6 times
c. 15.6 times
d. 16.7 times

Problems

1. Windsor Corporation shows the following data:

Common shares, 500,000 no par value shares	
authorized, 300,000 shares issued	$1,700,000
Retained earnings	3,200,000

REQUIRED: Please journalize the following transactions:
a. Sold 10,000 common shares for $9 per share (SO2).
b. Declared and distributed a 15% stock dividend. The fair market value of the shares on this date was $12 per share (SO5).
c. Sold 8,000 common shares for $15 per share (SO2).
d. Declared a 2-for-1 stock split. On this date the fair market value of the shares was $18 per share (SO5).
e. Declared and paid a $0.10 per share cash dividend (SO5).

Date	Account Titles	Debit	Credit

2. Please refer to Cognos' and JetForm's financial statements at the end of this study guide for information for answering the following questions. Don't forget to use the **Decision Toolkit** approach for help in the problem-solving.

(S01, S02) a. What type of shares do Cognos and JetForm have?

(S01, S02) b. On which financial statements is there information about shares?

(SO3) c. Are JetForm's preference shares cumulative or non-cumulative. Explain the difference.

(SO7) d. What is Cogno's basic earnings per share for the three years reported?

SOLUTIONS TO SELF-TEST

Completion

1. publicly held
2. authorized
3. share capital
4. cumulative
5. Preferred, common
6. record
7. stock dividend
8. deficit
9. share capital, retained earnings
10. 1.25% ($1.00 ÷ $80.00)

Multiple Choice

1. d The other three are considered to be advantages.
2. c There is no such thing as legal capital shares. Par value shares have a specified (legal) value. Stated value shares are no par value shares assigned a stated value by the board of directors.
3. a Par value is an arbitrary amount listed in the corporate charter, and market value is the selling price of a shares on a given day. Stated value is a value assigned to no par value shares by the board of directors. The legal capital is whatever is specified in the corporate charter, or by the board of directors—par value, no par value, or stated value.
4. d The journal entry is:

Cash	18,000	
Common Shares		18,000

5. a $23,000 + $40,000 = $63,000
6. b Preferred receives $20,000 for each of the past two years and $20,000 in the current year for a total of $60,000; common receives the difference of $90,000 and $60,000.
7. c Dividends may not be paid on common shares as long as preferred dividends are in arrears.
8. a The journal entry is:

Dividends Payable	500,000	
Cash		500,000

9. b 500,000 shares x 10% = 50,000 new shares
10. c The journal entry is:

Retained Earnings or Stock Dividend	40,000	
Common Stock Div. Distributable		40,000

    20,000 x 5% = 1,000 new shares; 1,000 x $40 fair market value = $40,000
11. a With a 2-for-1 stock split, one old share is exchanged for two new ones. The number of shares double (200,000) and fair market value is reduced by half ($40).
12. a A loss reduces Retained Earnings, requiring a debit to that account, and it is never closed to a share capital account.
13. d
14. d $10,000 + $20,000 + $255,000 = $285,000
15. a   ($800,000 – $50,000) ÷ 500,000 shares = $1.50
16. d $25.00 ÷ $1.50 = 16.7

Problems

1.

a. Cash   90,000

    Common Shares   90,000

    (To record issuance of shares —10,000

    shares at $9 per share)

b. Retained Earnings or Stock Dividend   558,000

    Common Stock Div. Distributable   558,000

    (To record declaration of stock dividend)

    Common Stock Dividends Distributable   558,000

    Common Shares   558,000

    (To distribute stock dividend)

    310,000 shares x 15% = 46,500 new shares x $12 fair market value per share = $558,000

c. Cash   120,000

    Common Shares   120,000

    (To record issuance of shares —8,000

    shares at $15 per share)

d. No entry required. The number of shares outstanding at this point, 364,500 (300,000 + 10,000 + 46,500 + 8,000), doubles to 729,000. The fair market value will be cut in half, $9.

e. Retained Earnings or Cash Dividend   72,900

    Dividends Payable   72,900

    (To declare a $0.10 per share cash

    dividend)

    Dividends Payable   72,900

    Cash   72,900

    (To pay the cash dividend)

    729,000 shares x $0.10 per share = $72,900.

2.

a. Cognos: Common Shares

    JetForm: Common and Preferred Shares

b. Balance Sheet, Statement of Shareholders' Equity and Statement of Cash Flow

c. The shares are non-cumulative. Note 7 describes the rights of the preferred shareholders. If the shares were cumulative the shareholders would have a right to both current year dividends as well as any prior years unpaid dividends.

d. From the Consolidated Statements of Income, 1998 $0.37, 1999 $0.67, 2000 $0.68.

<u>NOTES</u>

CHAPTER

12

REPORTING AND ANALYSING INVESTMENTS

CHAPTER OVERVIEW

In this chapter you will learn about the reasons that corporations invest in debt and equity securities and how to account for both. You will learn how debt and equity investments are valued and reported in the financial statements and, finally, how to distinguish between short-term and long-term investments.

REVIEW OF SPECIFIC STUDY OBJECTIVES

- **Corporations invest in debt or equity securities** for one of three reasons:

  1. They *have excess cash* that they do not need for immediate purposes. Excess cash may result from seasonal fluctuations in sales or from economic cycles. Excess cash is usually invested in low-risk, highly liquid securities, most often short-term government securities.

  2. Some companies *generate a significant portion of their earnings from investment income.*

  3. There may be *strategic reasons*, such as a corporation's desire to establish a presence in another company or to purchase a controlling interest in another company. A **vertical acquisition** is the *purchase of another company in the same industry*

STUDY OBJECTIVE

1

Identify the reasons corporations invest in debt and equity securities.

but which is involved in another activity. A **horizontal acquisition** is the *purchase of another company which performs the same activity as the purchasing company.*

- **Debt investments** are *investments in government and corporation bonds.*
- **Acquisition costs** include *all expenditures necessary to acquire the investment, such as the price paid plus brokerage fees (commissions).* If a company **purchases bonds for $60,000 plus a commission of $2,000**, then the journal entry is:

Debt Investments	62,000	
Cash		62,000
(To record purchase of bonds)		

Note that *there is no separate account for fees or commissions:* The purchase price and the commission are debited to the asset account.

- When **bond interest is received**, the debit is to Cash and the credit is to Interest Revenue (an Other Revenues and Gains item on the statement of earnings). If interest is accrued, then the entry is a debit to Interest Receivable and a credit to Interest Revenue.
- When **bonds are sold**, *any difference between net proceeds (sales price less fees) and the cost of the bonds is recorded as a gain or loss.* If **bonds with a cost of $20,000 are sold for a net amount of $18,000**, then the entry is as follows:

Cash	18,000	
Loss on Sale of Debt Investments	2,000	
Debt Investments		20,000
(To record sale of bonds at a loss)		

The **Loss account** appears *on the statement of earnings as an Other Expenses and Losses item.* A **gain** appears *on the statement of earnings as an Other Revenues and Gains item.*

- **Equity investments** are *investments in the share capital of corporations.* An **investment portfolio** consists of *securities (shares and/or debt) of several different corporations.*
- **Accounting for equity investments** is *based on the extent of the investor's influence over the operating and financial affairs of the issuing corporation (the investee).* **Guidelines are as follows**:
  1. If the **investor holds less than 20% of the investee's shares**, then there is an insignificant influence on the investee, and the *cost method* is used.
  2. If the **investor holds between 20% and 50% of the investee's shares**, then there is a presumption of significant influence on the investee, and the *equity method* is used.
  3. If the **investor holds more than 50% of the investee's shares**, then the investor has a controlling influence. The equity method is used for accounting and *consolidated financial statements* are prepared for reporting purposes.
- For **holdings less than 20%**, the cost method is used. The *investment is recorded at cost, and revenue is recognized only when dividends are received.* As is true for debt investments, cost includes all expenditures necessary to acquire the investments, including the price paid plus brokerage fees (commissions). If **a corporation acquires 2,000 common shares at $50 per share plus $2,000 in commissions**, then the journal entry is:

Equity Investments	102,000	
Cash		102,000
(To record purchase of common shares)		

Note that once again *there is no separate account for fees or commissions:* The purchase price and the commissions are debited to the asset account.

If **dividends of $3.00 per share are received**, then the journal entry is:

Cash	6,000	
Dividend Revenue		6,000
(To record receipt of dividends: 2,000 x $3 = $6,000)		

Dividend Revenue is reported separately, often in an *Other Revenues and Gains section in the statement of earnings.*

If **the shares are sold** for net proceeds of $105,000, then the journal entry is:

Cash	105,000	
Equity Investments		102,000
Gain on Sale of Equity		
Investments		3,000
(To record sale of common shares)		

A **loss account** appears *on the statement of earnings as an Other Expenses and Losses item.* A **gain** appears *on the statement of earnings as an Other Revenues and Gains item.*

- For **holdings of more than 20%**, *the equity method is used if significant influence exists. The investment is recorded initially at cost* and is *adjusted annually to show the investor's equity in the investee.* The investor debits the investment account and increases revenue for its share of the investee's net earnings. The investor debits Cash and credits the investment account for the amount of dividends received. With this method, the **investor is essentially purchasing part of the investee's Retained Earnings account.** Anything which makes that account increase, such as net earnings, is reflected in the investor's investment account as an increase, and anything which makes that account decrease, such as net loss or payment of dividends, is reflected in the investor's investment account as a decrease.

Reiher Corporation purchased 40% of the common shares of Ott Corporation for $250,000. The journal entry is:

Equity Investments	250,000	
Cash		250,000
(To record purchase of Ott shares)		

For the year, **Ott reported $200,000 of net earnings and paid dividends of $50,000.** The journal entries for Reiher are:

Equity Investments	80,000	
Revenue from Investment		
in Ott Corporation		80,000
(To record 40% equity in Ott's earnings: $200,000 x 40% = $80,000)		

Cash	20,000	
Equity Investments		20,000
(To record dividends received: $50,000 x 40% = $20,000)		

After these entries, the **balance in Equity Investments totals $310,000**:
$250,000 + $80,000 – $20,000.

- A **parent company** is a *company who controls, or owns more than 50% of, the common shares of another entity.* A **subsidiary (affiliated) company** is the *entity whose shares are owned by the parent company.* The parent company has a **controlling interest** in the subsidiary company.

STUDY OBJECTIVE

Describe the purpose and usefulness of consolidated financial statements.

- **Consolidated financial statements** are prepared. These statements *present the assets and liabilities controlled by the parent company and the aggregate profitability of the subsidiary companies.* They are presented in addition to the financial statements for each of the individual parent and subsidiary companies.
- **Consolidated financial statements** are *especially useful to the shareholders, board of directors, and management of the parent company.*

STUDY OBJECTIVE

5

Distinguish between short-term and long-term investments.

- For balance sheet presentation, **investments must be classified as either short-term or long-term**.
- **Short-term investments** are those which are *readily marketable* (can be sold easily whenever the need for cash arises) *and intended to be converted into cash within the next year or operating cycle, whichever is longer.* Short-term investments are **listed immediately below Cash or combined with Cash (as Cash Equivalents) on the balance sheet** because of their high liquidity (nearness to cash).
- **Long-term investments** are *reported in a separate section of the balance sheet immediately below current assets.*
- In the statement of earnings, **gains and losses, as well as interest and dividend revenue**, are *reported in the nonoperating section.* On the balance sheet, investments must be classified as either short- or long-term.

STUDY OBJECTIVE

6

Indicate how debt and equity investments are valued and reported in the financial statements.

- Investments are valued and reported at the **lower of cost and market (LCM)**. The application of this rule depends on whether the investments are classified as short-term or long-term.
- **Short-term investments**: The lower of cost and market value rule is applied to the total (not individual) investment portfolio at the end of the period. The investments are reported at cost unless market is lower. If market values are lower than cost, the loss in the decline in the value of the investments is recognized in the period of decline (an example of **conservatism**). The difference between the cost and market values is debited to a loss account and credited to a contra asset account, Allowance to Reduce Cost to Market Value.
- In a subsequent period, if the market value recovers above cost, the Allowance account would be written up to a nil value. In no circumstances, are short-term investments ever reported at an amount greater than cost.
- Because of the importance of market values, both cost and market values are reported for short-term investments in the current asset section of the balance sheet.
- **Long-term investments**: The lower of cost and market value rule is applied to individual investments, not the total portfolio. Investments are reported at cost unless market is lower and the **decline is permanent**. Long-term investments are not written down for short-term fluctuations in market values.
- If market values are lower than cost, the permanent loss in the decline in the value of the long-term investments is debited to a loss account and credited directly to the investment account. No contra asset account is used, because recovery in value is not anticipated.
- Classification of investments as short-term or long-term can help a company manage gains and losses. Such **window-dressing of earnings** often makes it difficult for an outsider to determine why companies choose to sell or hold a security, or classify it as they do.

CHAPTER SELF-TEST

As you work the exercises and problems, remember to use the **Decision Toolkit** discussed and used in the text:
1. *Decision Checkpoints*: At this point you ask a question.
2. *Info Needed for Decision*: You make a choice regarding the information needed to answer the question.
3. *Tool to Use for Decision*: At this point you review just what the information chosen in step 2 does for the decision-making process.
4. *How to Evaluate Results*: You perform evaluation of information for answering the question.

Note: The notation (SO1) means that the question was drawn from study objective number one.

Matching

Please write the letters of the following terms in the spaces to the left of the definitions.
a. Consolidated financial statements
b. Cost method
c. Equity method
d. Long-term investments
e. Parent company
f. Short-term investments
g. Subsidiary (affiliated) company
h. Lower of cost and market

(SO4)   _____ 1. A company that controls the common shares of another entity.

(SO4)   _____ 2. Financial statements which present the assets and liabilities controlled by the parent company and the aggregate profitability of the affiliated companies.

(SO3)   _____ 3. Method in which the investment in common shares is recorded at cost and revenue is recognized only when cash dividends are received.

(SO4)   _____ 4. A company whose shares are controlled by another company.

(SO5)   _____ 5. Investments that are not readily marketable or that management does not intend to convert into cash within the next year or operating cycle, whichever is longer.

(SO5)   _____ 6. Investments which are readily marketable and intended to be converted into cash within the next year or operating cycle, whichever is longer.

(SO3)   _____ 7. Method in which the investment in common shares is recorded at cost, and the investment account is then adjusted periodically to show the investor's equity in the investee.

(SO6)   _____ 8. Investments are valued using this rule, an application of conservatism, at year-end.

Multiple Choice

Please circle the correct answer.

(SO1)   1. If a corporation purchases a company in its industry but which is involved in a different activity, then the acquisition is a:
a. horizontal acquisition.
b. vertical acquisition.
c. leveraged acquisition.
d. equity acquisition.

(SO2)   2. Meyers Corporation acquired 20 of New Company's 5-year, 10%, $1,000 bonds for $22,000. Brokerage fees were $500. The entry to record the acquisition of the bonds includes a debit to:
a. Brokerage Fee Expense for $500.
b. Debt Investments for $22,000.
c. Debt Investments for $22,500.
d. Cash for $22,500.

(SO2)   3. Meyers Corporation sells its New Company bonds (from number 2 above) for $25,000. The journal entry to record the sale includes a:
a. credit to Debt Investments for $25,000.
b. credit to Cash for $25,000.
c. debit to Loss on Sale of Debt Investments for $2,500.
d. credit to Gain on Sale of Debt Investments for $2,500.

(SO3)   4. Mack Corporation owns 10% of the common shares of Knife Corporation. When Mack receives $5,000 in cash dividends, the journal entry is:

a. Cash	5,000	
Dividend Revenue		5,000
b. Cash	5,000	
Equity Investments		5,000
c. Equity Investments	5,000	
Dividend Revenue		5,000
d. Equity Investments	5,000	
Cash		5,000

(SO3)   5. Mack Corporation owns 40% of the common shares of Knife Corporation. When Mack receives $5,000 in cash dividends, the journal entry is:

a. Cash	5,000	
Dividend Revenue		5,000
b. Cash	5,000	
Equity Investments		5,000
c. Equity Investments	5,000	
Dividend Revenue		5,000
d. Equity Investments	5,000	
Cash		5,000

(SO3)   6. Ross Corporation owns 40% of the common shares of Searcy Corporation. When Searcy reports net earnings of $200,000, the journal entry on Ross's books is:

a. Equity Investments	80,000	
Dividend Revenue		80,000
b. Cash	80,000	
Equity Investments		80,000

c. Equity Investments	200,000	
Revenue from Investment		200,000
d. Equity Investments	80,000	
Revenue from Investment		80,000

(SO4)   7. Trice Corporation purchased 80% of the common shares of Waters Corporation. Trice is
the _____ company, and Waters is the _____ company.
   a. subsidiary, controlling
   b. controlling, subsidiary
   c. subsidiary, parent
   d. parent, subsidiary

(SO4)   8. With respect to the Trice purchase of Waters Corporation shares in number 7 above, which
of the following is true?
   a. Only consolidated financial statements are prepared.
   b. Trice and Waters each prepare their own financial statements. Trice uses the equity
      method to account for its investment in Waters in its own financial statements.
      Consolidated financial statements are also prepared.
   c. Trice and Waters each prepare their own financial statements, and consolidated finan-
      cial statements are not prepared.
   d. Since Trice is the purchaser, it prepares its own financial statements, Waters does not,
      and consolidated financial statements are also prepared.

(SO5)   9. A portfolio of shares which will be liquidated in six months is reported:
   a. in the shareholders' equity section of the balance sheet.
   b. in the current assets section of the balance sheet.
   c. as an operating item on the statement of earnings.
   d. as a nonoperating item on the statement of earnings.

(SO5)   10. Shares of another corporation purchased to gain some influence are reported:
   a. in the shareholders' equity section of the balance sheet.
   b. in the current assets section of the balance sheet.
   c. immediately below current assets.
   d. as a nonoperating item on the statement of earnings.

(SO6)   11. Caissie Corporation has a short-term equity investment portfolio with a total cost of
$75,000. On the financial statement date, the total fair market value is $72,000. The adjusting entry required to report these investments at the lower of cost and market is:

a. Loss on Decline in Value of Investments	3,000	
Equity Investments		3,000
b. Loss on Decline in Value of Investments	3,000	
Allowance to Reduce Cost		
to Market Value		3,000
c. Equity Investments	3,000	
Gain		3,000
d. No adjusting journal entry is required.		

(SO6)   12. Caissie Corporation has a long-term equity investment portfolio with a total cost of
$75,000. On the financial statement date, the total fair market value is $72,000. The decline
is thought to be temporary only. The adjusting entry required to report these investments
at the lower of cost and market is:

a. Loss on Decline in Value of Investments	3,000	
Equity Investments		3,000

  b. Loss on Decline in Value of Investments   3,000
    Allowance to Reduce Cost
     to Market Value   3,000
  c. Equity Investments   3,000
    Gain   3,000
  d. No adjusting journal entry is required.

Problems

1. Floss Corporation has purchased 10% of the common shares of Georgia Corporation for $50,000 plus brokerage fees of $1,000. At the end of the accounting period, Georgia reported $300,000 of net earnings and paid cash dividends of $80,000.

  a. Please record Floss Corporation's purchase of the shares and any other necessary journal entries.

   Date   *Account Titles*   *Debit*   *Credit*

  b. Assume the same data as in "a" above, but the shares purchased represents 30% of the common shares of Georgia Corporation. Please record the purchase of the investment and any other necessary journal entries.

   Date   *Account Titles*   *Debit*   *Credit*

c. Floss Corporation's portfolio of short-term investments has a total cost of $225,000. At the end of the accounting period the fair market value of the total portfolio is $215,000. Please record the necessary adjusting entry.

Date	Account Titles	Debit	Credit

Please refer to Cognos Incorporated financial statements at the end of this workbook for information for answering the following questions. Don't forget to use the Decision Toolkit approach to help in the problem-solving.

(SO4) 2. a. Does Cognos own any subsidiary companies?

(SO4)   b. What information is given about consolidation in the first note to the financial statements?

SOLUTIONS TO SELF-TEST

Matching

1. e
2. a
3. b
4. g
5. d
6. f
7. c
8. h

Multiple Choice

1. b In a horizontal acquisition, the company purchased does the same activity as your company. The terms "leveraged acquisition" and "equity acquisition" are not used in this context.
2. c The journal entry is:

Debt Investments	22,500	
Cash		22,500

   Brokerage fees are included in the asset account.
3. d The journal entry is:

Cash	25,000	
Debt Investments		22,500
Gain on Sale of Debt Investments		2,500

4. a The cost method is used.
5. b The equity method is used.
6. d The equity method is used.
7. d "Controlling" refers to the interest the parent has in the subsidiary.
8. b
9. b
10. c It does not appear in the current assets section or the equity section of the balance sheet, and it is not a statement of earnings item.
11. b A contra asset account is used to record the decline: $75,000 – $72,000 = $3,000.
12. d Only permanent declines in value are recorded for long-term investments.

Problems

1.
a. The cost method is used because the purchase is of 10% of the shares of Georgia Corporation. Only dividends are recognized.

Equity Investments	51,000	
Cash		51,000
(To record purchase of Floss Corporation shares—10%)		

Cash	8,000	
Dividend Revenue		8,000
(To record dividends:		
10% x $80,000 = $8,000)		

b. The equity method is used because the purchase is of 30% of the shares of Georgia Corporation. Floss's percentage of net earnings is recognized, as are dividends.

Equity Investments	51,000	
Cash		51,000
(To record purchase of Floss		
Corporation shares—30%)		

Equity Investments	90,000	
Revenue from Investment		90,000
(To record 30% equity in Georgia		
Corp. shares—$300,000 x 30% = $90,000)		

Cash	24,000	
Equity Investments		24,000
(To record dividends received:		
30% x $80,000 = $24,000)		

c. A loss of $10,000 must be recorded.

Loss on Decline in Value of Investments	10,000	
Allowance to Reduce Cost to Market Value		10,000
(To record decline in value of investment)		

Short-term investments are recorded at the lower of cost and market.

2.

  a. Note 5 of the financial statement identifies the acquisitions made during 1998, 1999 and 2000.

  b. Note 1 indicates all but one of the subsidiaries are wholly owned.

NOTES

13

STATEMENT OF CASH FLOWS

CHAPTER OVERVIEW

In this chapter you will learn in great depth about the statement of cash flows. You will learn about the three types of activities of a business, about the primary purpose of the statement, and how to prepare the statement using either the direct or the indirect method. You will learn how to evaluate a company using the statement of cash flows and about the impact of the product life cycle on a company's cash flows.

REVIEW OF SPECIFIC STUDY OBJECTIVES

- The **primary purpose of the statement of cash flows** is to *provide information about cash receipts, cash payments, and the net change in cash resulting from the operating, investing, and financing activities of a company during the accounting period.*

- The **statement answers the following questions**:
    1. Where did cash come from?
    2. What was cash used for?
    3. What was the change in the cash balance?

- **Operating activities**, the *most important category* because it shows the cash provided or used by company operations, include the *cash effects of transactions that create revenues and expenses* and thus enter determination of net earnings.

STUDY OBJECTIVE

1

Indicate the primary purpose of the statement of cash flows.

STUDY OBJECTIVE

2

Distinguish among operating, investing, and financing activities.

- **Investing activities** include _purchasing and disposing of investments and productive capital assets using cash and lending money and collecting the loans._
- **Financing activities** include _obtaining cash from issuing debt and repaying the borrowed amounts_ and _obtaining cash from shareholders and paying them dividends._
- In general:

  Operating activities involve _statement of earnings items and current assets and current liabilities._

  Investing activities involve _investments and other capital asset items._

  Financing activities involve _long-term liabilities and shareholders' equity items._
- A **company may also have significant noncash activities**, such as the _issuance of common shares for_ the _purchase of assets_, the _conversion of bonds into common shares_, the _issuance of debt to purchase assets_, and the _exchange of capital assets_. These are **not reported in the body of the statement of cash flows** but instead are reported in a _separate note to the financial statements_. Reporting of such activities satisfies the full disclosure principle.
- With respect to **format of the statement**, _cash flows from operating activities are reported first, followed by cash flows from investing and financing activities._ Individual inflows and outflows from investing and financing activities are reported separately, not netted against each other. Net cash provided or used by each class of activities is reported. The three numbers are totaled to show the net increase or decrease in cash for the period; and the net increase or decrease is added to or subtracted from the beginning cash balance to yield the ending cash balance. Significant noncash activities are shown separately in a note to the financial statements.

STUDY OBJECTIVE

3

Explain the impact of the product life cycle on a company's cash flows.

- The **product life cycle** is a _series of phases experienced by all products._
  1. The **introductory phase** occurs when the company is purchasing productive assets and beginning to produce and sell.
  2. The **growth phase** occurs while the company strives to expand production and sales.
  3. The **maturity phase** occurs when sales and production level off.
  4. The **decline phase** is marked by falling sales due to weak consumer demand.
- A company can be characterized as being in one phase because the majority of its products are in a particular phase.
  1. In the **introductory phase**, cash from operating activities is negative, cash from investing activities is negative, and cash from financing activities is positive. The company spends to purchase productive assets. To support its asset purchases, the company will have to issue equity or securities. The company is not generating significant cash from operating activities.
  2. In the **growth phase**, cash from operating activities is less than net earnings, cash from investing activities is negative because of asset acquisitions, and cash from financing activities is positive.
  3. In the **maturity phase**, cash from operating activities and net earnings are approximately the same, and the company can start to retire debt or buy back shares.
  4. In the **decline phase**, cash from operating activities decreases, cash from investing activities may be positive as the firm sells off excess assets, and cash from financing activities may be negative as the company buys back shares and retires debt.
- The **information in the statement of cash flows can help investors, creditors, and others to evaluate the following**:
  1. The entity's ability to generate future cash flows.
  2. The entity's ability to pay dividends and meet obligations.
  3. The reasons for the difference between net earnings and net cash provided or used by operating activities.
  4. The cash investing and financing transactions during the period.

- The **statement of cash flows** is *not prepared from the adjusted trial balance. The accrual concept is not used in its preparation.*
- **Information for preparation of the statement** comes from *three sources:* the *comparative balance sheet,* the *current period statement of earnings,* and *selected additional information.*
- The **three steps in the preparation of the statement** are as follows: *determine the increase or decrease in cash, determine net cash provided or used by operating activities,* and *determine net cash provided or used by investing and financing activities.*
- In the **operating activities section,** *accrual basis net earnings is converted to cash basis net earnings.* Either the **indirect or the direct method can be used** to accomplish this conversion: Both methods arrive at the same number, just in different manners. The **indirect method is used by the majority of companies** because it is easier to prepare, focuses on the differences between net earnings and net cash flow from operating activities, and tends to reveal less company information to competitors. While the CICA prefers the direct method, it allows either approach.

STUDY OBJECTIVE

4

Prepare a statement of cash flows using one of two approaches: (a) the indirect method or (b) the direct method.

- The following are the **three steps in the preparation of the statement of cash flows** regardless of whether the indirect or the direct method is used: *determine the increase or decrease in cash, determine net cash provided or used by operating activities,* and *determine net cash provided or used by investing and financing activities.*

4a.
- Use of the **indirect method** *affects only the operating activities section* of the statement. The investing and the financing activities sections are prepared in the same way under both methods. **Accrual basis net earnings is converted to cash basis net earnings** by *adjusting it for items that affected reported net earnings but did not affect cash.* There are various expenses and losses which reduce net earnings but which do not involve cash and revenues and gains which increase net earnings but which do not involve cash. The expenses and losses are added back to net earnings, and the revenues and gains are subtracted from net earnings to convert it to net cash provided by operating activities.
- Your textbook's discussion of the individual mechanics is very solid and clear, and the following is a **summary of conversion to net cash provided by operating activities with respect to current assets and current liabilities:**

Change in Account Balance	Add to Net Earnings	Deduct from Net Earnings
Accounts receivable	Decrease	Increase
Inventory	Decrease	Increase
Prepaid expenses	Decrease	Increase
Accounts payable	Increase	Decrease
Accrued expenses payable	Increase	Decrease

- **Noncash charges which must be added back to accrual basis net earnings** include *amortization expense,* intangible asset *amortization expense,* and *loss on sale of assets.* These items all reduce net earnings but have nothing to do with cash flow, and they must be added back to produce net cash flows from operating activities.
- **Noncash credits which must be deducted from accrual basis net earnings** include *gain on sale of assets.* This item increases net earnings but has nothing to do with cash flow, and it must be deducted to produce net cash flows from operating activities.
- The noncash charges and credits are frequently listed as the first adjustments to net earnings.
- The **investing activities section** deals with **long-term assets**, and the **financing activities section** deals with *long-term debt and shareholders' equity items.* All items are to be listed separately, not netted against one another. For example, if a company purchases one asset for $80,000 and sells another asset for $20,000, each cash flow must be listed, not just the net outflow of $60,000.

- Use of the **direct method** *affects only the operating activities section* of the statement. The investing and the financing activities sections are prepared in the same way under both methods. Under the direct method, **net cash provided by operating activities** is *calculated by adjusting each item in the statement of earnings from the accrual basis to the cash basis.* Only major classes of operating cash receipts and cash payments are reported. An **efficient way to apply the direct method** is to *analyse the revenues and expenses reported in the statement of earnings in the order in which they are listed.*

- Your textbook's discussion of the individual mechanics is very solid and clear, and the following is a **summary of the formulas for calculating the various cash inflows and outflows in order to arrive at net cash provided by operating activities:**

  Revenues from sales
  Deduct: Increase in accounts receivable OR
  Add: Decrease in accounts receivable
  Cash receipts from customers

  Purchases**
  Deduct: Increase in accounts payable OR
  Add: Decrease in accounts payable
  Cash payments to suppliers

  **To solve for purchases:
  Cost of goods sold
  Deduct: Decrease in inventory OR
  Add: Increase in inventory
  Purchases

  Operating expenses
  Deduct: Decrease in prepaid expenses OR
  Add: Increase in prepaid expenses AND
  Deduct: Increase in accrued expenses payable OR
  Add: Decrease in accrued expenses payable
  Cash payments for operating expenses

  Income tax expense
  Deduct: Increase in income taxes payable OR
  Add: Decrease in income taxes payable
  Cash payments for income taxes

- The **following do not appear on a statement of cash flows under the direct method because they are noncash charges**: *amortization expense, loss on sale of assets.* A gain on sale of assets likewise will not appear because it is a noncash credit.

- **Net earnings is not reported in the statement of cash flows under the direct method.** In the operating activities section, cash payments are subtracted from cash receipts to arrive at net cash provided by operating activities.

- The **investing activities section** deals with **long-term assets**, and the **financing activities section deals** with *long-term debt and shareholders' equity items.* All items are to be listed separately, not netted against one another. For example, if a company purchases one asset for $80,000 and sells another asset for $20,000, each cash flow must be listed, not just the net outflow of $60,000.

- While traditional ratios are based on accrual basis accounting, **cash-based ratios are gaining acceptance among analysts.**

- **Free cash flow** is calculated by *subtracting capital expenditures and dividends paid from cash provided by operating activities*. It is a measure of a company's ability to generate sufficient cash to finance new capital assets. Analysts often estimate the capital expenditures amount by using the reported expenditures for the purchase of new capital assets shown in the investing activities section of the statement of cash flows.

STUDY OBJECTIVE

5

Use the statement of cash flows to evaluate a company.

- Another measure of a company's ability to generate sufficient cash to finance new capital assets is the **capital expenditure ratio**, calculated by *dividing cash provided by operating activities by capital expenditures*. This ratio provides a relative measure of cash provided by operating activities compared to cash used for the purchase of productive assets. If the ratio is calculated as 5 times, then this means that the company could have purchased five times as much property, plant, and equipment as it did without requiring any additional outside financing.

- A **traditional measure of liquidity (a company's ability to meet its current obligations) is the current ratio**: current assets divided by current liabilities. A disadvantage of this ratio is that it uses only year-end balances. A ratio that partially corrects this problem is the **cash current debt coverage ratio**: *cash provided by operating activities divided by average current liabilities*. Cash provided by operating activities involves the entire year and is often considered a better representation of liquidity on the average day.

- A **measure of solvency (the ability of a company to survive over the long term) which uses cash figures** is the **cash total debt coverage ratio**: *cash provided by operating activities divided by average total liabilities*. It indicates a company's ability to repay its liabilities from cash generated by operating activities.

- A **measure of profitability (a company's ability to generate a reasonable return) which uses cash figures** is the **cash return on sales ratio**: *cash provided by operating activities divided by net sales*. This ratio indicates the company's ability to turn sales into dollars for the firm.

CHAPTER SELF-TEST

As you work the exercises and problems, remember to use the **Decision Toolkit** discussed and used in the text:

1. *Decision Checkpoints*: At this point you ask a question.
2. *Info Needed for Decision*: You make a choice regarding the information needed to answer the question.
3. *Tool to Use for Decision*: At this point you review just what the information chosen in step 2 does for the decision-making process.
4. *How to Evaluate Results*: You perform evaluation of information for answering the question.

Note: The notation (SO1) means that the question was drawn from study objective number one.

Completion

Please write in the word or words which will complete the sentence.

(SO1)   1. The primary purpose of the statement of cash flows is to _____ _____ about cash receipts, cash payments, and the net change in cash during the accounting period.

(SO2)   2. The issuance of long-term bonds for cash is an example of a/an _____ activity.

(SO2)   3. Significant _____ activities are not reported in the body of the statement of cash flows.

(SO3)   4. All products go through a series of phases called the _____ _____ _____.

(SO3)   5. During the _____ phase of a company, cash from operating activities decreases, and the firm sells off excess assets and buys back shares and retires debt.

(SO4a)   6. With the _____ method of preparing the statement of cash flows, net earnings is adjusted for items that did not affect cash.

(SO4a)   7. With the indirect method of preparing the statement of cash flows, _____ expense is an example of noncash charge which is added back to net earnings.

(SO4b)   8. If a company uses the _____ method of preparing the statement of cash flows, then net earnings is not reported in the operating activities section.

(SO4b)   9. If a company uses the direct method of preparing the statement of cash flows, then _____ _____ do not appear in any section.

(SO5)   10. If cash provided by operating activities is $200,000 and average current liabilities are $125,000, then the cash current debt coverage ratio is _____.

Multiple Choice

Please circle the correct answer.

(SO2)   1. What type of activity is the purchase of a piece of equipment?
   a. Operating activity
   b. Investing activity
   c. Financing activity
   d. Balance sheet activity

(SO2)   2. Which of the following is the most important category of activity?
a. Operating activity
b. Investing activity
c. Financing activity
d. Manufacturing activity

(SO2)   3. Which of the following statements is correct?
a. Significant noncash activities are never reported in a company's annual report.
b. Significant noncash activities are reported in the body of the statement of cash flows.
c. Significant noncash activities are reported in a separate note to the financial statements.
d. Significant noncash activities are always reported on the company's statement of earnings.

(SO3)   4. During the introductory phase of a company, which of the following is expected?
a. Cash from operating activities is positive.
b. Cash from investing activities is positive.
c. Cash from financing activities is negative.
d. Cash from operating activities is negative.

(SO3)   5. During the growth phase of a company, which of the following is expected?
a. Cash from investing activities is negative.
b. Cash from investing activities is positive.
c. Cash from financing activities is negative.
d. Cash from operating activities is more than net earnings.

(SO4)   6. Which of the following is a source of information for preparation of the statement of cash flows?
a. Comparative balance sheet
b. Current period statement of earnings
c. Selected additional information
d. All of the above are needed for preparation of the statement.

(SO4a)   7. If the indirect method is used for preparation of the statement of cash flows, then a decrease in accounts receivable is accounted for as a(n):
a. cash inflow in the investing activities section.
b. cash inflow in the financing activities section.
c. addition to net earnings in the operating activities section.
d. deduction from net earnings in the operating activities section.

(SO4a)   8. If the indirect method is used for preparation of the statement of cash flows, then an increase in prepaid expenses is accounted for as a(n):
a. cash inflow in the investing activities section.
b. cash inflow in the financing activities section.
c. addition to net earnings in the operating activities section.
d. deduction from net earnings in the operating activities section.

(SO4a)   9. If a company purchases land through the issuance of long-term bonds, then this is accounted for as a(n):
a. operating activity.
b. investing inflow.
c. financing outflow.
d. significant noncash investing and financing activity that merits disclosure.

(SO4b) 10. A company has $200,000 of net earnings, $500,000 of revenues from sales, and an increase in accounts receivable of $50,000. If the company uses the direct method of preparing the statement of cash flows, then cash receipts from customers total:
   a. $500,000.
   b. $450,000.
   c. $300,000.
   d. $150,000.

(SO4b) 11. A company has cost of goods sold of $300,000, an increase in inventory of $100,000, and an increase in accounts payable of $30,000. If it uses the direct method of preparing the statement of cash flows, then purchases total:
   a. $400,000.
   b. $370,000.
   c. $300,000.
   d. $200,000.

(SO4b) 12. A company has cost of goods sold of $300,000, an increase in inventory of $100,000, and an increase in accounts payable of $30,000. If it uses the direct method of preparing the statement of cash flows, then cash payments to suppliers total:
   a. $400,000.
   b. $370,000.
   c. $300,000.
   d. $200,000.

Please use the following data to answer questions 13, 14, and 15.
Clark Corporation shows the following:

Cash provided by operating activities	$500,000
Capital expenditures	125,000
Dividends paid	40,000
Average total liabilities	300,000

(SO5) 13. What is the company's free cash flow?
   a. $335,000
   b. $375,000
   c. $415,000
   d. $500,000.

(SO5) 14. What is the company's capital expenditure ratio?
   a. 0.25 times
   b. 0.60 times.
   c. 1.67 times
   d. 4.00 times

(SO5) 15. What is Clark's cash total debt coverage ratio?
   a. 0.25 times
   b. 0.60 times.
   c. 1.67 times
   d. 4.00 times

Problems

1. Condensed financial data of Fortress, Inc. appears below.

FORTRESS, INC.
Comparative Balance Sheet
December 31

Assets	2003	2002
Cash	$89,000	$34,200
Accounts receivable	86,100	29,000
Inventories	107,350	99,450
Prepaid expenses	15,250	13,000
Investments	105,000	91,000
Capital assets	266,900	238,000
Accumulated amortization	(50,000)	(51,000)
	$619,600	$453,650
Liabilities and Shareholders' Equity		
Accounts payable	$87,300	$62,350
Accrued expenses payable	12,500	14,000
Bonds payable	80,000	105,000
Common shares	210,000	170,000
Retained earnings	229,800	102,300
	$619,600	$453,650

FORTRESS, INC.
Statement of Earnings
For the Year Ended December 31, 2003

Sales		$348,780
Less:		
Cost of goods sold	$123,060	
Operating expenses (excluding amortization)	15,410	
Amortization expense	43,100	
Income taxes	9,280	
Interest expense	5,730	
Loss on sale of capital assets	5,500	202,080
Net earnings		$146,700

Additional information:
1. New capital assets costing $81,000 were purchased for cash during the year.
2. Old capital assets with an original cost of $52,100 were sold for $2,500 cash.
3. Bonds matured and were paid off at face value for cash.
4. A cash dividend of $19,200 was declared and paid during the year.
5. Accounts payable pertains solely to merchandise creditors.

Instructions
(a) Prepare a statement of cash flows, using the indirect method.
(b) Required: Using the direct method, please prepare a statement of cash flows for Fortress, Inc. for the year ended December 31, 2003. Make assumptions as appropriate.

Fortress Inc.
Statement of Cash Flows
For the Year Ended December 31, 2003

2. Please refer to Cognos Incorporated annual report at the end of this workbook for information for answering the following questions. Don't forget to use the **Decision Toolkit** approach to help in the problem-solving.

(SO4a)   a. What method does Cognos use in its preparation of the statement of cash flows?

b. In 2000 did Cognos have a net increase or decrease in cash?

c. In 2000 what is Cognos' largest use of cash?

SOLUTIONS TO SELF-TEST

Completion

1. provide information
2. financing
3. noncash
4. product life cycle
5. decline
6. indirect
7. amortization
8. direct
9. noncash charges
10. 1.6 times ($200,000 ÷ $125,000)

Multiple Choice

1. b Operating activities deal with statement of earnings items and with current assets and current liabilities. Financing activities deal with long-term liabilities and with shareholders' equity items. "Balance sheet activity" is a fabricated term.
2. a It is critical that a company generate its cash flow from operating activities, not from investing and financing activities.
3. c Significant noncash activities are reported but not in the body of the statement of cash flows. They do not appear on the statement of earnings.
4. d In the introductory phase the company does not generate positive cash from operating activities. Cash from investing activities is negative, and cash from financing activities is positive.
5. a Cash from investing activities is negative, and cash from financing activities is positive. Cash from operating activities is less than net earnings.
6. d
7. c A change in a current asset is an operating activity, not an investing or a financing activity. The decrease in receivables is not a deduction from net earnings.
8. d A change in a current asset is an operating activity, not an investing or a financing activity. The increase in prepaid expenses is not an addition to net earnings.
9. d Cash is not involved in this transaction; therefore, it is not an operating, an investing, or a financing activity. It is a noncash transaction.
10. b $500,000 − $50,000 = $450,000
11. a $300,000 + $100,000 = $400,000
12. b $300,000 + $100,000 − $30,000 = $370,000
13. a $500,000 − $125,000 − $40,000 = $335,000
14. d $500,000 ÷ $125,000 = 4.00
15. c $500,000 ÷ $300,000 = 1.67

FORTRESS, INC.
Statement of Cash Flows
For the Year Ended December 31, 2003

1 (a)

Cash flows from operating activities

Net earnings		$146,700
Adjustments to reconcile net income to net cash provided by operating activities:		
Amortization expense	$ 43,100	
Loss on sale of capital assets	5,500	
Increase in accounts receivable	(57,100)	
Increase in inventory	(7,900)	
Increase in accounts payable	24,950	
Decrease in accrued expenses payable	(1,500)	
Decrease in prepaid expenses	(2,250)	4,800
Net cash provided by operating activities		151,500

Cash flows from investing activities

Purchase of investments	(14,000)	
Sale of capital assets	2,500	
Purchase of capital assets	(81,000)	
Net cash used by investing activities		(92,500)

Cash flows from financing activities

Sale of common shares	40,000	
Redemption of bonds	(25,000)	
Payment of cash dividends	(19,200)	
Net cash used by financing activities		(4,200)

Net increase in cash	54,800
Cash at beginning of period	34,200
Cash at end of period	$89,000

Recap of sale of capital assets:

Cost of capital assets sold	$52,100
Accumulated amortization on capital assets sold ($51,000 ɪ $43,100 $50,000)	44,100
Book value of capital assets sold	8,000
Cash received from sale	2,500
Loss on sale of capital assets	$ 5,500

Problems

FORTRESS, INC.
Statement of Cash Flows
For the Year Ended December 31, 2003

1 (b)

Cash flows from operating activities

Cash receipts from customers		$291,680(1)
Cash paid		
To suppliers	$106,010(2)	
For operating expenses	19,160(3)	
For income taxes	9,280	
For interest	5,730	140,180
Net cash provided by operating activities		151,500
Cash flows from investing activities		
Purchase of investments	(14,000)	
Sale of capital assets	2,500	
Purchase of capital assets	(81,000)	
Net cash used by investing activities		(92,500)
Cash flows from financing activities		
Sale of common shares	40,000	
Redemption of bonds	(25,000)	
Payment of cash dividends	(19,200)	
Net cash used by financing activities		(4,200)
Net increase in cash		54,800
Cash at beginning of period		34,200
Cash at end of period		$ 89,000

Calculations:

(1) Cash receipts from customers

Sales	$348,780
Deduct: Increase in accounts receivable	57,100
	$291,680

(2) Cash payments to merchandise suppliers

Cost of goods sold	$123,060
Add: Increase in inventory	7,900
Cost of purchases	130,960
Deduct: Increase in accounts payable	24,950
	$106,010

(3) Cash payments for operating expenses

Operating expenses, exclusive of amortization		$ 15,410
Add: Increase in prepaid expenses	$2,250	
Decrease in accrued expenses payable	1,500	3,750
		$ 19,160

Recap of sale of capital assets:

Cost of capital assets sold	$ 52,100
Accumulated amortization on capital assets sold	
($51,000 + $43,100 - $50,000)	44,100
Book value of capital assets sold	8,000
Cash received from sale	2,500
Loss on sale of capital assets	$ 5,500

2. a. In order to answer this question you need to look at the operating section of the cash flow statement. Cognos reports net income and add non cash items and changes in working capital items. This would indicate the use of the indirect method. The direct method does not include net income (loss). Net cash provided by operating activities is computed by adjusting each item on the income statement from an accrual to a cash basis.

   b. Cognos had a net increase in cash of $38,818.

   c. Cognos' largest use of cash was in investing activities. This would be normal for a healthy growing firm.

NOTES

14

FINANCIAL ANALYSIS: THE BIG PICTURE

CHAPTER OVERVIEW

This chapter is essentially a capstone chapter for the textbook. You will learn about several new items: earning power and irregular items such as discontinued operations, extraordinary items, and changes in accounting principle; and horizontal and vertical analysis. You will revisit ratios learned in prior chapters, focusing on what the ratios indicate, and will learn about the limitations of financial analysis.

REVIEW OF SPECIFIC STUDY OBJECTIVES

- **Earning power** is *net earnings adjusted for irregular items*. It is the most likely level of earnings to be obtained in the future, to the extent that this year's net earnings is a good predictor of future years' net earnings. There are **three types of irregular items**: *discontinued operations, extraordinary items,* and *changes in accounting principle*. All three items are **reported net of income taxes**. If there is an extraordinary loss of $100,000 and the tax rate is 30%, then the loss is reported at its net amount of $70,000 (the $30,000 of income taxes is actually a tax savings in the case of a loss).

- **Discontinued operations** refer to the *disposal of a significant segment of a business, such as the elimination of a major class of customers or an entire activity*. The statement of earnings should report earnings from continuing operations and earnings (or loss) from

STUDY OBJECTIVE

1

Understand the concept of earning power and indicate how irregular items are presented.

discontinued operations. (It is important to distinguish infrequently occurring items from routine, recurring operations and in general makes sense to eliminate irregular items in estimating future earning power.) The **earnings (loss) from discontinued operations consists of the earnings (loss) from operations and the gain (loss) on disposal of the segment**. Remember that both the operating earnings or loss and the disposal gain or loss are *reported net of income taxes*.

- **Extraordinary items** are *events and transactions that meet three conditions: They are unusual in nature, infrequent in occurrence and not the result of a management decision*. These conditions are necessarily influenced by the judgment of the accountants dealing with the items. Extraordinary items are *reported net of income taxes* in a separate section of the statement of earnings immediately below discontinued operations. If a transaction meets only one or two of the criteria, then it is treated as a line item in the upper half of the statement of earnings under Other Expenses and Losses or Other Revenues and Gains: It is shown at the gross amount, not net of tax. It will go into the determination of earnings from continuing operations, and income taxes are calculated for that number.

- A **change in accounting principle** occurs when the *principle used in the current year is different from the one used in the preceding year*. Remember that consistency is desirable but that changes can be made as long as their occurrence and effects are disclosed. **Examples** of changes include changes in the *method used for amortization* and in the *method used for inventory costing*. While discontinued operations and extraordinary items are reported in the statement of earnings, changes in accounting principle are reported as an adjustment to opening retained earnings in the statement of retained earnings.

STUDY OBJECTIVE

2

Discuss the need for comparative analysis and identify the tools of financial statement analysis.

For data to be meaningful, they must be compared to something. Comparisons may be:
1. *Intracompany comparisons*. Comparisons may be made within a company on a year-to-year basis to detect changes in financial relationships and significant trends. "Intra" is a Latin preposition which means "within."
2. *Intercompany comparisons*. Comparisons with other companies provide insight into a company's competitive position. "Inter" is a Latin preposition which means "between."
3. *Industry comparisons*. Comparisons with industry averages provide information about a company's relative position within the industry.
- **Three basic tools** are used in *financial statement analysis: horizontal analysis, vertical analysis, and ratio analysis*.

STUDY OBJECTIVE

3

Explain and apply horizontal analysis.

- **Horizontal analysis** is a *technique for evaluating a series of financial statement data over a period of time*. Its **purpose** is to *determine the increase or decrease that has taken place, expressed as either an amount or a percentage*.
- A company has net sales of $100,000 in 2000, $110,000 in 2001, and $116,000 in 2002. The **formula for calculating changes since the base period** is:

$$\frac{\text{Current-Year Amount} - \text{Base-Year Amount}}{\text{Base-Year Amount}}$$

In our example, $\frac{\$110,000 - \$100,000}{\$100,000}$ = 10% increase in 2001's net sales over 2000's.

For the year 2002:

$\frac{\$116,000 - \$100,000}{\$100,000}$ = 16%

Note that the base year amount is always $100,000. Net sales in 2002 have increased by 16% over 1998's net sales, not over 2001's net sales.

- An **advantage of horizontal analysis** is that it *helps to highlight the significance of a change by reducing the change to a percentage.* Sometimes it is difficult to see the magnitude of a change when only the dollar amount is examined.
- **Several complications can arise using horizontal analysis**. If an item has no value in a base year or preceding year and a value in the next year, then no percentage change can be calculated. If a negative number appears in the base year or preceding year and a positive amount exists the next year, or vice versa, then no percentage change can be calculated.

- **Vertical analysis** is a *technique for evaluating financial statement data that expresses each item in a financial statement as a percent of a base amount.* On the balance sheet, assets are usually expressed as a percentage of total assets, and liability and shareholders' equity items are usually expressed as a percentage of total liabilities and shareholders' equity. On the statement of earnings, items are usually expressed as a percentage of net sales.
- When comparative balance sheets statements of earnings are presented, **vertical analysis shows not only the relative size of each category in each year on the balance sheet and on the statement of earnings but also the percentage change in the individual items on the two financial statements**.
- If current assets are $2,200 and total assets are $9,000, then current assets are 24.4% of total assets ($2,200 ÷ $9,000).
- Just as is true with horizontal analysis, an **advantage of vertical analysis** is that it *helps to highlight the significance of a change by reducing the change to a percentage.* It also helps when making comparisons between companies of different sizes.

STUDY OBJECTIVE 4

Explain and apply vertical analysis.

- **Ratios can be classified into three types**: *liquidity,* which measure the short-term ability of the company to pay its debts and to meet unexpected needs for cash; *solvency,* which measure a company's ability to survive over a long period of time; and *profitability,* which measure the earnings or operating success of a company for a given period of time.
- A **single ratio is not meaningful but must be compared with something**. As noted above, there may be intracompany comparisons, *intercompany comparisons, and comparisons with industry averages.*
- The following are **liquidity ratios**:
  1. **Current ratio**, calculated by *dividing current assets by current liabilities.* If the current ratio is 1.25 to 1, then the company has $1.25 of current assets for every $1.00 of current liabilities. This ratio can also be expressed as an equation. The difference between current assets and current liabilities is called **working capital**.
  2. **Acid-test (or quick) ratio**, calculated by *dividing the sum of cash, short-term investments, and net receivables by current liabilities.* Inventories and prepaid expenses are excluded from the numerator. If the acid-test ratio is 0.65 to 1, then the company has $0.65 of quick assets for every $1.00 of current liabilities.
  3. **Cash current debt coverage ratio**, calculated by *dividing cash provided by operating activities by average current liabilities.* Instead of using in the numerator and denominator balances from just one point in time, this ratio uses numbers covering a period of time and thus may provide a better representation of liquidity. If the ratio is 0.5 times, then the company has $0.50 of cash provided by operating activities for every $1.00 of current liabilities. This ratio is cash basis, not accrual basis.
  4. **Credit risk ratio**, calculated by *dividing the allowance for doubtful accounts by accounts receivables.* This ratio measures the quality of receivables. If the ratio is 15.6, then 15.6% of the receivables may not be collected.
  5. **Receivables turnover ratio**, calculated by *dividing net credit sales by average net receivables.* This ratio measures the number of times, on average, receivables are collected during the period. If the ratio is 12.5 times, then the company collects its receivables 12.5 times during the accounting period.

STUDY OBJECTIVE 5

Identify and calculate ratios, describe their purpose, and use them to analyse a firm's liquidity, solvency, and profitability.

6. **Average collection period**, calculated by *dividing 365 days by the receivables turnover ratio*. Using the 12.5 times from the previous ratio, the average collection period for this company is 29.2 days (365 ÷ 12.5). The general rule is that the collection period should not greatly exceed the credit term period (the time allowed for payment).

7. **Inventory turnover ratio**, calculated by *dividing cost of goods sold by average inventory*. If the ratio is 8 times, then the company sold its inventory 8 times during the accounting period. Since the business of a merchandiser is to sell inventory, this ratio is very closely monitored. If it shows significant change in either direction, then action is taken. This ratio varies widely among industries.

8. **Days in inventory**, calculated by *dividing 365 days by the inventory turnover ratio*. Using the 8 times from the previous ratio, the average days in inventory number is 45.6 days. The company takes approximately 46 days to sell its inventory.

- The following are **solvency ratios**:

1. **Debt to total assets ratio**, calculated by *dividing total liabilities by total assets*. It measures the percentage of the total assets provided by creditors and provides some indication of the company's ability to withstand losses without impairing the interests of its creditors. If the ratio is 65%, then creditors have provided financing sufficient to cover 65% of the company's total assets. The higher the percentage of liabilities to total assets, the greater the risk that the company may be unable to pay its debts; therefore, creditors usually like to see a low ratio. The *debt to equity ratio* shows the relative use of borrowed funds compared with resources invested by the owners.

2. **Times interest earned ratio**, calculated by *dividing earnings before interest expense and income taxes (EBIT) by interest expense*. It indicates the company's ability to meet interest payments as they come due. If the ratio is 13 times, then the company has earnings before interest and taxes that is 13 times the amount needed for interest expense.

3. **Cash interest coverage ratio**, calculated by *dividing earnings before interest, tax and amortization expense (EBITDA) by interest expense*. It indicates the cash flow available to cover interest payments. It is similar to the times interest earned ratio but excludes the non-cash item, amortization, in the numerator.

4. **Cash total debt coverage ratio**, calculated by *dividing cash provided by operating activities by average total liabilities*. It indicates a company's ability to repay its debts from cash generated from operating activities without having to liquidate the assets used in its operations. If the ratio is 0.24 times, then net cash generated from 1 year of operations is sufficient to pay off 24% of the company's total liabilities. This ratio is cash basis, not accrual basis.

5. **Free cash flow**, calculated by *subtracting the sum of capital expenditures and dividends paid from cash provided by operating activities*. It indicates the cash available for paying additional dividends or expanding operations.

6. **Capital expenditure ratio**, calculated by *dividing cash provided by operating activities by capital expenditures*. Indicates ability to generate sufficient cash to finance new capital assets.

- The following are **profitability ratios**, (profitability is used frequently as the ultimate test of management's operating effectiveness):

1. **Average useful life of capital assets**, calculated by *dividing average cost of capital assets by amortization expense*. Indicates the average useful life of capital assets.

2. **Average age of capital assets**, calculated by *dividing accumulated amortization by amortization expense*. Indicates average age of capital assets.

3. **Return on common shareholders' equity ratio**, calculated by *dividing earnings available to common shareholders by average common shareholders' equity*. It shows how many dollars of net earnings were earned for each dollar invested by the owners. Two factors affect this ratio: the return on assets ratio and the degree of leverage.

4. **Return on assets ratio**, calculated by *dividing net earnings by average total assets*. It measures the rate earned on each dollar invested in assets. **Leveraging** (or trading on the

equity at a gain) means that the *company has borrowed money by issuing bonds or notes at a lower rate of interest than it is able to earn by using the borrowed money*: The company borrows at 10% but is able to earn 15%. Note that the opposite could be true: The company borrows at 10% but is able to earn only 8%. This is called trading on the equity at a loss. Two factors affect this ratio: the profit margin ratio and the asset turnover ratio.

5. **Profit margin ratio**, calculated by *dividing net earnings by net sales*. This is a measure of the percentage of each dollar of sales that results in net earnings. If the ratio is 12%, then each dollar of sales results in $0.12 of net earnings. High-volume enterprises (grocery stores) generally have low profit margins, whereas low-volume enterprises (jewellery stores) usually have high profit margins. Two factors strongly influence this ratio: the gross profit rate and the operating expenses to sales ratio.

6. **Asset turnover ratio**, calculated by *dividing net sales by average total assets*. It measures how efficiently a company uses its assets to generate sales. This ratio varies widely among industries.

7. **Gross profit rate**, calculated by *dividing gross profit by net sales*. It indicates a company's ability to maintain an adequate selling price above its costs. The more competition in an industry, the lower the gross profit rates. If the gross profit rate is 58%, then each dollar of net sales generates gross profit of $0.58.

8. **Operating expenses to sales ratio**, calculated by *dividing operating expenses (selling and administrative expenses) by net sales*. It measures the costs incurred to support each dollar of sales.

9. **Cash return on sales ratio**, calculated by *dividing net cash provided by operating activities by net sales*. This is another cash basis ratio.

10. **Earnings per share (EPS)**, calculated by *dividing earnings available to common shareholders by average number of outstanding common shares*. The numerator is the difference between net earnings and preferred dividends declared for the period, if any. It is a measure of the net earnings earned on common shares. If earnings per share is $2.05, then $2.05 of net earnings was earned on each common share

11. **Book value per share**, calculated by *dividing common shareholders' equity by the average number of outstanding common shares*. The numerator is total shareholders' equity less the legal capital of the preferred shareholders, if any. Book value per share is not an indicator of market value per share.

12. **Cash flow per share**, calculated by *dividing net cash flow from all activities by the average number of outstanding common shares*. This ratio is the cash based equivalent to earnings per share.

13. **Price-earnings ratio**, calculated by *dividing the market price per common share by earnings per share*. It measures the ratio of the market price of each share to the earnings per share. If the price-earnings ratio is 23, then each share sold for 23 times the amount that was earned on each share.

14. **Payout ratio**, calculated by *dividing cash dividends declared on common shares by net earnings*. It measures the percentage of earnings distributed in the form of cash dividends. Growth companies have low payout ratios because they reinvest earnings in the business.

15. **Dividend yield**, calculated by *dividing cash dividends per common share by year end share price*. Indicates the rate of return earned from dividends. This is a supplement to the payout ratio.

* **Availability of information** is not a problem in financial statement analysis. The goal is to perform relevant analysis and select pertinent comparative data. The goal is knowing what ratio will give the answer to the question being asked.

STUDY OBJECTIVE

Discuss the limitations of financial statement analysis.

- Some of the **limitations of financial statement analysis** are:
  1. _Estimates are used in financial statements,_ and if the estimates are inaccurate, then the analysis will be faulty.
  2. _Financial statements are based on historical cost_ and not adjusted for price-level changes.
  3. _Variations in the application of generally accepted accounting principles_ may make it difficult to compare results of different companies.
  4. The choice by companies of year-ends which coincide with the low point in operating activity or inventory level may yield account balances which are not representative of the entire period.
  5. _Many firms are so diversified that they cannot be classified by industry._ Companies are required to report segmental data in a note to the financial statements when they have significant operations in different lines of business.

CHAPTER SELF-TEST

As you work the exercises and problems, remember to use the **Decision Toolkit** discussed and used in the text:

1. *Decision Checkpoints*: At this point you ask a question.
2. *Info Needed for Decision*: You make a choice regarding the information needed to answer the question.
3. *Tool to Use for Decision*: At this point you review just what the information chosen in step 2 does for the decision-making process.
4. *How to Evaluate Results*: You perform evaluation of information for answering the question.

Note: The notation (SO1) means that the question was drawn from study objective number one.

Matching

Please write the letters of the following terms in the spaces to the left of the definitions.

a. Asset turnover ratio
b. Cash total debt coverage ratio
c. Cash current debt coverage ratio
d. Earnings per share
e. Free cash flow
f. Horizontal analysis
g. Price-earnings ratio
h. Profit margin ratio
i. Return on common shareholders' equity ratio
j. Vertical analysis

(SO5) _____ 1. Cash provided by operating activities divided by average total liabilities.

(SO3) _____ 2. A technique for evaluating a series of data over a period of time to determine the increase or decrease that has taken place, expressed as either an amount or a percentage.

(SO5) _____ 3. Earnings available to common shareholders divided by average common shareholders' equity.

(SO5) _____ 4. Earnings available to common shareholders divided by average common shares outstanding.

(SO5) _____ 5. Net sales divided by average total assets.

(SO4) _____ 6. A technique for evaluating data that expresses each item in a financial statement as a percent of a base amount.

(SO5) _____ 7. Cash provided by operating activities minus the sum of capital expenditures and dividends paid.

(SO5) _____ 8. Market price of a share divided by the earnings per share.

(SO5) _____ 9. Cash provided by operating activities divided by average current liabilities.

(SO5) _____ 10. Net earnings divided by net sales.

Multiple Choice
....

Please circle the correct answer.

(SO1) 1. To be classified as extraordinary, an item must:
a. result from an act of God.
b. be only unusual in nature.
c. be only infrequent in occurrence.
d. be unusual in nature, infrequent in occurrence, and not influenced by management.

(SO1) 2. Discontinued operations and extraordinary items appear on the:
a. statement of earnings as part of earnings from continuing operations.
b. statement of earnings net of income taxes, below "Earnings from Continuing Operations."
c. statement of earnings at their gross amount, below "Earnings from Continuing Operations."
d. balance sheet in the shareholders' equity section.

(SO1) 3. A change in accounting principle appears on the:
a. statement of earnings net of income taxes, below "Earnings from Continuing Operations."
b. statement of retained earnings.
c. balance sheet in the shareholders' equity section.
d. statement of cash flows.

(SO2) 4. Which of the following is a type of comparison providing decision usefulness of financial information?
a. Industry averages
b. Intercompany basis
c. Intracompany basis
d. All of the above provide decision usefulness

(SO3) 5. Total current liabilities are $10,000 in 2001, $18,000 in 2002, and $22,000 in 2003. What is the percentage increase from 2001 to 2003?
a. 22% (rounded)
b. 80%
c. 120%
d. It cannot be calculated from the data given.

(SO4) 6. Consider the following data for Elizabeth Corporation:

Net sales	$100,000
− Cost of goods sold	30,000
Gross profit	70,000
− Operating expenses	50,000
Net earnings	$ 20,000

Performing vertical analysis and using net sales as the base, what percentage of net sales is cost of goods sold?
a. 20%
b. 30%
c. 70%
d. 333% (rounded)

(SO5) 7. Measures of a company's ability to survive over a long period of time are called:
a. liquidity ratios.
b. solvency ratios.
c. profitability ratios.
d. acid-test ratios.

(SO5)   8. _____ is frequently used as the ultimate test of management's operating effectiveness.
a. Net earnings
b. Liquidity
c. Solvency
d. Profitability

Please use the following data for questions 9 through 11:

Current assets	$150,000
Total assets	500,000
Current liabilities	125,000
Total liabilities	200,000
Net credit sales	600,000
Cost of goods sold	160,000
Average receivables	50,000
Average inventory	40,000

(SO5)   9. What is the receivables turnover ratio?
a. 3.2 times
b. 4.0 times
c. 12 times
d. 15 times

(SO5)   10. What is the inventory turnover ratio?
a. 3.2 times
b. 4.0 times
c. 12 times
d. 15 times

(SO5)   11. What is the debt to total assets ratio?
a. 25.0%
b. 40.0%
c. 62.5%
d. 83.3%

(SO5)   12. Net sales are $6,000,000, net earnings is $800,000, earnings available to common shareholders is $700,000, and the average number of outstanding common shares is 300,000. What is the profit margin ratio?
a. 13.3%
b. 11.7%
c. $2.67
d. $2.33

(SO5)   13. Net sales are $6,000,000, net earnings is $800,000, earnings available to common shareholders is $700,000, and the average number of outstanding common shares is 300,000. What is earnings per share?
a. 13.3%
b. 11.7%
c. $2.67
d. $2.33

(SO5)   14. Which of the following is considered a profitability ratio?
a. Price-earnings ratio
b. Times interest earned ratio
c. Average collection period
d. Cash current debt coverage ratio

(SO5)   15. Which of the following is considered a solvency ratio?
- a. Price-earnings ratio
- b. Times interest earned ratio
- c. Average collection period
- d. Cash current debt coverage ratio

Problems

(SO6)   1.   What are some of the limitations of horizontal, vertical, and ratio analysis?

2. Please refer to both Cognos financial statements at the end of this workbook for information for answering the following questions. Don't forget to use the **Decision Toolkit** approach for help in the problem-solving.

(SO3)   a. How much did Cognos selling and administrative expenses increase from 1998 to 1999? From 1998 to 2000? Calculate in percentage terms.

(SO4)   b. What percentage of 2000 net sales is selling and administrative expenses? What percentage of 2000 total assets is current assets?

(SO5)   c. In 2000 and 1999 what percentage of each dollar of sales resulted in net income?

(SO1)   d. For the three years shown, did Cognos change any of its accounting policies?

SOLUTIONS TO SELF-TEST

Matching

1. b
2. f
3. i
4. d
5. a
6. j
7. e
8. g
9. c
10. h

Multiple Choice

1. d An act of God may be extraordinary or ordinary. An item must be *all* of the following to be classified as extraordinary: unusual, infrequent, and not subject to a management determination.
2. b They are shown net of tax in the bottom half of the statement of earnings, below earnings from continuing operations. They never appear on the balance sheet.
3. b Changes in accounting principle are reported net of tax as an adjustment to opening retained earnings in the statement of retained earnings.
4. d
5. c ($22,000 − $10,000) ÷ $10,000 = 120%
6. b $30,000 ÷ $100,000 = 30%
7. b Liquidity refers to a company's short-term ability to pay obligations as they arise, and profitability measures the operating success of a business for a given period of time. The acid-test ratio is a measure of liquidity.
8. d Net earnings is simply the difference between revenues and expenses, and liquidity and solvency refer to the company's ability to survive on a short-term and on a long-term basis, respectively.
9. c $600,000 ÷ $50,000 = 12
10. b $160,000 ÷ $40,000 = 4
11. b $200,000 ÷ $500,000 = 40.0%
12. a $800,000 ÷ $6,000,000 = 13.3%
13. d $700,000 ÷ 300,000 shares = 2.33
14. a Times interest earned is a solvency ratio, and average collection period and the cash current debt coverage ratio are liquidity measures.
15. b The price-earnings ratio is a profitability ratio.

Problems

1. a. Financial statements are based on estimates, and analysis is only as good as the estimates on which the statements and analysis are based.

   b. Financial statements are based on historical cost and are not adjusted for price-level changes. Fair market value, for the most part, is not reflected in the values of assets and liabilities.

   c. Trying to compare companies is made difficult by the fact that companies may use different methods and approaches in some areas, such as amortization and inventory. Straight-line amortization and double-declining-balance amortization give very different numbers, as do FIFO and average inventory methods. Trying to compare the inventory turnover ratios for two companies, one of which uses FIFO and one of which uses average, will be problematic.

   d. Many of the numbers used in ratios are year-end balances and may not be representative of balances in the accounts during the year. For example, companies typically try to choose a year-end when inventory levels are low, and ratios based on year-end inventory balances may not give a completely accurate picture.

   e. Many companies are very diversified, making it difficult to classify them by industry. It helps that companies must report segmental data which break out the results of the various segments of the company.

2. a. To answer this you must perform a horizontal analysis to determine the increase of decrease in percentage.
   1998-1999 $172,482 − $140,882 = $31,600 ÷ $140,882 = 22.4%
   1998-2000 $238,147 − $140,882 = $97,265 ÷ $140,882 = 69%
   In each case the base year is 1998.

   b. To answer this you must perform a vertical analysis in which each expense is calculated as a percent of sales for the income statement and total assets or total liabilities on the balance sheet.
   Selling and administrative expenses to sales $238,147 ÷ $385,640 = 61.7%
   Current assets to total assets $313,188 ÷ $379,886 = 82.4%

   c. To answer this question you must calculate the profit margin ratio for each year, calculated by dividing net income by net sales.
   2000: $58,815 ÷ $385,640 = 15.2%
   1999: $58,434 ÷ $301,125 = 19.4%
   Cognos' profit margin is decreasing and would warrant further investigation.

   d. To answer this question you must look at the Consolidated Statement of Stockholders' Equity to see if there is an item related to changes in accounting principle. No such item is indicated therefore you can assume there were no changes in accounting policies for the years shown.

<u>NOTES</u>

_____

_____

_____

_____

_____

_____

_____

_____

_____

_____

_____

_____

_____

_____

_____

_____

_____

_____

_____

_____

_____

<u>NOTES</u>

Annual Report **2000**

LEVERAGING **LEADERSHIP**

MANAGEMENT'S STATEMENT OF RESPONSIBILITY

Management is responsible for the preparation of the financial statements and all other information in the Form 10-K filing with the U.S. Securities and Exchange Commission. The financial statements have been prepared in accordance with generally accepted accounting principles and reflect management's best estimates and judgements. The financial information presented elsewhere in the annual report is consistent with the consolidated financial statements.

Management has developed and maintains a system of internal controls to provide reasonable assurance that all assets are safeguarded and to facilitate the preparation of relevant, reliable and timely financial information. Consistent with the concept of reasonable assurance, the Company recognizes that the relative cost of maintaining these controls should not exceed their expected benefits.

The Audit Committee, which is made up of independent directors, reviews the consolidated financial statements, considers the report of the external auditor, assesses the adequacy of the Company's internal controls and recommends to the Board of Directors the independent auditors for appointment by the shareholders. The financial statements were reviewed by the Audit Committee and approved by the Board of Directors.

The financial statements were audited by PricewaterhouseCoopers LLP, the external auditors, in accordance with generally accepted auditing standards on behalf of the shareholders.

A. Kevin Francis
President,
Chief Executive Officer
and Director

Jeff McMullen
Vice-President,
Finance
and Chief Financial Officer

AUDITORS' REPORT
To the Shareholders of JetForm Corporation

We have audited the consolidated balance sheets of JetForm Corporation as of April 30, 2000 and 1999, and the consolidated statements of operations, comprehensive income, shareholders' equity and cash flows for the years ended April 30, 2000, 1999 and 1998. These financial statements are the responsibility of the Company's management. Our responsibility is to express an opinion on these financial statements based on our audits.

We conducted our audits in accordance with auditing standards generally accepted in Canada. Those standards require that we plan and perform an audit to obtain reasonable assurance whether the financial statements are free of material misstatement. An audit includes examining, on a test basis, evidence supporting the amounts and disclosures in the financial statements. An audit also includes assessing the accounting principles used and significant estimates made by management, as well as evaluating the overall financial statement presentation.

In our opinion, these consolidated financial statements present fairly, in all material respects, the financial position of the Company as of April 30, 2000 and 1999, and the results of its operations and its cash flows for the years ended April 30, 2000, 1999 and 1998, in accordance with accounting principles generally accepted in the United States.

On June 20, 2000, we reported separately to the shareholders of JetForm Corporation on financial statements for the same period, prepared in accordance with accounting principles generally accepted in Canada.

PricewaterhouseCoopers LLP

PricewaterhouseCoopers LLP
Chartered Accountants
Ottawa, Canada
June 20, 2000

CONSOLIDATED BALANCE SHEETS

(in thousands of Canadian dollars except share amounts)	April 30, 2000	April 30, 1999
Assets		
Current assets		
Cash and cash equivalents	$ 42,092	$ 47,262
Accounts receivable (Note 2)	21,416	29,274
Term accounts receivable (Note 2)	5,224	13,486
Unbilled receivables	4,492	3,455
Inventory	1,084	1,139
Prepaid expenses	2,956	3,727
Asset held for sale	—	3,417
	77,264	101,760
Term accounts receivable (Note 2)	242	6,090
Deferred income tax assets	5,604	4,364
Fixed assets (Note 3)	16,556	18,620
Other assets (Note 4)	21,670	25,871
	$ 121,336	$ 156,705
Liabilities and shareholders' equity		
Current liabilities		
Accounts payable	$ 7,423	$ 7,874
Accrued liabilities	10,685	15,656
Unearned revenue	15,588	12,463
Term loan (Note 6)	10,000	—
Current portion of Delrina obligation (Note 14)	—	22,023
	43,696	58,016
Accrued liabilities (Note 15)	1,338	3,225
Term loan (Note 6)	—	9,998
Delrina obligation (Note 14)	—	536
	45,034	71,775
Commitments (Note 10)		
Shareholders' equity		
Capital stock (Issued and outstanding —19,592,314 Common Shares and 450,448 Preference Shares at April 30, 2000; 19,421,428 Common Shares, 450,448 Preference at April 30, 1999) (Note 7)	248,210	247,119
Cumulative translation adjustment	(2,670)	(1,052)
Deficit	(169,238)	(161,137)
	76,302	84,930
	$ 121,336	$ 156,705

(the accompanying notes are an integral part of these consolidated financial statements)

Signed on behalf of the board:

A. Kevin Francis
President,
Chief Executive Officer and Director

Abraham Ostrovsky
Chairman, Board of Directors

CONSOLIDATED STATEMENTS OF OPERATIONS

(in thousands of Canadian dollars except share and per share amounts)

		Year ended April 30,	
	2000	1999	1998
Revenues			
Product	$ 52,583	$ 66,662	$ 74,781
Service	41,734	47,550	36,446
	94,317	114,212	111,227
Costs and expenses			
Cost of product	12,053	9,164	7,539
Cost of service	12,373	19,058	15,259
Sales and marketing	45,097	53,315	40,214
General and administrative	12,168	10,722	9,846
Research and development (Note 5)	15,423	15,384	10,620
Depreciation and amortization	10,300	11,568	11,631
Restructuring (Note 15)	(1,106)	30,503	—
Gain on sale of assets	(1,813)	—	—
	104,495	149,714	95,109
Operating income (Loss)	(10,178)	(35,502)	16,118
Net investment income (expense) (Note 12)	2,868	3,826	(3,564)
Other income (expense)	295	(11)	—
Income (Loss) before taxes	(7,015)	(31,687)	12,554
Provision for current taxes (Note 9)	(1,086)	(2,073)	(2,045)
Recovery of deferred taxes (Note 9)	—	4,625	355
Net income (Loss)	$ (8,101)	$ (29,135)	$ 10,864
Basic income (loss) per share (Note 8)			
Net income (loss) per share	$ (0.41)	$ (1.47)	$ 0.65
Weighted average number of shares	19,915,893	19,826,057	16,622,835
Fully diluted income (loss) per share (Note 8)			
Net income (loss) per share	$ (0.41)	$ (1.47)	$ 0.62
Weighted average number of shares	19,915,893	19,826,057	17,615,595

(the accompanying notes are an integral part of these consolidated financial statements)

CONSOLIDATED STATEMENTS OF COMPREHENSIVE INCOME

(in thousands of Canadian dollars)

| | | Year ended April 30, | |
	2000	1999	1998
Net income (loss)	$ (8,101)	$ (29,135)	$ 10,864
Other comprehensive income (loss):			
Cumulative translation adjustment	(1,618)	(1,052)	—
Comprehensive income (loss)	$ (9,719)	$ (30,187)	$ 10,864

(the accompanying notes are an integral part of these consolidated financial statements)

CONSOLIDATED STATEMENTS OF SHAREHOLDERS' EQUITY

(in thousands of Canadian dollars except share amounts)

| | Number Issued and Outstanding | | | Stated Value | | | | | | |
	Common Stock	Special Warrants	Preference Stock	Common Stock	Special Warrants	Preference Stock	Total Capital Stock	Cumulative Translation Adjustment	Retained Earnings (Deficit)	Total Shareholders' Equity
Balance as at April 30, 1997	15,693,623	—	450,448	$ 154,016	$ —	$ 4,939	$ 158,955	$ —	$ (142,866)	$ 16,089
Issuance of Common Shares:										
Pursuant to acquisitions	6,918	—	—	144	—	—	144	—	—	144
Repayment of Delrina obligation	715,654	—	—	15,485	—	—	15,485	—	—	15,485
Exercise of stock options	611,946	—	—	5,917	—	—	5,917	—	—	5,917
Issuance of Special Warrants	—	2,200,000	—	—	63,650	—	63,650	—	—	63,650
Net income for the year	—	—	—	—	—	—	—-	—	10,864	10,864
Balance as at April 30, 1998	17,028,141	2,200,000	450,448	175,562	63,650	4,939	244,151	—	(132,002)	112,149
Issuance of Common Shares:										
Pursuant to acquisitions	6,918	—	—	242	—	—	242	—	—	242
Share purchase plan	20,768	—	—	375	—	—	375	—	—	375
Exercise of stock options	165,601	—	—	2,259	—	—	2,259	—	—	2,259
Conversions of Special Warrants	2,200,000	(2,200,000)	—	63,742	(63,650)	—	92	—	—	92
Cumulative translation adjustment	—	—	—	—	—	—	—	(1,052)	—	(1,052)
Net loss for the year	—	—	—	—	—	—	—	—	(29,135)	(29,135)
Balance as at April 30, 1999	19,421,428	—	450,448	242,180	—	4,939	247,119	(1,052)	(161,137)	84,930
Issuance of Common Shares:										
Pursuant to acquisitions	6,918	—	—	44	—	—	44	—	—	44
Share purchase plan	49,141	—	—	282	—	—	282	—	—	282
Exercise of stock options	114,827	—	—	765	—	—	765	—	—	765
Cumulative translation adjustment	—	—	—	—	—	—	—	(1,618)	—	(1,618)
Net loss for the year	—	—	—	—	—	—	—	—	(8,101)	(8,101)
Balance as at April 30, 2000	19,592,314	—	450,448	$ 243,271	—	$ 4,939	$ 248,210	$ (2,670)	$ (169,238)	$ 76,302

(the accompanying notes are an integral part of these consolidated financial statements)

CONSOLIDATED STATEMENTS OF CASH FLOWS

(in thousands of Canadian dollars)

	Year ended April 30,		
	2000	1999	1998
Cash provided from (used in)			
Operating activities			
Net income (loss)	$ (8,101)	$ (29,135)	$ 10,864
Items not involving cash:			
Depreciation and amortization	13,941	14,838	13,629
Deferred income taxes	—	(4,615)	(338)
Other non-cash items	(246)	(3,368)	4,034
Gain on sale of assets	(1,813)	—	—
Gain on sale of securities	(1,497)	—	—
Restructuring (Note 15)	(1,106)	21,611	—
Net change in operating components			
of working capital (Note 11)	17,083	8,055	(6,520)
	18,261	7,386	21,669
Investing activities			
Proceeds from sale of assets	5,000	—	—
Proceeds from sale of securities	2,854	—	—
Purchase of fixed assets	(4,990)	(8,503)	(8,467)
Increase in other assets	(3,774)	(5,949)	(9,263)
	(910)	(14,452)	(17,730)
Financing activities			
Proceeds from issuance of shares	1,091	2,968	69,567
Issuance of debt	—	9,998	—
Repayment of Delrina obligation	(22,560)	(50,845)	(16,663)
	(21,469)	(37,879)	52,904
Effect of exchange rate changes on cash	(1,052)	603	311
Increase (decrease) in cash and cash equivalents	(5,170)	(44,342)	57,154
Cash and cash equivalents, beginning of year	47,262	91,604	34,450
Cash and cash equivalents, end of year	$ 42,092	$ 47,262	$ 91,604

(the accompanying notes are an integral part of these consolidated financial statements)

Notes to Consolidated Financial Statements

NOTES TO CONSOLIDATED FINANCIAL STATEMENTS

1. SIGNIFICANT ACCOUNTING POLICIES

(a) Basis of presentation

These consolidated financial statements have been prepared by management in accordance with accounting principles generally accepted in the United States ("US GAAP"), and include all assets, liabilities, revenues and expenses of JetForm Corporation ("JetForm") and its wholly-owned subsidiaries: JetForm Corporation (a Delaware corporation), JetForm Pacific Pty Limited ("JetForm Pacific"), JetForm Scandinavia AB ("JetForm Nordic"), JetForm France SA ("JetForm France"), JetForm UK Limited ("JetForm UK"), JetForm Deutschland GmbH ("JetForm Germany"), JetForm Technologies Limited ("JetForm Ireland"), JetForm Japan K.K. ("JetForm Japan") and JetForm PTE Ltd ("JetForm Singapore"). JetForm and its wholly-owned subsidiaries are collectively referred to herein as the "Company." Investments in businesses that the Company does not control, but over which it can exert significant influence, are accounted for using the equity method. Such investments are periodically evaluated for impairment and appropriate adjustments are recorded, if necessary.

(b) Nature of operations

The Company develops Web-based software solutions for the e-business market in the electronic processes, electronic document presentment and electronic forms arenas. The Company's e-process, e-document presentment and e-forms technologies provide organizations with the capability to adopt e-business models, giving them a competitive advantage in their respective industries. These solutions are complemented by the Company's professional services team, which facilitates product implementation, and its customer services team, which provides ongoing training and support. The Company sells its products and services internationally through multiple channels which include direct sales to end users, strategic partnerships with system integrators, solution partners, international distributors and original equipment manufacturers.

(c) Use of estimates

The preparation of financial statements in conformity with generally accepted accounting principles requires management to make estimates and assumptions that affect the reported amounts of assets and liabilities and disclosure of contingent assets and liabilities at the dates of the financial statements and the reported amounts of revenues and expenses during the reporting periods. Actual results could differ from those estimates.

(d) Revenue recognition

The Company recognizes revenue in accordance with Statement of Position ("SOP") 97-2, "Software Revenue Recognition", issued by the American Institute of Certified Public Accountants ("AICPA") in October 1997 and SOP 98-9 issued in December 1998.

The Company records product revenue from packaged software and irrevocable commitments to purchase products when persuasive evidence of an arrangement exists, the software product has been shipped, there are no significant uncertainties surrounding product acceptance, the fees are fixed and determinable and collection is considered probable. Revenues from irrevocable commitments to purchase products with payment terms exceeding the Company's customary trade terms are recorded at the amount receivable less deemed interest. The Company amortizes the difference between the face value of the receivable and the discounted amount over the term of the receivable and records the discount as interest income.

Revenue from software product licenses which include significant customization and revenue from services are recognized on a percentage of completion basis, whereby revenue is recorded, based on labor input hours, at the estimated realizable value of work completed to date.

Estimated losses on contracts are recognized when they become probable. Unbilled receivables represent consulting work performed under contract and not yet billed.

Revenue from maintenance agreements is recognized ratably over the term of the agreement. Unearned revenue represents payments received from customers for services not yet performed.

(e) Income taxes

The Company accounts for income taxes under the asset and liability method that requires the recognition of deferred tax assets and liabilities for the expected future tax consequences of temporary differences between the carrying amounts and tax basis of assets and liabilities. The Company provides a valuation allowance on net deferred tax assets when it is more likely than not that such assets will not be realized.

(f) Investment tax credits

Investment tax credits ("ITCs"), which are earned as a result of qualifying research and development expenditures, are recognized when the expenditures are made and their realization is more likely than not, and are applied to reduce research and development expenses in the year.

(g) Fixed assets

Fixed assets are recorded at cost. Computer software purchased by the Company is recorded as fixed assets when acquired. Costs for internal use software that are incurred in the preliminary project stage and in the post implementation/operation stage are expensed as incurred. Costs incurred during the application development stage, including appropriate Web site development costs, are capitalized and amortized over the estimated useful life of the software.

Depreciation and amortization are calculated using the following rates and bases.

Computer equipment	30% declining balance and straight-line over 2 to 4 years
Software	30% declining balance
Furniture and fixtures	20% declining balance
Software licenses and purchased rights to improve, market and/or distribute products	Straight-line over the lesser of the lives of the license or right and 15 years
Leasehold improvements	Straight-line over the term of the lease

The carrying value of fixed assets is periodically reviewed by management, and impairment losses, if any, are recognized when the expected non-discounted future operating cash flow derived from the fixed asset is less than the carrying value of such asset. In the event of an impairment in fixed assets, the discounted cash flows method is used to arrive at the estimated fair value of such asset.

(h) Goodwill and other intangibles

Goodwill, which represents the purchase price paid for an acquired business in excess of the fair values assigned to identifiable assets, is amortized on a straight-line basis over its expected useful life. In general, goodwill has been expected to have a useful life of seven years.

Depreciation and amortization are calculated using the following rates and bases.

Delrina technology	Straight-line over 3 to 5 years
Trademarks, trade names, workforce and other assets	Straight-line or declining balance over the useful lives of the assets which range from 3 to 15 years

The carrying value of goodwill and enterprise goodwill is periodically reviewed by management, and impairment losses, if any, are recognized when the expected non-discounted future operating cash flows derived from the related business acquired are less than the carrying value of such

Notes to Consolidated Financial Statements

goodwill. In the event of an impairment in goodwill, the discounted cash flows method is used to arrive at the estimated fair value of such goodwill.

(i) Software development costs

Costs related to the development of proprietary software are expensed as incurred unless the costs relate to technically feasible and complete products and can reasonably be regarded as assured of recovery through future revenues in which case the costs are deferred and amortized, based on estimated future revenues, on a straight-line basis over the useful life of the product, not to exceed three years.

(j) Foreign currency translation

The financial statements of the parent company and its subsidiaries have been translated into Canadian dollars in accordance with Statement of Financial Accounting Standards ("SFAS") No. 52, "Foreign Currency Translation." The Company's subsidiaries use their local currency as their functional currency. All balance sheet amounts with the exception of Shareholders' Equity have been translated using the exchange rates in effect at year end. Income statement amounts have been translated using the average exchange rate for the year. The gains and losses resulting from the translation of foreign currency statements into the Canadian dollar are reported in comprehensive income and as a separate component of Shareholders' Equity.

(k) Cash equivalents

Cash equivalents are defined as liquid investments which have a term to maturity at the time of purchase of less than ninety days.

(l) Stock-based compensation

The Company has elected to continue to follow Accounting Principles Board Opinion No. 25, "Accounting for Stock Issued to Employees" ("APB 25"), and to present the pro forma information that is required by SFAS No. 123 — "Accounting for Stock-Based Compensation" ("SFAS 123").

2. ACCOUNTS RECEIVABLE

Accounts receivable and term accounts receivable are net of an allowance for doubtful accounts of $2.4 million at April 30, 2000, and $1.9 million at April 30, 1999.

The Company records revenues from irrevocable commitments to purchase products which do not conform to the Company's customary trade terms at the minimum amount receivable less deemed interest ("Term Accounts Receivable"). The Company uses a discount rate equal to its net cost of borrowing at the time the revenue is recorded, which is 6.5% at April 30, 2000. Under an irrevocable commitment to purchase product, the customer commits to pay a minimum amount over a specified period of time in return for the right to use or resell up to a specific number of copies of a delivered product.

The Company records Term Accounts Receivable as non-current to the extent that management estimates payment will be received more than one year from the balance sheet date. Payment of Term Accounts Receivable is generally due the earlier of: (i) delivery of the Company's products by the customer to its customers or end users; and (ii) specific dates in the license agreement ("Minimum Payment Dates"). The gross amount of these receivables at April 30, 2000, and April 30, 1999 was $7.2 million and $22.0 million, respectively. As at April 30, 2000, total Term Accounts Receivable with Minimum Payment Dates exceeding one year were approximately $242,000. As at April 30, 1999, total Term Accounts Receivable with Minimum Payment Dates exceeding one year were approximately $6.1 million.

The Company's customer base consists of large numbers of diverse customers dispersed across many industries and geographies. As a result, concentration of credit risk with respect to accounts receivable and term accounts receivable is not significant.

3. FIXED ASSETS

(in thousands of Canadian dollars)

	Cost	Accumulated depreciation and amortization	Net book value
		April 30, 2000	
Computer equipment	$ 16,407	$ 10,852	$ 5,555
Furniture and fixtures	8,600	4,258	4,342
Software	9,896	5,864	4,032
Leasehold improvements	4,053	1,426	2,627
	$ 38,956	$ 22,400	$ 16,556

(in thousands of Canadian dollars)

	Cost	Accumulated depreciation and amortization	Net book value
		April 30, 1999	
Computer equipment	$ 15,051	$ 8,030	$ 7,021
Furniture and fixtures	8,410	2,961	5,449
Software	7,916	4,065	3,851
Leasehold improvements	3,270	971	2,299
	$ 34,647	$ 16,027	$ 18,620

4. OTHER ASSETS

(in thousands of Canadian dollars)

	Cost	Accumulated amortization	Net book value
		April 30, 2000	
Delrina technology, trademarks, trade names and workforce	$ 16,081	$ 9,425	$ 6,656
Goodwill	1,216	512	704
Licenses, marketing and distribution rights	6,857	2,632	4,225
Deferred development costs	14,724	7,905	6,819
Other assets	5,618	2,352	3,266
	$ 44,496	$ 22,826	$ 21,670

(in thousands of Canadian dollars)

	Cost	Accumulated amortization	Net book value
		April 30, 1999	
Delrina technology, trademarks, trade names and workforce	$ 16,081	$ 7,510	$ 8,571
Goodwill	1,159	226	933
Licenses, marketing and distribution rights	8,482	3,244	5,238
Deferred development costs	11,125	4,784	6,341
Other assets	6,624	1,836	4,788
	$ 43,471	$ 17,600	$ 25,871

Notes to Consolidated Financial Statements

5. RESEARCH AND DEVELOPMENT EXPENSE

The following table provides a summary of development costs deferred and the related amortization charged to cost of product in the years ended April 30, 2000, 1999 and 1998.

(in thousands of Canadian dollars)	Year ended April 30,		
	2000	1999	1998
Research and development costs	$ 20,713	$ 20,559	$ 14,123
Investment tax credits	(1,690)	(1,575)	(728)
Deferred development costs	(3,600)	(3,600)	(2,775)
Net research and development expense	$ 15,423	$ 15,384	$ 10,620
Amortization of development costs charged to cost of product	$ 3,121	$ 2,636	$ 1,726

6. FINANCIAL INSTRUMENTS AND CREDIT FACILITIES

For certain of the Company's financial instruments, including accounts receivable, unbilled receivables, accounts payable, and short-term accrued liabilities, the carrying amount approximates the fair value due to their short maturities. The carrying amount of term accounts receivable, after applying an appropriate discount rate, approximates their fair value. Cash and cash equivalents, term loan, the Delrina obligation and long-term accrued liabilities are carried at cost, which approximate their fair value.

The Company has entered into receivable purchase agreements with third-party purchasers. Under the agreements, the Company has the option to sell certain accounts receivable on a recourse basis. The Purchasers have recourse in the event of a trade dispute as defined in the receivables purchase agreements and upon the occurrence of other specified events. As at April 30, 2000, and April 30, 1999, the outstanding balance of accounts receivable sold under these agreements was approximately US$9.7 million and US$6.9 million, respectively. The Company believes that none of the receivables sold are at risk of recourse. These sales meet all of the requirements of SFAS No. 125 "Accounting for Transfers and Servicing of Financial Assets and Extinguishments of Liabilities," for off balance sheet reporting.

The Company has a committed $20 million credit facility with the Royal Bank of Canada. The credit facility is made up of (i) a $10 million term loan facility which bears interest at a rate of 1.5% over the Bankers Acceptance rate of the Bank from time to time and is payable on February 1, 2001; and (ii) a $10 million revolving line of credit which bears interest at the prime rate of the Canadian Bank from time to time. As at April 30, 2000, the Company had drawn all of the $10 million term loan facility and fixed in the interest rate until July 19, 2000, at 7.11%. The effective rate of Interest on this term loan facility for the year ended April 30, 2000, was approximately 6.51%. The Company had no borrowings against its revolving line of credit as at April 30, 2000. The Company has granted as collateral for the $20 million credit facility a general security agreement over JetForm's assets, including a pledge of the shares of certain subsidiaries.

7. CAPITAL STOCK

The authorized capital stock of the Company consists of an unlimited number of Common Shares ("Common Shares") and 2,263,782 Convertible Preference Shares ("Preference Shares").

Holders of Common Shares are entitled to one vote for each share held on all matters submitted to a vote of shareholders and do not have cumulative voting rights. Holders of Common

Shares are entitled to receive ratably such dividends, if any, as may be declared by the Board of Directors at its discretion from funds legally available therefor. Upon the liquidation, dissolution or winding up of the Company the holders of Common Shares are entitled to receive ratably, together with the Preference Shares, the net assets of the Company available after the payment of debts and other liabilities. Holders of Common Shares have no pre-emptive, subscription, redemption or conversion rights.

Holders of the Preference Shares are not entitled to receive a fixed dividend but are entitled to receive a dividend as and when declared by the Board of Directors of the Company equal to the dividend declared on its Common Shares. The holders of the Preference Shares are entitled to convert such shares into fully paid and non-assessable Common Shares at a rate equal to one Common Share per Preference Share held (subject to adjustment for share re-classification, reorganizations or for other changes). In the event of the liquidation, dissolution or winding-up of the Company, the holders of the Preference Shares shall rank pari passu, share for share, with the holders of the Common Shares.

During the year ended April 30, 1998, the Company issued 2,200,000 special warrants ("Special Warrants") to Canadian investors at a price of US$21.25 per Special Warrant. The net proceeds from the offering after deducting underwriting discounts, fees and expenses were $63.7 million. The Special Warrants were deemed to have been exercised by the holders thereof on June 26, 1998, without payment of additional consideration on the basis of one Common Share for each Special Warrant so held. On June 19, 1998, the Company filed a final prospectus with Canadian securities regulators to register the 2,200,000 Common Shares issuable on exercise of the Special Warrants. The Company does not intend to register such Common Shares under the United States Securities Act of 1933.

In June 1990, the Company adopted an Employee Stock Option Plan (the "1990 Plan") pursuant to which 400,000 Common Shares were reserved for the grant of options. On March 4, 1993, the Board of Directors voted to terminate the 1990 Plan effective as of the consummation of the Company's initial public offering dated April 20, 1993, at which time the 1993 Employee Stock Option Plan (the "1993 Plan") became effective.

On March 4, 1993, the Board of Directors adopted the 1993 Plan. The 1993 Plan is administered by the Compensation Committee of the Board of Directors and options are not granted at less than the fair market value of the Common Shares on the date of grant. Options outstanding under the 1993 Plan remain in effect pursuant to their terms. Options granted under the 1993 Plan generally have a term of five years and vest at the rate of one-third of the shares covered on each of the first three anniversary dates of the date of grant. Options granted under the 1993 Plan are not transferable and are exercisable only by the optionee during the optionee's lifetime.

The Company established the 1995 Plan on June 28, 1995, to replace the 1993 Plan. The 1995 Plan is administered by the Compensation Committee of the Board of Directors and provides for the grant to all eligible full-time employees, directors, officers and others of options to purchase Common Shares at a price based upon the last trading price of the Common Shares on the NASDAQ National Market on the trading day immediately preceding the date of grant. Pursuant to the 1995 Plan, the aggregate number of Common Shares available to be issued is 4,425,763, of which 656,000 are still available for grant as at April 30, 2000. Options granted under the 1995 Plan have a term of four, five or seven years and vest ratably during the first three years following grant. Options also vest automatically on a change in control of the Company. Options granted are non-transferable.

Notes to Consolidated Financial Statements

On September 11, 1997, the Shareholders of the Company approved the 1997 Employee Stock Purchase Plan (the "Stock Purchase Plan"). A total of 400,000 Common Shares of the Company have been reserved for issuance pursuant to the Stock Purchase Plan. Shares may be purchased under the Stock Purchase Plan by employees through payroll deduction. The purchase price of Common Shares issued under the Stock Purchase Plan is the lower of 95% of the fair market of the Common Shares of the Company at the beginning of each six-month offering period and 95% of the fair market value of the Common Shares of the Company at the end of each six-month offering period.

The following table presents the number of options and warrants outstanding and exercisable, and the weighted average exercise price:

	1995 Plan	1993 Plan	1990 Plan	IPO underwriter's warrants	Moore	Other options and warrants	Total	Weighted average exercise price in US dollars
Number of outstanding options and warrants								
Balance at April 30, 1997	1,152,054	781,139	84,250	77,478	116,216	90,000	2,301,137	12.70
Grants	2,048,905	–	–	–	–	5,000	2,053,905	13.39
Cancellations and forfeitures	(164,557)	(31,830)	–	–	–	(2,219)	(198,606)	15.25
Exercises	(60,261)	(342,176)	(84,250)	(77,478)	–	(47,781)	(611,946)	6.95
Balance at April 30, 1998	2,976,141	407,133	–	–	116,216	45,000	3,544,490	13.95
Grants	1,037,960	63,550	–	–	–	–	1,101,510	4.50
Cancellations and forfeitures	(360,813)	(175,059)	–	–	–	–	(535,872)	12.49
Exercises	(47,485)	(98,116)	–	–	–	(20,000)	(165,601)	9.38
Balance at April 30, 1999	3,605,803	197,508	–	–	116,216	25,000	3,944,527	11.71
Grants	775,112	–	–	–	–	–	775,112	6.00
Cancellations and forfeitures	(725,759)	(99,259)	–	–	–	–	(825,018)	12.60
Exercises	(38,910)	(75,917)	–	–	–	–	(114,827)	4.71
Balance at April 30, 2000	3,616,246	22,332	–	–	116,216	25,000	3,779,794	10.63
Weighted average exercise price at April 30,1998, in US dollars	$ 14.73	$ 7.70	N/A	N/A	$ 16.50	$ 11.54	$ 13.95	
Weighted average exercise price at April 30, 1999, in US dollars	$ 11.78	$ 6.93	N/A	N/A	$ 16.50	$ 15.98	$ 11.71	
Weighted average exercise price at April 30, 2000, in US dollars	$ 10.39	$ 13.15	N/A	N/A	$ 16.50	$ 15.98	$ 10.63	
Number of exercisable options and warrants								
April 30, 1998	509,854	397,974	–	–	77,478	38,334	1,023,640	12.88
April 30, 1999	1,397,776	180,759	–	–	116,216	25,000	1,719,751	14.44
April 30, 2000	1,958,369	22,332	–	–	116,216	25,000	2,121,917	13.52
Range of exercise prices in US dollars at April 30, 2000								
From	$ 3.75	$ 11.75	N/A	N/A	$ 16.50	$ 15.25	$ 3.75	
To	$ 22.00	$ 16.00	N/A	N/A	$ 16.50	$ 18.88	$ 22.00	
Range of expiry dates at April 30, 2000								
From	February 2001	June 2000	N/A	N/A	March 2001	August 2000	June 2000	
To	December 2004	June 2000	N/A	N/A	March 2001	October 2001	December 2004	

The following table presents the exercise prices and average remaining life of the outstanding options as at April 30, 2000:

Range of exercise prices			Options outstanding			Options exercisable	
From	To	Number	Weighted average exercise price	Weighted average remaining life	Number	Weighted average exercise price
(US dollars)			(US dollars)	(Years)		(US dollars)
$ 3.75	$ 3.94	871,877	$ 3.81	2.97	279,124	$ 3.81
4.06	12.88	739,500	6.30	3.80	26,420	11.04
13.00	13.50	1,313,604	13.32	2.57	992,136	13.32
14.31	22.00	854,813	17.12	2.33	824,237	17.12
		3,779,794	10.61	2.85	2,121,917	13.52

Options and warrants outstanding at April 30, 1999, had a weighted average remaining contractual life of approximately 3.53 years. The exercise price of all options granted during the years ended April 30, 2000, 1999 and 1998 was equal to the fair market value of the underlying shares at the date of grant. No compensation expense has been recorded in the Consolidated Statements of Operations for stock-based compensation.

The following table presents net income and earnings per share for the periods presented on a pro forma basis after recording the pro forma compensation expense relating to stock options granted to employees, in accordance with SFAS No. 123:

(in thousands of Canadian dollars except per share amounts)

	Year ended April 30,		
	2000	1999	1998
Net income (loss) reported	$ (8,101)	$ (29,135)	$ 10,864
Pro forma compensation expense	(1,384)	(6,770)	(5,430)
Pro forma net income (loss)	$ (9,485)	$ (35,905)	$ 5,434
Pro forma basic income (loss) per share	$ (0.48)	$ (1.81)	$ 0.33
Pro forma fully diluted income (loss) per share	$ (0.48)	$ (1.81)	$ 0.31

SFAS No.123 requires that pro forma compensation expense be recognized over the vesting period, based on the fair value of options granted to employees. The pro forma compensation expense presented above has been estimated using the Black Scholes option pricing model. Assumptions used in the pricing model include: (i) risk-free interest rates for the periods of between 4.80% and 6.27%; (ii) expected volatility of 40% for the year ended April 30, 2000; 40% for the year ended April 30, 1999; and 35% for the year ended April 30, 1998; (iii) expected dividend yield of nil; and (iv) an estimated average life of three to four years.

SFAS No. 123 requires that pro forma compensation expense be reported for options granted in fiscal years beginning after December 15, 1994, which in the case of the Company, was the year ended April 30, 1996. Since the compensation expense is recognized over the vesting period, the pro forma

compensation expense presented above is not necessarily indicative of the pro forma compensation expense that will be reported in future periods if the Company continues to grant options.

8. EARNINGS PER SHARE

In February 1997, the Financial Accounting Standards Board ("FASB") issued SFAS No. 128, "Earnings Per Share," which was required to be adopted on December 31, 1997. As a result, the Company has changed the method used to compute income per share and has restated all prior periods.

The Common Shares and Preference Shares represent equivalent residual interests and have been included in the computation of weighted average number of shares outstanding for purposes of the earnings per share computation.

Notes to Consolidated Financial Statements

The reconciliation of the numerator and denominator for the calculation of net income per share and diluted net income per share is as follows:

(in thousands of Canadian dollars except share and per share amount)		Year ended April 30,	
	2000	1999	1998
Basic income (loss) per share			
Net income (loss)	$ (8,101)	$ (29,135)	$ 10,864
Weighted average number of shares outstanding	19,915,893	19,826,057	16,622,835
Net income (loss) per share	$ (0.41)	$ (1.47)	$ 0.65
Fully diluted income (loss) per share			
Net income (loss)	$ (8,101)	$ (29,135)	$ 10,864
Weighted average number of shares outstanding	19,915,893	19,826,057	16,622,835
Dilutive effect of stock options*	—	—	992,760
Adjusted weighted average number of shares outstanding	19,915,893	19,826,057	17,615,595
Net income (loss) per share	$ (0.41)	$ (1.47)	$ 0.62

*All anti-dilutive options have been excluded

9. INCOME TAXES

The Company operates in several tax jurisdictions. Its income is subject to varying rates of tax, and losses incurred in one jurisdiction cannot be used to offset income taxes payable in another.

The income (loss) before income taxes consisted of the following:

(in thousands of Canadian dollars)		Year ended April 30,	
	2000	1999	1998
Domestic income (loss)	$ (2,980)	$ (12,664)	$ 8,584
Foreign income (loss)	(4,035)	(19,023)	3,970
Income (loss) before income taxes	$ (7,015)	$ (31,687)	$ 12,554

The provision (recovery) for income taxes consisted of the following:

(in thousands of Canadian dollars)		Year ended April 30,	
	2000	1999	1998
Domestic:			
Current income taxes	$ 375	$ 771	$ 587
Deferred income taxes	—	220	(355)
	375	991	232
Foreign:			
Current income taxes	711	1,302	1,458
Deferred income taxes	—	(4,845)	—
	711	(3,543)	1,458
Provision (recovery) for income taxes	$ 1,086	$ (2,552)	$ 1,690

The Company has domestic non-capital loss carry forwards of $107.0 million which expire between 2003 and 2006. In addition, the Company has approximately $6.0 million in domestic investment tax credits which begin to expire in 2006.

A reconciliation of the combined Canadian federal and provincial income tax rate with the Company's effective income tax rate is as follows

(in thousands of Canadian dollars)	Year ended April 30,		
	2000	1999	1998
Expected statutory rate (recovery)	(44.52%)	(44.62%)	44.62%
Expected provision for (recovery of) income tax	$ (3,130)	$ (14,134)	$ 5,601
Effect of foreign tax rate differences	711	2,816	(313)
Non-taxable portion of capital gain	(372)	—	—
Income tax rate change	573	—	—
Provincial tax incentive	(426)	—	—
Non-deductible restructuring charges	—	1,372	—
Change in valuation allowance	3,393	6,884	(3,824)
Other items	337	510	226
Provision for income taxes	$ 1,086	$ (2,552)	$ 1,690

The primary temporary differences which gave rise to deferred taxes at April 30, 2000 and 1999 are:

(in thousands of Canadian dollars)	Year ended April 30,	
	2000	1999
Deferred tax assets:		
Scientific research and experimental development expenditures	$ 6,762	$ 3,195
Net operating loss carryforwards	20,773	18,670
Depreciation and amortization	(4,075)	(5,616)
Restructuring	1,081	3,331
In-process research and development	29,866	31,147
Investment tax credits	3,288	2,954
Marketing and distribution rights	(69)	(164)
Accrued severance and other	524	—
Total deferred tax asset	58,150	53,517
Less, valuation allowance	(52,546)	(49,153)
	$ 5,604	$ 4,364

The valuation allowance for deferred taxes is required due to the Company's operating history and management's assessment of various uncertainties related to their future realization. Since the realization of deferred tax assets is dependent upon generating sufficient taxable income in the tax jurisdictions which gave rise to the deferred tax asset, the amount of the valuation allowance for deferred taxes may be reduced if it is demonstrated that positive taxable income in the various tax jurisdictions is sustainable in the future.

Notes to Consolidated Financial Statements

10. COMMITMENTS

As at April 30, 2000, the Company was committed under certain operating leases for rental of office premises and equipment as follows:

(in thousands of Canadian dollars)
Years ending April 30,

2001	$ 4,861
2002	$ 4,555
2003	$ 4,629
2004 $	4,470
2005 and beyond	$ 15,723

Total rent expense for the years ended April 30, 2000, 1999 and 1998 was $4.9 million, $5.9 million and $3.6 million, respectively.

11. NET CHANGE IN OPERATING COMPONENTS OF WORKING CAPITAL

The net change in operating components of working capital is made up of:

(in thousands of Canadian dollars)	Year ended April 30,		
	2000	1999	1998
Decrease (increase) in:			
Accounts receivable and term accounts receivable	$ 21,176	$ (6,658)	$ (8,095)
Unbilled receivables	(1,124)	2,984	(3,908)
Inventory	55	(14)	(47)
Prepaid expenses and deferred charges	715	(569)	438
Other	(1,231)	(1,605)	(727)
Increase (decrease) in:			
Accounts payable	(116)	3,759	(330)
Accrued liabilities	(5,671)	6,449	3,967
Unearned revenue	3,279	3,709	2,182
	$ 17,083	$ 8,055	$ (6,520)

12. NET INVESTMENT INCOME

The net investment income is comprises of:

(in thousands of Canadian dollars)	Year ended April 30,		
	2000	1999	1998
Interest income	$ 2,853	$ 5,910	$ 853
Interest expense	(1,482)	(2,084)	(4,417)
Gain on sale of securities	1,497	—	—
Net investment income (expense)	$ 2,868	3,826	(3,564)

13. SEGMENTED INFORMATION

In June 1997, FASB issued SFAS No. 131, "Disclosures about Segments of an Enterprise and Related Information", that was effective for fiscal years beginning after December 15, 1997. The Company adopted this new Statement in fiscal year 1999 and has restated all prior periods.

Operating segments are defined as components of an enterprise about which separate financial information is available that is evaluated regularly by the Company's chief decision maker in deciding how to allocate resources and assess performance. The Company's chief decision maker is the Chief Executive Officer.

The Company's reportable segments include Product, Consulting and Customer Support. The Product segment engages in business activities from which it earns license revenues from the Company's software products. The Consulting segment earns revenues from assisting customers in configuring, implementing and integrating the Company's products and, when required, customizing products and designing automated processes to meet the customers' specific business needs as well as providing all necessary training. The Customer Support segment earns revenues through after-sale support for software products as well as providing software upgrades under the Company's maintenance and support programs.

The accounting policies of the Company's operating segments are the same as those described in Note 1. The Company evaluates performance based on the contribution of each segment. The Product segment costs include all costs associated with selling product licenses, consulting services and customer support. The costs of the Consulting and Customer Support segments include all costs associated with the delivery of the service to the customer. Inter-segment revenues as well as charges such as depreciation and amortization, interest expense and overhead allocation are not included in the calculation of segment profit. The Company does not use a measure of segment assets to assess performance or allocate resources. As a result, segment asset information is not presented.

Notes to Consolidated Financial Statements

	Year ended April 30, 2000			
	Product	Consulting	Customer Support	Total
Revenues	$ 52,583	$ 17,549	$ 24,185	$ 94,317
Costs	35,402	8,920	3,453	47,775
Contribution	$ 17,181	$ 8,629	$ 20,732	$ 46,542
Research and development				(15,423)
Other expenses				(41,053)
Recovery of restructuring costs				1,106
Gain on sale of assets				1,813
Provision for income taxes				(1,086)
Net loss				$ (8,101)

	Year ended April 30, 1999			
	Product	Consulting	Customer Support	Total
Revenues	$ 66,662	$ 25,612	$ 21,938	$ 114,212
Costs	43,756	8,843	3,904	56,503
Contribution	$ 22,906	$ 16,769	$ 18,034	$ 57,709
Research and development				(15,384)
Other expenses				(43,509)
Restructuring				(30,503)
Provision for income taxes				2,552
Net loss				$ (29,135)

	Year ended April 30, 1998			
	Product	Consulting	Customer Support	Total
Revenues	$ 74,781	$ 18,959	$ 17,487	$ 111,227
Costs	38,974	6,947	1,874	47,795
Contribution	$ 35,807	$ 12,012	$ 15,613	63,432
Research and development				(10,620)
Other expenses				(40,258)
Provision for income taxes				(1,690)
Net income				$ 10,864

The following table details the revenue and assets attributable to Canada (the Company's country of domicile), the United States and all other foreign jurisdictions. The Company attributes revenue to geographic areas based on the location of the customer to which the products or services were sold.

(in thousands of Canadian dollars)	Year ended April 30,					
	2000		1999		1998	
	Revenue	Fixed and other assets	Revenue	Fixed and other assets	Revenue	Fixed and other assets
Canada	$ 5,611	$ 31,800	$ 6,584	$ 35,110	$ 15,637	$ 41,815
United States	55,831	2,592	72,616	3,299	65,915	4,343
Other	32,875	3,834	35,012	6,082	29,675	20,678
	$ 94,317	$ 38,226	$ 114,212	$ 44,491	$ 111,227	$ 66,836

14. DELRINA OBLIGATION

On September 10, 1996, the Company acquired certain
assets, including title to intellectual property, related to the
forms software group (the "Delrina Assets") of Delrina
Corporation ("Delrina"), a subsidiary of Symantec Corporation
of Cupertino, California, USA, for a non-interest bearing
obligation of US$100.0 million. This non-interest bearing
obligation was originally valued using a discount rate of 6%.

Under the asset purchase agreement, the Company was
required to make unequal quarterly payments to Delrina, from
September 27, 1996 to June 27, 2000.

On February 12, 1998, the Company and Delrina renegotiated
certain terms of the asset purchase agreement whereby
the Company agreed to accelerate payment of its obligation
in consideration for a reduction in the effective interest
rate, resulting in a reduction in imputed interest charges.

As at April 30, 2000, the Company had satisfied its payment
obligation to Delrina and no further amount was outstanding
under the Delrina debt.

Notes to Consolidated Financial Statements

15. RESTRUCTURING

On March 17, 1999, the Corporation announced a restructuring plan directed at reducing costs.The key restructuring actions included:

- Consolidation of management responsibilities and reduction in headcount.
- Closure of redundant facilities.
- Reduction in the carrying value of certain capital assets primarily related to past acquisitions.
- Cancellation of certain commitments and other costs.

The following table summarizes the activity in the provision for restructuring costs during the years ended April 30, 1999, and April 30, 2000:
(in thousands of Canadian dollars)

	Employee Termination	Total Facilities	Other	Costs	Non-Cash Costs	Total Restructuring
Restructuring provision	$ 5,252	$ 2,914	$ 726	$ 8,892	$ 21,611	$ 30,503
Cash payments	(1,175)	(36)	(207)	(1,418)	—	(1,418)
Non-cash items	—	—	—	—	(21,611)	(21,611)
Balance, April 30, 1999	$ 4,077	$ 2,878	$ 519	$ 7,474	$ —	$ 7,474
Cash payments	(2,921)	(1,092)	(124)	(4,137)	—	(4,137)
Reductions	(566)	(540)	—	(1,106)	—	(1,106)
Balance, April 30, 2000	$ 590	$ 1,246	$ 395	$ 2,231	$ —	$ 2,231
Long-term balance	$ —	$ 1,059	$ 279	$ 1,338	$ —	$ 1,338

Employee terminations totalled 105 and included 46 in sales and marketing, 40 in research and development, 12 in internal corporate services and seven in systems and consulting services. All employees were terminated on or before April 30, 1999. Employee terminations include salary continuance for which the Company is contractually obligated to pay. During the year ended April 30, 2000, the Company's liability for bonuses and other compensation to terminated employees was reduced by $566,000.

Facilities costs consisted primarily of $2.1 million and $780,000 related to the closure of the Company's U.K. and Toronto facilities, respectively. The provision for redundant facilities includes management's best estimates of the total future operating costs of these vacant facilities for the remainder of their respective lease terms. Actual costs could differ from these estimates. During the year ended April 30, 2000, the Company bought out its lease obligation of its vacant Toronto facilities for $420,000 and was successful in subleasing one of its vacant facilities in the United Kingdom. The Company has not been successful in finding alternative arrangements, the lease for which extends to 2010. During the year ended April 30, 2000, the Company's liability for vacant facilities was reduced by $540,000.

Other cash costs related primarily to the cancellation of trade shows and other commitments.

Non-cash costs include impairment losses of $21.6 million related to assets held for use. The losses comprise $16.6 million related to marketing and distribution rights, $3.1 million related to goodwill and $1.9 million related to other capital assets.

16. RECENT ACCOUNTING PRONOUNCEMENTS

In June 1998, the Financial Accounting Standards Board ("FASB") issued the Statement of Financial Accounting Standard ("SFAS") No. 133, "Accounting for Derivative Instruments and Hedging Activities" ("SFAS 133"). This statement establishes accounting and reporting standards for derivative instruments and hedging activities and is effective for all fiscal quarters of fiscal years beginning after June 15, 1999. In June 1999, the FASB issued SFAS No. 137 which delays the effective date of SFAS No. 133 until fiscal years beginning after June 15, 2000. Currently, as the Company has no derivative instruments, the adoption of SFAS No. 133 would have no impact on the Company's financial condition or results of operations. To the extent the Company begins to enter into such transactions in the future, the Company will adopt the Statement's disclosure requirements in the quarterly and annual financial statements for the year ending April 30, 2002.

On March 31, 2000, the Financial Accounting Standards Board (FASB) issued Interpretation No. 44, Accounting for Certain Transactions involving Stock Compensation — an interpretation of APB Opinion No. 25 (FIN 44), providing new accounting rules for stock-based compensation under APB Opinion No. 25, Accounting for Stock Issued to Employees (APB 25). FIN 44 does not change FASB Statement No. 123, Accounting for Stock-Based Compensation (FAS 123). The new rules are significant and will result in compensation expense in several situations in which no expense is typically recorded under current practice, including option repricings, purchase business combinations and plans that permit tax withholdings. FIN 44 is generally effective for transactions occurring after July 1, 2000, but apply to repricings and some other transactions after December 15, 1998. The Company does not expect the adoption of this Interpretation to have a material impact on its results of operations or financial position.

In December 1999, the Securities and Exchange Commission (SEC) issued Staff Accounting Bulletin (SAB) No. 101, Revenue Recognition in Financial Statements, which was amended in March 2000 by SAB 101A. The SAB summarizes certain of the SEC staff views in applying generally accepted accounting principles to revenue recognition in financial statements. This SAB is effective beginning the Company's first quarter of fiscal 2001. The Company does not expect the adoption of this SAB to have a material impact on its results of operations or financial position.

2000
ANNUAL
REPORT

Management's Discussion and Analysis of Financial Condition and Results of Operations

(in United States dollars, unless otherwise indicated, and in accordance with U.S. GAAP)

The following discussion should be read in conjunction with the audited consolidated financial statements and notes included in this Annual Report. The Corporation prepares and files its consolidated financial statements and the Management's Discussion and Analysis of Financial Condition and Results of Operations (MD&A) in United States (U.S.) dollars and in accordance with U.S. Generally Accepted Accounting Principles (GAAP). The consolidated financial statements and MD&A in accordance with Canadian GAAP, in U.S. dollars, are made available to all shareholders and led with various regulatory authorities.

On April 6, 2000, subsequent to the year-end, the Board of Directors of the Corporation authorized a two-for-one stock split, effected in the form of a stock dividend, payable on or about April 27, 2000 to shareholders of record at the close of business on April 20, 2000. Share and per-share amounts in this MD&A, and the audited consolidated financial statements and notes thereto included in this Annual Report, have been adjusted retroactively for this split.

OVERVIEW

The Corporation develops, markets, and supports complementary lines of software tools that are designed to satisfy business-critical needs for the extended enterprise within traditional and e-business markets. The Corporation's business intelligence products are designed to give individual users the ability to independently access, explore, analyze, and report corporate data. The Corporation's client/server application development tools are designed to increase the productivity of system analysts and developers. Cognos products are distributed both directly and through resellers worldwide.

Revenue is derived from the licensing of software and the provision of related services, which include product support and education, consulting, and other services. The Corporation generally licenses software and provides services subject to terms and conditions consistent with industry standards. Customers may elect to contract with the Corporation for product support, which includes product and documentation enhancements, as well as telephone support, by paying either an annual fee or fees based on usage of support services.

The Corporation operates internationally, with a substantial portion of its business conducted in foreign currencies. Accordingly, the Corporation's results are affected by year-over-year exchange rate fluctuations of the United States dollar relative to the Canadian dollar, to various European currencies, and to a lesser extent, other foreign currencies.

RESULTS OF OPERATIONS

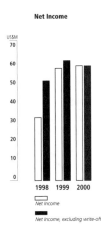

Net Income

US$M

Net Income

Net Income, excluding write-offs

Total revenue for the year ended February 29, 2000 (fiscal 2000) was $385.6 million, which was 28% more than the fiscal 1999 revenue of $301.1 million which, in turn, was 23% more than the fiscal 1998 revenue of $244.8 million. Net income for fiscal 2000 was $58.8 million and diluted net income per share was $0.67, compared to fiscal 1999 net income of $58.4 million and diluted net income per share of $0.66, and net income of $32.6 million and diluted net income per share of $0.36 for fiscal 1998.

The results for the prior fiscal year, fiscal 1999 include the write-off of $3.8 million of acquired in-process technology as a result of the acquisitions of Relational Matters and LEX2000 Inc., both of which occurred in the last fiscal quarter of fiscal 1999. The results for fiscal 1998 include the write-off of $18.0 million of acquired in-process technology as a result of the acquisitions of Right Information Systems Limited and Interweave Software, Inc. during the year. Excluding the effect of these write-offs, net income and diluted net income per share for fiscal 1999 would have been $61.8 million and $0.69, respectively, and net income and diluted net income per share for fiscal 1998 would have been $50.6 million and $0.55, respectively.

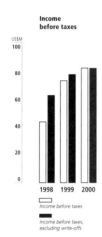

**Income
before taxes**

US$M
100

80

60

40

20

0

1998 1999 2000

☐
Income before taxes

■
*Income before taxes,
excluding write-offs*

Basic net income per share was $0.68, $0.67, and $0.37 in fiscal 2000,1999, and 1998, respectively. Excluding the effect of the write-offs in fiscal 1999 and fiscal 1998, basic net income per share would have been $0.71 and $0.57, respectively.

The Corporation experienced a decrease in net income as a percentage of revenue in fiscal 2000 as a result of increases in selling, general, and administrative expenses and an increase in the provision for income taxes. During fiscal 2000 the Corporation increased its investment in its sales channels to focus on revenue growth and expand global market coverage. The provision for income taxes increased in fiscal 2000 from the prior fiscal years as the Corporation recognized the benefits of previously unrecorded tax benefits during fiscal 1999 and 1998.

The following table sets out, for each fiscal year indicated, the percentage that each income and expense item bears to revenue, and the percentage change in the dollar amount of each item as compared to the prior fiscal year.

	PERCENTAGE OF REVENUE			PERCENTAGE CHANGE FROM FISCAL	
	2000	1999	1998	1999 to 2000	1998 to 1999
Revenue	**100.0%**	100.0%	100.0%	28.1%	23.0%
Operating expenses					
Cost of product license	**1.3**	1.9	1.5	(8.8)	49.9
Cost of product support	**3.5**	3.7	4.0	23.2	15.2
Selling, general, and administrative	**61.8**	57.3	57.5	38.1	22.4
Research and development	**13.9**	14.0	13.7	26.7	26.1
Acquired in-process technology	**0.0**	1.3	7.4	(100.0)	(78.9)
Total operating expenses	**80.5**	78.2	84.1	31.9	14.3
Operating income	**19.5**	21.8	15.9	14.1	68.8
Interest expense	**(0.2)**	(0.2)	(0.2)	36.2	9.6
Interest income	**1.9**	2.2	2.2	15.9	20.4
Income before taxes	**21.2**	23.8	17.9	14.1	63.6
Income tax provision	**5.9**	4.4	4.6	74.2	18.1
Net income	**15.3%**	19.4%	13.3%	0.7%	79.0%

The following table sets out, for each fiscal year indicated, the percentage that specific items bear to revenue, and the percentage change in the dollar amount of each item as compared to the prior fiscal year, when the effect of the write-offs of acquired in-process technology is excluded.

	PERCENTAGE OF REVENUE			PERCENTAGE CHANGE FROM FISCAL	
	2000	1999	1998	1999 to 2000	1998 to 1999
Revenue	**100.0%**	100.0%	100.0%	28.1%	23.0%
Total operating expenses	**80.5**	76.9	76.8	34.1	23.3
Operating income	**19.5**	23.1	23.2	7.9	22.1
Net income	**15.3%**	20.5%	20.7%	(4.8)%	22.0%

REVENUE

The Corporation's total revenue (consisting of product license, product support, and services revenue) was $385.6 million in fiscal 2000, compared to $301.1 million in fiscal 1999 and $244.8 million in fiscal 1998. The Corporation operates internationally, with a substantial portion of its business conducted in foreign currencies. Accordingly, the Corporation's results are affected by year-over-year exchange rate fluctuations of the United States dollar relative to the Canadian dollar, to various European currencies, and to a lesser extent, other foreign currencies. The effect of foreign exchange rate fluctuations decreased the overall revenue growth by two percentage points in fiscal 2000 from fiscal 1999 and by one percentage point in fiscal 1999 from fiscal 1998.

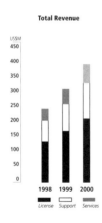

Total Revenue

The Corporation's growth in total revenue was derived primarily from the increase in revenue from the Corporation's business intelligence products, principally Web versions of PowerPlay®, Impromptu® and to a lesser extent, the addition of revenue from Cognos Visualizer and DecisionStream™, which were released during fiscal 2000. The bundling of these products for facilitated and flexible deployment contributed to the growth of Web versions of the Corporation's business intelligence products. Total revenue for all business intelligence products was $328.0 million, $230.9 million, and $176.2 million in fiscal 2000, 1999, and 1998, respectively, which resulted in year-over-year increases of 42% and 31%, respectively. Total revenue from the Corporation's business intelligence products represented 85%, 77%, and 72% of total revenue in fiscal 2000, 1999, and 1998, respectively. As described in the following section on Product License Revenue, the Corporation believes that its business intelligence products address the current market need for distributing corporate information to the end user's desktop in an extended enterprise environment of corporate intranets, extranets and client/server networks.

Total revenue from the Corporation's application development tools, PowerHouse® and Axiant®, was $57.6 million in fiscal 2000, compared to $70.2 million in fiscal 1999, and $68.6 million in fiscal 1998, which resulted in year-over-year changes of (18)% and 2%, respectively. While the Corporation experienced an increase in total revenue from these products during fiscal 1999, as described in the following section on Product License Revenue, the Corporation believes that, in the long term, revenues from these products will continue to decline.

The growth in total revenue from the three revenue categories in fiscal 2000 from fiscal 1999 was as follows: a 28% increase in product license revenue, a 27% increase in product support revenue, and a 30% increase in services revenue. This compares to an increase for the same categories for fiscal 1999 from fiscal 1998 as follows: 25%, 28%, and 9%, respectively.

Fiscal 2000 Total Revenue
by geography

Europe 32%   Asia/Pacific 7%

North America 61%

The Corporation's operations are divided into three main geographic regions: (1) North America (includes Latin America), (2) Europe (consists of the U.K. and Continental Europe), and (3) Asia/Pacific (consists of Australia and countries in the Far East). In fiscal 2000, the percentage of total revenue from North America, Europe, and Asia/Pacific was 61%, 32%, and 7%, respectively, compared to 59%, 34%, and 7%, respectively, in fiscal 1999, and 60%, 33%, and 7%, respectively, in fiscal 1998. In fiscal 2000, total revenue from North America, Europe, and Asia/Pacific increased from fiscal 1999 by 32%, 20%, and 32%, respectively, compared to increases of 22%, 25%, and 23%, respectively, in fiscal 1999 from fiscal 1998. The increase in growth for fiscal 2000 compared to growth in fiscal 1999 in North America and Asia/Pacific is attributable to the increase in revenue from the business intelligence products. The decrease in growth for Europe was attributable to slower growth in the U.K. where the Corporation experienced a relatively larger decline in revenue from application development tools and relatively less growth in business intelligence products.

Product License Revenue

Total product license revenue was $203.3 million, $158.4 million, and $126.8 million in fiscal 2000, 1999, and 1998, respectively, and accounted for 53%, 53%, and 52% of the Corporation's revenue for the respective time periods.

Business Intelligence

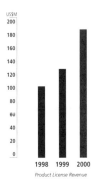

US$M

Product License Revenue

The increase in all periods occurred predominantly as a result of the performance of the Corporation's business intelligence products. Product license revenue from these products was $186.6 million, $131.9 million, and $102.3 million in fiscal 2000, 1999, and 1998, respectively. The Corporation derived approximately 92% of its product license revenue in fiscal 2000 from these products, compared to 83% in fiscal 1999, and 81% in fiscal 1998.

The Corporation believes that its business intelligence products address the current market need for distributing corporate information to the end user's desktop in an extended enterprise environment of corporate intranets, extranets and client/server networks. The Corporation continues to address the emerging market for Web or intranet-based products with the release in the current fiscal year of PowerPlay 6.6, and the launch of the Cognos enterprise BI Platform and in fiscal 1999, the release of Impromptu Web Reports. While the Corporation believes that there is a market opportunity for Web-based decision support solutions, there can be no assurance of the rate or extent of growth of this market, or that the Corporation will be successful in continuing to develop products that will effectively address this market.

Application Development

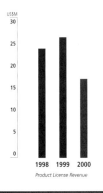

US$M

Product License Revenue

Product license revenue from the Corporation's application development tools, PowerHouse and Axiant, was $16.7 million, $26.5 million, and $24.5 million in fiscal 2000, 1999, and 1998, respectively. Over several of the past fiscal years, the Corporation has experienced a decline in product license revenue in this market which is consistent, in the Corporation's view, with the market trend away from proprietary systems and host-based computing toward industry-standard systems, corporate intranets, extranets, client/server technology, and packaged application products. The Corporation believes the increase during scal 1999 w as partially the result of expanded use of PowerHouse applications or upgrades to customer computers, and testing of legacy systems to ensure Year 2000 compliance. The Corporation believes that the maximum revenue potential from the activity around Year 2000 compliance occurred during fiscal 1999 and expects that, in the long term, the trend of decreasing product license revenue from these products will continue.

The Corporation's sales and marketing strategy includes multi-tiered channels ranging from a direct sales force to various forms of third-party distributors, resellers, and original equipment manufacturers. In fiscal 2000, the Corporation increased product license revenue derived from third-party channels to $62.2 million from $49.2 million in fiscal 1999, and from $39.6 million in fiscal 1998. The majority of the increase in product license revenue derived from third parties in fiscal 2000 from fiscal 1999 was attributable to the activity in Asia/Pacific and Europe and to a lesser extent activity in North America. The increase in product license revenue derived from third parties in fiscal 1999 from fiscal 1998 was mainly attributable to an increase in activity in North America.

Total product license revenue from third-party channels represented 31% of total product license revenue in each of fiscal 2000, 1999 and 1998.

Within the Corporation's business intelligence market, product license revenue from third-party channels was $57.3 million in fiscal 2000, compared to $42.3 million in fiscal 1999, and $33.0 million in fiscal 1998. Product license revenue within this market, from third-party channels represented 31% of the Corporation's product license revenue in fiscal 2000, compared to 32% in fiscal 1999 and 1998.

The Corporation expects to continue to enhance its combined sales and marketing strategies to further develop the potential within the business intelligence products market. The Corporation expects to continue to utilize a multi-tiered channel strategy, as outlined above. With respect to the marketing strategy, the Corporation intends to continue to form alliances with system integrators, the larger accounting and consulting firms, packaged application providers, and various other strategic partners. In addition, the Corporation plans to continue to utilize marketing and promotional programs to generate awareness of extended enterprise business intelligence solutions and interest in the Corporation's products.

There can be no assurance that increases in total product license revenue will continue to occur, or occur to the same extent to which they have historically occurred.

Product Support Revenue
Product support revenue was $118.1 million, $93.3 million, and $72.8 million in fiscal 2000, 1999, and 1998, respectively. Product support revenue accounted for 31% of the Corporation's total revenue for fiscal 2000 and 1999 and 30% for fiscal 1998. The increase in the dollar amounts was the result of new support contracts from the expansion of the Corporation's customer base, as well as the renewal of existing support contracts. The rate of growth in product support revenue associated with the expansion of the Corporation's customer base exceeds the rate of non-renewals of support contracts.

Total product support revenue from the business intelligence products was $78.8 million, $52.0 million, and $31.9 million in fiscal 2000, 1999, and 1998, respectively and comprised 67%, 56%, and 44% of the total product support revenue in fiscal 2000, 1999, and 1998, respectively. In fiscal 2000, total product support revenue from the business intelligence products increased by 52% from fiscal 1999, and total product support revenue from the application development tools decreased by 5% over the same period. In fiscal 1999, total product support revenue from the business intelligence products increased by 63% from fiscal 1998, and total product support revenue from the application development tools increased by 1% over the same period. Consistent with the discussion in product license revenue, the Corporation believes that, despite the product support revenue growth from the application development tools in fiscal 1999, in the long term, the trend of decreasing revenue from these products will continue.

There can be no assurance that increases in total product support revenue will continue to occur, or occur to the same extent to which they have historically occurred.

Services Revenue

Revenue from education, consulting, and other services was $64.3 million, $49.4 million, and $45.2 million in fiscal 2000, 1999, and 1998, respectively. Services revenue accounted for 17%, 16%, and 18% of the Corporation's total revenue for the same time periods. During fiscal 2000 the Corporation began to offer a broader range of consulting and education services in line with the shift in the demand for Web-based products. As a result, during fiscal 2000 the Corporation experienced both an increase in growth of services revenue, and an increase in the percentage of total revenue generated by services. The decline in fiscal 1999 services revenue as a percentage of total revenue was the result of relatively larger increases in both product support and product license revenue.

The increase in services revenue was predominantly the result of an increase in consulting revenue and to a lesser extent, increases in education revenue associated with the business intelligence products, consistent with the trend in product license revenue in this market. Services revenue associated with the business intelligence products contributed approximately 97%, 95%, and 93% to this revenue category in fiscal 2000, 1999, and 1998, respectively.

There can be no assurance that increases in total services revenue will continue to occur, or occur to the same extent to which they have historically occurred.

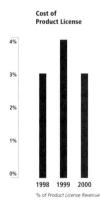

Cost of Product License

% of Product License Revenue

COST OF PRODUCT LICENSE

The cost of product license consists primarily of royalties for technology licensed from third parties and the costs of materials and distribution related to licensed software.

Product license costs in fiscal 2000 were $5.2 million compared to $5.7 million in fiscal 1999, and $3.8 million in fiscal 1998. Product license costs represented 3% of product license revenue for fiscal 2000, compared to 4% and 3% of product license revenue for fiscal 1999 and 1998, respectively.

The decrease, in dollar terms in fiscal 2000 from fiscal 1999 is principally due to decreases in both royalty costs and materials and distribution costs associated with product offerings. The increase in fiscal 1999 from fiscal 1998 was predominantly the result of a relatively larger increase in royalties; manufacturing and distribution costs remained constant between the two years.

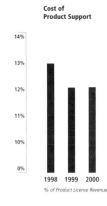

**Cost of
Product Support**

% of Product License Revenue

COST OF PRODUCT SUPPORT

The cost of product support includes the costs associated with resolving customer telephone inquiries and other telesupport activities, royalties in respect of technological support received from third parties, and the cost of materials delivered in connection with enhancement releases.

The cost of product support was $13.8 million, $11.2 million, and $9.7 million in fiscal 2000,1999, and 1998, respectively. These costs represented 12% of product support revenue for fiscal 2000 and 1999, and 13% for fiscal 1998.

The increase in fiscal 2000 from fiscal 1999 was associated predominantly with increases in customer telesupport costs; enhancement release costs contributed to a lesser extent to the increase. The increase in fiscal 1999 from fiscal 1998 was primarily associated with increases in telesupport costs.

SELLING, GENERAL, AND ADMINISTRATIVE

Selling, general, and administrative expenses were $238.1 million, $172.5 million, and $140.9 million in fiscal 2000, 1999, and 1998, respectively. These costs were 62% of revenue in fiscal 2000 compared to 57% and 58% in fiscal 1999 and 1998.

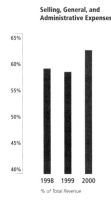

**Selling, General, and
Administrative Expenses**

% of Total Revenue

The increase in the selling, general, and administrative expenses in fiscal 2000 was substantially the result of increases in staffing and related compensation expenses, and to a lesser extent increases in subcontracting, facilities and marketing costs. During fiscal 2000 the Corporation increased its investment in its sales channels to focus on revenue growth and expand global market coverage. The average number of employees within the selling, general, and administrative areas grew by 30% in fiscal 2000 predominantly as the result of additions to sales staff. The increase in the selling, general, and administrative expenses in fiscal 1999 was mainly the result of increased staffing and related compensation expense as the average number of employees within this area grew by approximately 15%. The costs per employee increased 6% in both fiscal 2000 and fiscal 1999.

Foreign exchange rate fluctuations reduced the overall percentage increase in fiscal 2000 over 1999 by approximately one percentage point, whereas they reduced the overall percentage increase in fiscal 1999 over 1998 by approximately three percentage points.

RESEARCH AND DEVELOPMENT

The following table sets out the components of the Corporation's research and development, as well as the percentages of revenue for the periods indicated.

	2000	1999	1998
	($000s)	*($000s)*	*($000s)*
Gross research and development costs	**$54,244**	$42,746	$33,997
Government allowances	**(696)**	(527)	(897)
Amortization of previously capitalized amounts	**–**	55	430
Research and development	**$53,548**	$42,274	$33,530
Percentage of total revenue			
Gross research and development	**14%**	14%	14%
Research and development	**14%**	14%	14%

Gross research and development costs have continued to increase, in dollar terms, over the last several fiscal years but have remained relatively constant as a percentage of total revenue. The growth in both fiscal 2000 and fiscal 1999 was predominantly the result of increases associated with higher staffing levels in this area. The increase in the average number of employees in this area was 26% in fiscal 2000 from fiscal 1999, and was 27% in fiscal 1999 from fiscal 1998. Foreign exchange rate fluctuations improved the overall percentage increase in fiscal 2000 by approximately one percentage point whereas it reduced the overall increase by eight percentage points for fiscal 1999.

Software development costs are expensed as incurred unless they meet generally accepted accounting criteria for deferral and amortization. Software development costs incurred prior to the establishment of technological feasibility do not meet these criteria, and are expensed as incurred. Capitalized costs are amortized over a period not exceeding 36 months. Costs were not deferred in any of fiscal 2000, 1999, or 1998 because either no projects met the criteria for deferral or the period between (i) achieving technological feasibility and (ii) the general availability of the product was short, and the associated costs were immaterial.

The Corporation believes there is a business opportunity for distributing corporate information to the end user's desktop in an extended enterprise environment of corporate intranets, extranets and client/server networks. In earlier years the Corporation addressed this opportunity with the release of Web-based products: PowerPlay Web, Impromptu Web Reports, and Cognos Query (formerly Impromptu Web Query).

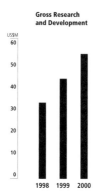

Gross Research and Development

During fiscal 2000 the Corporation launched a platform for Enterprise Business Intelligence. This platform, which includes DecisionStream, provides a single user interface or portal to support access to all Cognos business intelligence products in an extended enterprise environment. During fiscal 2000 the Corporation released PowerPlay 6.6, which provides Web managed reporting and analysis functions for intranet, extranet and Internet access to OLAP (online analytical processing) data. Also, during fiscal 2000 the Corporation released Cognos Visualizer, a business management and measurement product that extends the capabilities of PowerPlay and Impromptu with advanced visual reporting and analysis. The Corporation also released new versions of Impromptu Web Reports, DataMerchant™, and Cognos Finance (formerly LEX2000).

The Corporation continues to support its application development tools and to that end released a new version of PowerHouse during fiscal 2000 which enables Web deployment of PowerHouse applications.

During fiscal 2001 the Corporation will invest in research and development of business intelligence solutions, particularly those solutions that support the Corporation's strategy to meet the needs of the extended enterprise customers within the e-business economy. These investments will include the development of e-application packages which include pre-defined data marts, key reports and analysis solutions. The Corporation will continue the development of business-to-business solutions using BI which extend the enterprise to incorporate the supply chain, and the relationship with an enterprise's customers.

ACQUIRED IN-PROCESS TECHNOLOGY

Fiscal 2000

During fiscal 2000 the Corporation completed two acquisitions. Neither the acquisition of Information Tools AG, nor the acquisition of the minority interest in Cognos Far East Pte Limited involved the purchase of acquired in-process technology.

The Corporation acquired Information Tools AG, the Corporation's distributor in Switzerland. The shareholders of Information Tools AG are to receive total consideration of approximately $657,000, of which $458,000 was received in cash during fiscal 2000. The remainder of the consideration ($199,000) is payable equally on the first and second anniversaries of the closing of the transaction. An amount, not to exceed $500,000 could also be paid in contingent consideration. Of that amount, approximately $120,000 will be paid in fiscal 2001 relating to fiscal 2000 results. This amount has been recorded as additional purchase price.

The Corporation purchased the entire outstanding minority interest in the Corporation's subsidiary in Singapore, Cognos Far East Pte Limited. The former minority shareholders of Cognos Far East Pte Limited received approximately $1,688,000 in cash upon completion of the purchase. No further consideration is due to the former minority shareholders of the subsidiary.

Fiscal 1999

The Corporation acquired substantially all the assets of Relational Matters including DecisionStream software. DecisionStream aggregates and integrates large volumes of transaction data with multidimensional data structures. Relational Matters will receive approximately $7,550,000 over three years and 250,980 shares of the Corporation's common stock valued at $1,823,000 over the same time period. The shares, all of which were issued, are being held in escrow by the Corporation and will be released on the second (40%) and third (60%) anniversaries of the closing of the transaction. For valuation purposes, the deferred payments and shares were appropriately discounted. An independent appraisal valued the in-process research and development at $2,400,000. In the opinion of management and the appraiser, the acquired in-process research and development had not yet reached technological feasibility and had no alternative future uses. Accordingly, the Corporation recorded a special charge of $2,400,000 ($0.02 per share on a diluted basis) in the fourth quarter ended February 28, 1999, to write off the acquired in-process technology.

The Corporation acquired LEX2000 Inc., a developer of financial data mart and reporting software, for a combination of cash and the Corporation's common stock. The shareholders of LEX2000 Inc. will receive approximately $7,444,000 over three years and 252,118 shares of the Corporation's common stock valued at $1,940,000 over the same time period. Approximately 14,200 shares were issued at closing; the remainder, all of which were issued, are being held in escrow by the Corporation and will be released equally on the second (50%) and third (50%) anniversaries of the closing of the transaction. For valuation purposes, the deferred payments and shares were appropriately discounted. An independent appraisal valued the in-process research and development at $1,400,000. In the opinion of management and the appraiser, the acquired in-process research and development had not yet reached technological feasibility and had no alternative future uses. Accordingly, the Corporation recorded a special charge of $1,400,000 ($0.02 per share on a diluted basis) in the fourth quarter ended February 28, 1999, to write off the acquired in-process technology.

Fiscal 1998

During the first quarter ended May 31, 1997, the Corporation completed the acquisition of Right Information Systems Limited (RIS) of London, England. RIS was the provider of 4Thought™, business modeling and forecasting software. The shareholders of RIS received $4,500,000 and 180,000 shares of the Corporation's common stock, valued at $1,607,000. These shares are being held in escrow by the Corporation until April 9, 2000. An independent appraisal valued the in-process research and development at $5,000,000. In the opinion of management and the appraiser, the acquired in-process research and development had not yet reached technological feasibility and had no alternative future uses. Accordingly, the Corporation recorded a special charge of $5,000,000 ($0.05 per share on a diluted basis) in the first quarter ended May 31,1997, to write off the acquired in-process technology.

During the third quarter ended November 30, 1997, the Corporation completed the acquisition of Interweave Software, Inc. (Interweave) of Santa Clara, California, U.S.A. Interweave was the developer and marketer of the Interweave software product line, which allows information technology organizations to deploy intranet- and extranet-based business intelligence applications more broadly within and across enterprises. The acquisition agreement called for the Corporation to pay approximately $12,415,000 cash to the shareholders of Interweave, most of which was paid upon completion of the acquisition. An independent appraisal valued the in-process research and development at $13,000,000. In the opinion of management and the appraiser, the acquired in-process research and development had not yet reached technological feasibility and had no alternative future uses. Accordingly, the Corporation recorded a special charge of $13,000,000 ($0.14 per share on a diluted basis) in the third quarter ended November 30, 1997, to write off the acquired in-process technology.

The acquisitions in fiscal 2000,1999 and 1998 have been accounted for using the purchase method. The results of operations of all acquired companies prior to their respective dates of acquisition were not material. The results of all acquired companies have been combined with those of the Corporation since their respective dates of acquisition. (See Note 5 of the Notes to the Consolidated Financial Statements.)

INTEREST INCOME AND EXPENSE

Interest income is earned on the Corporation's cash, cash equivalents, and short-term investments, and interest expense relates primarily to the interest on the Corporation's mortgage and capital leases.

Net interest income was $6.7 million, $5.9 million, and $4.9 million in fiscal 2000,1999, and 1998, respectively. The increase during fiscal 2000 was the result of a significant increase in the average size of the investment portfolio, and to a lesser extent the impact of favorable exchange rate fluctuations. This increase was offset by a slight decrease in the average effective interest rates during fiscal 2000. The increase in fiscal 1999 was primarily attributable to higher average effective interest rates, and to a lesser extent, a larger average portfolio, which was partially offset by the impact of adverse exchange rate fluctuations.

TAX EXPENSE

The Corporation's tax rate is affected by the relative profitability of its operations in various geographic regions. In fiscal 2000 the Corporation recorded an income tax provision of $22.9 million on $81.7 million of pre-tax income. This tax expense represents an effective income tax rate of 28% for the year as compared to 18% for 1999. In fiscal 1999 the Corporation recorded an income tax provision of $13.1 million on $75.4 million of pre-tax income, excluding the $3.8 million write-off of acquired in-process technology, some of which was not tax deductible. This tax expense represented an effective income tax rate of 18% for the year, excluding the aforementioned non-deductible items, which was consistent with the effective tax rate for fiscal 1998. The rate for fiscal 2000 has increased from the prior year as the Corporation recognized the benefits of previously unrecorded tax benefits during fiscal 1999 and 1998. (See Note 9 of the Notes to the Consolidated Financial Statements.)

LIQUIDITY AND CAPITAL RESOURCES

As of February 29, 2000, the Corporation held $196.7 million in cash, cash equivalents, and short-term investments, an increase of $47.0 million from February 28, 1999. In addition, the Corporation has arranged an unsecured credit facility that includes an operating line and foreign exchange conversion facilities. The operating line permits the Corporation to borrow funds or issue letters of credit or guarantee up to Cdn$15.0 (US$10.4) million, subject to certain covenants. As of February 29, 2000, there were no direct borrowings under this operating line. As discussed further below, the Corporation has foreign exchange conversion facilities that allow it to hold foreign exchange contracts of approximately Cdn$130.0 (US$89.7) million outstanding at any one time.

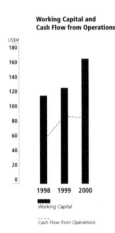

Working Capital and Cash Flow from Operations

US$M

Working Capital

Cash Flow from Operations

As of February 29, 2000, the Corporation had a total of $4.9 million of long-term liabilities (including the current portion of long-term debt), consisting of a mortgage, other long-term liabilities, and certain capital leases. As of February 29, 2000, working capital was $166.5 million, an increase of $43.1 million from February 28, 1999, primarily because of higher levels of cash, accounts receivable, and short-term investments, which were partially offset by increases in deferred revenue and other current liabilities. Working capital increased in fiscal 2000 even though the Corporation used $26.0 million for share repurchases and $2.1 million for acquisitions during the year.

Cash provided by operating activities (after changes in non-cash working capital items) for fiscal 2000 was $83.2 million, a decrease of $1.4 million compared to the prior fiscal year. This fluctuation was due to a net increase in non-cash working capital as compared to a net decrease in non-cash working capital during fiscal 1999, which was offset by an increase in net income after adjustments for depreciation, amortization and other non-cash items.

Cash used in investing activities was $37.7 million for fiscal 2000, a decrease in investment of $11.9 million compared to the prior fiscal year. The majority of the fluctuation stems from a decrease in net investment in short-term investments and decreases in acquisition costs; these decreases were offset by an increase in fixed asset additions. The increase in fixed asset additions was primarily the result of computer equipment and software purchases. Further, during fiscal 2000 the Corporation began the construction of a second building on the site of its corporate headquarters in Ottawa. The Corporation has invested approximately $3.4 million in the current year and it is anticipated that costs will total $21 million when the construction is substantially complete in fiscal 2001. (See Note 7 of the Notes to the Consolidated Financial Statements.) During fiscal 1999, the Corporation purchased the remaining interest in its head office building in Ottawa, Canada for approximately $4.8 million. In fiscal 2000, the Corporation spent $7.4 million related to the activity in short-term investments compared to $19.2 million (both net of maturities) in fiscal 1999. In addition, the Corporation spent $2.1 million in fiscal 2000 on acquisitions, compared to $9.2 million in fiscal 1999. (See Note 5 of the Notes to the Consolidated Financial Statements.)

Cash used in financing activities was $9.1 million for fiscal 2000, compared to $28.7 million in fiscal 1999. The Corporation's financing activities for both fiscal years were centered around the repurchase of its own shares in the open market, and the issuance of shares pursuant to the Corporation's stock purchase plan and the exercise of stock options. During fiscal 2000, the Corporation repurchased 2,286,000 shares at a cost of $26.0 million, compared to 3,006,000 shares repurchased at a cost of $34.1 million in fiscal 1999. Offsetting this activity, the Corporation issued 2,093,000 common shares for consideration of $16.5 million during fiscal 2000, compared to 1,146,000 shares for consideration of $5.0 million in fiscal 1999. The issuance of shares in both periods was pursuant to the Corporation's stock purchase plan and the exercise of stock options by employees, officers, and directors. In fiscal 1999, the Corporation also issued 503,000 shares for a value of $3.8 million in conjunction with the acquisition of Relational Matters and LEX2000 Inc. In fiscal 1998 the Corporation issued 180,000 shares for a value of $1.6 million in conjunction with the acquisition of RIS. (See Note 5 of the Notes to the Consolidated Financial Statements.)

The share repurchases made in the past three fiscal years were part of distinct open market share repurchase programs through the Nasdaq National Market. The share repurchases made in fiscal 2000 were part of two open market share repurchase programs. The program adopted in October 1998 expired on October 8, 1999. Under this program the Corporation repurchased 3,161,800 of its shares for $35.4 million; all repurchased shares were cancelled. In October 1999, the Corporation adopted a new program that will enable it to purchase up to 4,200,000 common shares (not more than 5% of those issued and outstanding) between October 9, 1999 and October 8, 2000. Under the current program the Corporation has repurchased 100,000 shares for $1.3 million during fiscal 2000; all repurchased shares were cancelled. This program does not commit the Corporation to make any share repurchases. Purchases will be made on The Nasdaq Stock Market at prevailing open market prices and paid out of general corporate funds. All repurchased shares will be cancelled. A copy of the *Notice of Intention to Make an Issuer Bid* is available from the Corporate Secretary. (See Note 10 of the Notes to the Consolidated Financial Statements.)

The Corporation's policy with respect to foreign currency exposure is to manage its financial exposure to certain foreign exchange fluctuations with the objective of neutralizing some of the impact of foreign currency exchange movements. To achieve this objective, the Corporation enters into foreign exchange forward contracts to hedge portions of the net investment in its various subsidiaries. The Corporation enters into these foreign exchange forward contracts with major Canadian chartered banks, and therefore does not anticipate non-performance by these counterparties. The amount of the exposure on account of any non-performance is restricted to the unrealized gains in such contracts. As of February 29, 2000, the Corporation had foreign exchange forward contracts, with maturity dates ranging from March 30, 2000 to May 25, 2000, to exchange various foreign currencies in the amount of $6.2 million.

The Corporation has never declared or paid any cash dividends on its common shares. The Corporation's current policy is to retain its earnings to finance expansion and to develop, license, and acquire new software products, and to otherwise reinvest in the Corporation.

The Corporation anticipates that through fiscal 2001 its operations will be financed by current cash balances and funds from operations. If the Corporation were to require funds in excess of its current cash position to finance its longer-term operations, the Corporation would expect to obtain such funds from, one or a combination of, the expansion of its existing credit facilities, or from public or private sales of equity or debt securities.

Inflation has not had a signicant impact on the Corporation's results of operations.

YEAR 2000 PROJECT

Beginning in fiscal 1998 the Corporation commenced an intensive effort to identify and categorize potential problem areas and develop action plans with respect to the Year 2000. This process involved an examination of its products, and its internal systems, hardware and software, as well as contacting its suppliers to obtain assurances regarding their Year 2000 readiness. The total project costs for both the Corporation's software products and its internal systems and processes were $2.4 million, of which approximately $0.1 million were capitalized. Of the total project costs, $0.7 million, were incurred during fiscal 2000, and $1.7 million during fiscal 1999.

EUROPEAN ECONOMIC AND MONETARY UNION

The introduction of the euro currency on January 1, 1999 has associated with it many potential implications for businesses operating in Europe including, but not limited to, products, information technology, pricing, currency exchange rate risk and derivatives exposure, continuity of material contracts, and potential tax consequences.

The Corporation is preparing for this new euro currency, which is scheduled to be introduced in stages over the course of a $3^{1}/_{2}$ year transition period. The Corporation believes the introduction of the euro will have limited longer-term implications on the Corporation's business. The Corporation is preparing for the introduction of the euro in the area of its internal processes and systems through identifying, modifying, and testing these processes and systems to handle transactions involving the euro in accordance with the regulations. The Corporation's financial application systems represent the most signicant internal systems that will be affected by the introduction of the euro. The Corporation upgraded these systems to a version that enables it, together with certain process changes and modications provided by the application vendor to its supported customers, to handle the initial requirements for transactions involving the euro. The Corporation continues to identify and, where necessary, modify its systems and processes in order to handle the various stages of the euro implementation. The Corporation is continuing to monitor its pricing in Europe, giving consideration to the introduction of the euro.

The Corporation believes that the costs relating to the conversion of its internal systems and processes will not have a material adverse effect on its business, results of operations, or financial condition.

MARKET RISK

Market risk represents the risk of loss that may impact our financial position due to adverse changes in financial market prices and rates. Our market risk exposure is primarily a result of fluctuations in interest rates and foreign currency exchange rates. We do not hold or issue financial instruments for trading purposes.

Further discussion of our investment and foreign exchange policies can be found in Notes 1 and 8 of the Notes to the Consolidated Financial Statements.

INTEREST RATE RISK

Our exposure to market rate risk for changes in interest rates relates primarily to our investment portfolio. The investment of cash is regulated by our investment policy of which the primary objective is security of principal. Among other selection criteria, the investment policy states that the term to maturity of investments cannot exceed one year in length. We do not use derivative financial instruments in our investment portfolio.

Interest income on our cash, cash equivalents, and short-term investments is subject to interest rate fluctuations, but we believe that the impact of these fluctuations does not have a material effect on our financial position due to the short-term nature of these financial instruments. The amount of our long-term debt is immaterial. Our interest income and interest expense are most sensitive to the general level of interest rates in Canada and the United States. Sensitivity analysis is used to measure our interest rate risk. For the fiscal year ending February 29, 2000, a 100 basis-point adverse change in interest rates would not have had a material effect on our consolidated financial position, earnings, or cash flows.

FOREIGN CURRENCY RISK

We operate internationally; accordingly, a substantial portion of our financial instruments are held in currencies other than the United States dollar. Our policy with respect to foreign currency exposure is to manage financial exposure to certain foreign exchange fluctuations with the objective of neutralizing some of the impact of foreign currency exchange movements. To achieve this objective, we enter into foreign exchange forward contracts to hedge portions of the net investment in various subsidiaries. The forward contracts are typically between the United States dollar and the British pound, the German mark, and the Australian dollar. Sensitivity analysis is used to measure our foreign currency exchange rate risk. As of February 29, 2000, a 10% adverse change in foreign exchange rates versus the U.S. dollar would not have had a material effect on our reported cash, cash equivalents, and short-term investments.

CERTAIN FACTORS THAT MAY AFFECT FUTURE RESULTS

We make certain statements in this report that constitute forward-looking statements. These statements include, but are not limited to, statements relating to our expectations concerning future revenues and earnings, including future rates of growth, from the licensing of our business intelligence and application development products and related product support and services, and relating to the sufficiency of capital to meet our working capital and capital expenditure requirements. Forward-looking statements are subject to risks and uncertainties that may cause future results to differ materially from those expected. There can be no guarantee that future results will turn out as expected. Factors that may cause such differences include, but are not limited to, the factors discussed below. Additional risks and uncertainties that we are unaware of or currently deem immaterial may also adversely affect our business operations.

OUR GROWTH MAY NOT CONTINUE AT HISTORICAL GROWTH RATES.

Although we have experienced signicant license revenue growth with respect to our business intelligence products over the past few fiscal years, we cannot assure you that we will continue to grow. If we do grow, we cannot assure you that we will be able to maintain the histor-ical rate or extent of such growth in the future. Despite product license revenue growth from our application development tools during fiscal 1999, we have been experiencing a decline in product license revenue from our application development tools over the past several years. In the long term, we expect declining revenues in these more established proprietary markets for our application development tools.

OUR QUARTERLY AND ANNUAL OPERATING RESULTS ARE SUBJECT TO FLUCTUATIONS, WHICH MAY CAUSE OUR STOCK PRICE TO FLUCTUATE OR DECLINE.

Historically, our quarterly operating results have varied from quarter to quarter, and we anticipate this pattern to continue. We typically realize a larger percentage of our annual revenue and earnings in the fourth quarter of each fiscal year, and lower revenue and earnings in the first quarter of the next fiscal year. Our quarterly operating results may be adversely affected by a wide variety of factors, including:

- our ability to maintain revenue growth at current levels or anticipate a decline in revenue from any of our products;
- changes in product mix and our ability to anticipate changes in shipment patterns;
- our ability to identify and develop new technologies and to commercialize those technologies into new products;
- our ability to accurately select appropriate business models and strategies;
- our ability to make appropriate decisions which will position us to achieve further growth;
- our ability to identify, hire, train, motivate, and retain highly qualified personnel, and to achieve targeted productivity levels;
- our ability to identify, develop, deliver, and introduce in a timely manner new and enhanced versions of our products which anticipate market demand and address customer needs;
- market acceptance of business intelligence software generally and of new and enhanced versions of our products in particular;
- timing of new product announcements;
- our ability to establish and maintain a competitive advantage;
- changes in our pricing policies or those of our competitors and other competitive pressures on selling prices;
- size, timing, and execution of customer orders and shipments, including delays, deferrals, or cancellations of customer orders;
- number and signicance of product enhancements and new product and technology announcements by our competitors;
- our reliance on third party distribution channels as part of our sales and marketing strategy;
- the timing and provision of pricing protections and exchanges from certain distributors;
- changes in foreign currency exchange rates and issues relating to the conversion to the euro; and
- our ability to enforce our intellectual property rights.

As a result of the foregoing and other factors, we may experience material fluctuations in future quarterly and annual operating results. These fluctuations could materially and adversely affect our stock price, as well as, our business, results of operations, and financial condition.

THE SOFTWARE MARKETS THAT WE TARGET ARE SUBJECT TO RAPID TECHNOLOGICAL CHANGE AND NEW PRODUCT INTRODUCTIONS AND ENHANCEMENTS.

The markets for our products are characterized by:

- rapid and signicant technological change;
- frequent new product introductions and enhancements;
- changing customer demands; and
- evolving industry standards.

We believe that our future success depends principally on our ability to continue to support a number of popular operating systems and databases; our ability to maintain and improve our product line; and our ability to rapidly develop new products that achieve market acceptance, maintain technological competitiveness, and meet an expanding range of customer requirements. If we are unable to achieve these factors, we may lose our competitive position. Successful product development and introduction depend upon a number of factors, including new product selection, timely and efficient completion of product design, product performance at customer locations, and whether our competitors develop similar products. In addition, the introduction of products embodying new technologies can quickly make existing products obsolete and unmarketable. We cannot assure you that our products will remain competitive, respond to market demands and developments and new industry standards, and not become obsolete. In particular, we cannot assure you that we have developed the appropriate products to respond effectively to the growing market interest in Web-based software, or if so, whether we can continue to bring those products to market in a timely and cost-effective basis and distribute those products in the face of competition from similar products developed by existing or new competitors. We cannot assure you that market interest in Web-based software will continue at the same rate, or that alternative methods of deploying software will not become more popular. If we are unable to identify a shift in the market demand quickly enough, we may not be able to develop products to meet those new demands, or bring them to market in a timely way.

WE RELY ON PARTNERS AND OTHER DISTRIBUTION CHANNELS TO MARKET AND DISTRIBUTE OUR PRODUCTS AND ANY FAILURE OF THESE PARTIES TO DO SO, COULD HAVE A MATERIAL ADVERSE EFFECT ON OUR BUSINESS.

Our sales and marketing strategy includes multi-tiered channels ranging from a direct sales force to various forms of third-party distributors, resellers, and original equipment manufacturers. We have developed a number of these relationships and intend to continue to develop new channel partner relationships. Our inability to attract important and effective channel partners, or these partners' inability to penetrate their respective market segments, or the loss of any of our channel partners as a result of competitive products offered by other companies or products developed internally by these channel partners or otherwise, could materially adversely affect our business, results of operations, and financial condition.

UNAUTHORIZED USED OF OUR INTELLECTUAL PROPERTY COULD DAMAGE OUR BUSINESS.

Our success depends in part on our ability to protect our proprietary rights in our intellectual property. We rely on certain intellectual property protections, including contractual provisions, patents, copyright, trademark and trade secret laws, to preserve our intellectual property rights. Despite our precautions, it may be possible for third parties to obtain and use our intellectual property without our authorization. Policing unauthorized use of software is difficult and some foreign laws do not protect proprietary rights to the same extent as Canada or the United States.

To protect our intellectual property, we may become involved in litigation, which could result in substantial expenses and materially disrupt the conduct of our business. Third parties could assert that our technology infringes their proprietary rights, which could adversely affect our ability to distribute our products and result in substantial litigation expenses and monetary liability. Any invalidation of our intellectual property rights or lengthy and expensive defense of those rights could have a material adverse affect on our business, results of operations, and financial condition.

THE LOSS OF OUR RIGHTS TO USE SOFTWARE LICENSED TO US BY THIRD PARTIES COULD HARM OUR BUSINESS.

In order to provide a complete solution, we license certain technologies used in our products from third parties, generally on a non-exclusive basis. The termination of such licenses, or the failure of the third-party licensors to adequately maintain or update their products, could delay our ability to ship certain of our products while we seek to implement alternative technology offered by other sources. In addition, alternative technology may not be available on commercially reasonable terms. In the future, it may be necessary or desirable to obtain other third-party technology licenses relating to one or more of our products or relating to current or future technologies to enhance our product offerings. We cannot assure you that we will be able to obtain licensing rights to the needed technology on commercially reasonable terms, if at all.

WE FACE INTENSE COMPETITION AND COULD BE AFFECTED BY THE ACTIONS OF OUR COMPETITORS.

We face substantial competition throughout the world, primarily from software companies located in the United States, Europe, and Canada. Some of our competitors have been in business longer than us and have substantially greater financial and other resources with which to pursue research and development, manufacturing, marketing, and distribution of their products. We expect our current competitors and potentially new competitors to continue to improve the performance of their current products and to introduce new products or new technologies that provide improved cost of ownership and performance characteristics. New product introductions by our competitors could cause a decline in sales, a reduction in the sales price, or a loss of market acceptance of our existing products. To the extent that we are unable to effectively compete against our current and future competitors, our ability to sell products could be harmed and our market share reduced. Any erosion of our competitiveness could have a material adverse effect on our business, results of operations, and financial condition.

WE HAVE MULTINATIONAL OPERATIONS THAT ARE SUBJECT TO RISKS INHERENT IN INTERNATIONAL OPERATIONS.

We derive a signicant portion of our total revenues from international sales. International sales are subject to signicant risks, including:

- unexpected changes in legal and regulatory requirements and policy changes affecting our markets;
- changes in tariffs and other trade barriers;
- fluctuations in currency exchange rates;
- political and economic instability;
- longer payment cycles and other difficulties in accounts receivable collection;
- difficulties in managing distributors and representatives;
- difficulties in staffing and managing foreign operations;
- difficulties in protecting our intellectual property; and
- potentially adverse tax consequences.

Each of these factors could adversely affect our business, results of operations, and financial condition.

OUR EXECUTIVE MANAGEMENT AND OTHER KEY PERSONNEL ARE ESSENTIAL TO OUR BUSINESS; WE MAY NOT BE ABLE TO RECRUIT AND RETAIN THE PERSONNEL WE NEED TO SUCCEED.

Our performance is substantially dependent on the performance of our key technical and management personnel. The loss of the services of any of these persons could have a material adverse effect on our business, results of operations, and financial condition. Our success is highly dependent on our continuing ability to identify, hire, train, motivate, and retain highly qualified management, technical, sales, and marketing personnel. Competition for such personnel is intense, and we cannot assure you that we will be able to attract, assimilate, or retain highly qualified technical and managerial personnel in the future. Our inability to attract and retain the necessary management, technical, sales, and marketing personnel could have a material adverse effect on our business, results of operations, and financial condition.

PURSUING AND COMPLETING RECENT AND POTENTIAL ACQUISITIONS COULD DIVERT MANAGEMENT ATTENTION AND FINANCIAL RESOURCES AND MAY NOT PRODUCE THE DESIRED BUSINESS RESULTS.

We completed the acquisitions of Information Tools AG, and the outstanding minority interest in Cognos Far East Pte Limited during scal 2000. In fiscal 1999, we acquired Relational Matters and LEX2000 Inc., and in fiscal 1998, Right Information Systems Limited and Interweave Software, Inc. We may in turn engage in additional selective acquisitions of other products or businesses that we believe are complementary to ours. We cannot assure you that we will be able to identify additional suitable acquisition candidates available for sale at reasonable prices, consummate any acquisition, or successfully integrate any acquired product or business into our operations. Further, acquisitions may involve a number of special risks, including:

- diversion of management's attention;
- disruption to our ongoing business;
- failure to retain key acquired personnel;
- difficulties in assimilating acquired operations, technologies, products, and personnel;
- unanticipated expenses, events, or circumstances;
- assumption of legal and other undisclosed liabilities; and
- the ability to appropriately value the acquired in-process research and development.

If we do not successfully address these risks or any other problems encountered in connection with an acquisition, the acquisition could have a material adverse effect on our business, results of operations, and financial condition. Problems with an acquired business could have a material adverse effect on our performance as a whole. In addition, if we proceed with an acquisition, our available cash may be used to complete the transaction, or shares may be issued which could cause a dilution to existing shareholders.

OUR STOCK PRICE WILL FLUCTUATE.

The market price of our common shares may be volatile and could be subject to wide fluctuations due to a number of factors, including:

- actual or anticipated fluctuations in our results of operations;
- announcements of technological innovations or new products by us or our competitors;
- changes in estimates of our future results of operations by securities analysts;
- general industry changes in the business intelligence tools or client/server development tools markets; or
- other events or factors.

In addition, the financial markets have experienced signicant price and volume fluctuations that have particularly affected the market prices of equity securities of many high technology companies and that often have been unrelated to the operating performance of these companies. Broad market fluctuations, as well as economic conditions generally and in the software industry specically, may adversely affect the market price of our common shares. In the past, following periods of volatility in the market price of a particular company's securities, securities class action litigation has often been brought against that company. Similar litigation may occur in the future with respect to us, which could result in substantial costs, divert management's attention and other company resources, and have a material adverse effect upon our business, results of operations, and financial condition.

Quarterly Results

The following table sets out selected unaudited consolidated financial information for each quarter in fiscal 1999 and fiscal 2000.

On April 6, 2000, subsequent to year-end, the Board of Directors of the Corporation authorized a two-for-one stock split, effected in the form of a stock dividend, payable on or about April 27, 2000 to shareholders of record at the close of business on April 20, 2000. All historic consolidated results have been restated for the split.

| | FISCAL 1999 | | | | FISCAL 2000 | | | |
	First Quarter	Second Quarter	Third Quarter	Fourth Quarter	First Quarter	Second Quarter	Third Quarter	Fourth Quarter
					($000s, except per share amounts, U.S. GAAP)			
Revenue	$67,309	$70,583	$76,308	$86,925	**$81,645**	**$88,128**	**$97,753**	**$118,114**
Operating expenses								
Cost of product license	942	1,137	1,354	2,305	**1,054**	**1,001**	**1,456**	**1,724**
Cost of product support	2,408	2,793	2,968	2,997	**3,095**	**3,336**	**3,608**	**3,719**
Selling, general, and administrative	41,706	40,708	43,355	46,713	**51,808**	**54,593**	**61,513**	**70,233**
Research and development	9,946	10,235	10,863	11,230	**12,197**	**12,845**	**13,574**	**14,932**
Acquired in-process technology	–	–	–	3,800	**–**	**–**	**–**	**–**
Total operating expenses	55,002	54,873	58,540	67,045	**68,154**	**71,775**	**80,151**	**90,608**
Operating income	$12,307	$15,710	$17,768	$19,880	**$13,491**	**$16,353**	**$17,602**	**$ 27,506**
Net income	$11,276	$14,122	$15,855	$17,181	**$10,865**	**$12,835**	**$13,851**	**$ 21,264**
Net income per share								
Basic	$0.13	$0.16	$0.18	$0.20	**$0.13**	**$0.15**	**$0.16**	**$0.25**
Diluted	$0.12	$0.16	$0.18	$0.19	**$0.12**	**$0.15**	**$0.16**	**$0.24**

The Corporation's sales cycle typically ranges from a few days up to twelve months, depending on factors such as the size of the transaction, the product involved, the length of the customer relationship, the timing of new product introductions by the Corporation and others, the level of sales management activity, and general economic conditions. Delays in closing product licensing transactions at or near the end of any quarter may have a materially adverse effect on the financial results for that quarter. While the Corporation takes steps to minimize the impact of such delays, there can be no assurance that such delays will not occur. See Certain Factors That May Affect Future Results.

Report of Management

The Corporation's management is responsible for preparing the accompanying consolidated financial statements in conformity with accounting principles generally accepted in the United States. In preparing these consolidated financial statements, management selects appropriate accounting policies and uses its judgment and best estimates to report events and transactions as they occur. Management has determined such amounts on a reasonable basis in order to ensure that the financial statements are presented fairly, in all material respects. Financial data included throughout this Annual Report is prepared on a basis consistent with that of the financial statements.

The Corporation maintains a system of internal accounting controls designed to provide reasonable assurance, at a reasonable cost, that assets are safeguarded and that transactions are executed and recorded in accordance with the Corporation's policies for doing business. This system is supported by written policies and procedures for key business activities; the hiring of qualified, competent staff; and by a continuous planning and monitoring program.

Ernst & Young LLP, the independent auditors appointed by the shareholders, have been engaged to conduct an examination of the consolidated financial statements in accordance with generally accepted auditing standards, and have expressed their opinion on these statements. During the course of their audit, Ernst & Young LLP reviewed the Corporation's system of internal controls to the extent necessary to render their opinion on the consolidated nancial statements .

The Board of Directors is responsible for ensuring that management fulfills its responsibility for financial reporting and internal control, and is ultimately responsible for reviewing and approving the consolidated financial statements. The Board carries out this responsibility principally through its Audit Committee; all members are outside Directors. The Committee meets four times annually to review audited and unaudited financial information prior to its public release. The Committee also considers, for review by the Board of Directors and approval by the shareholders, the engagement or reappointment of the external auditors. Ernst & Young LLP has full and free access to the Audit Committee.

Management acknowledges its responsibility to provide financial information that is representative of the Corporation's operations, is consistent and reliable, and is relevant for the informed evaluation of the Corporation's activities.

James M. Tory
Chairman

Ron Zambonini
President and
Chief Executive Ofcer

Donnie M. Moore
Senior Vice President,
Finance & Administration,
and Chief Financial Ofcer

March 30, 2000
[except Note 15, as to which
the date is April 6, 2000]

Auditors' Report

To the Board of Directors and Shareholders of Cognos Incorporated:

We have audited the consolidated balance sheets of Cognos Incorporated as at February 29, 2000 and February 28, 1999 and the consolidated statements of income, stockholders' equity, and cash flows for each of the years in the three-year period ended February 29, 2000. These financial statements are the responsibility of the Corporation's management. Our responsibility is to express an opinion on these financial statements based on our audits.

We conducted our audits in accordance with generally accepted auditing standards. Those standards require that we plan and perform an audit to obtain reasonable assurance whether the financial statements are free of material misstatement. An audit includes examining, on a test basis, evidence supporting the amounts and disclosures in the financial statements. An audit also includes assessing the accounting principles used and significant estimates made by management, as well as evaluating the overall financial statement presentation.

In our opinion, these consolidated financial statements present fairly, in all material respects, the financial position of the Corporation as at February 29, 2000 and February 28, 1999, and the results of its operations and its cash flows for each of the years in the three-year period ended February 29, 2000, in accordance with accounting principles generally accepted in the United States of America.

On March 30, 2000, we reported separately to the Board of Directors and Shareholders of Cognos Incorporated on financial statements for the same periods, prepared in accordance with accounting principles generally accepted in Canada.

Ernst & Young LLP

Ernst & Young LLP
Chartered Accountants

Ottawa, Canada
March 30, 2000
[except Note 15, as to which
the date is April 6, 2000]

Consolidated Statements of Income

(US$000s except share amounts, U.S. GAAP)

	Note	2000	1999	1998
			YEARS ENDED THE LAST DAY OF FEBRUARY	
Revenue				
Product license		$203,299	$158,393	$126,820
Product support		118,061	93,311	72,832
Services		64,280	49,421	45,182
Total revenue		385,640	301,125	244,834
Operating expenses				
Cost of product license		5,235	5,738	3,828
Cost of product support		13,758	11,166	9,694
Selling, general, and administrative		238,147	172,482	140,882
Research and development		53,548	42,274	33,530
Acquired in-process technology	5	–	3,800	18,000
Total operating expenses		310,688	235,460	205,934
Operating income		74,952	65,665	38,900
Interest expense	6	(718)	(527)	(481)
Interest income		7,454	6,430	5,340
Income before taxes		81,688	71,568	43,759
Income tax provision	9	22,873	13,134	11,117
Net income		$ 58,815	$ 58,434	$ 32,642
Net income per share	10, 15			
Basic		$0.68	$0.67	$0.37
Diluted		$0.67	$0.66	$0.36
Weighted average number of shares (000s)	10, 15			
Basic		85,972	87,416	88,414
Diluted		88,100	88,940	91,544

(see accompanying notes)

Consolidated Balance Sheets

(US$000s, U.S. GAAP)

	Note	FEBRUARY 29, 2000	FEBRUARY 28, 1999
Assets			
Current assets			
Cash and cash equivalents	8	**$132,435**	$ 93,617
Short-term investments	8	**64,284**	56,074
Accounts receivable	2	**107,823**	76,876
Inventories		**806**	807
Prepaid expenses		**7,840**	6,388
		313,188	233,762
Fixed assets	3	**44,835**	30,164
Intangible assets	4	**21,863**	25,203
		$379,886	$289,129
Liabilities			
Current liabilities			
Accounts payable		**$ 22,908**	$ 18,960
Accrued charges		**17,540**	13,148
Salaries, commissions, and related items		**24,024**	19,656
Income taxes payable		**3,548**	7,290
Current portion of long-term debt	6	**2,176**	123
Deferred revenue		**76,537**	51,242
		146,733	110,419
Long-term debt	6	**–**	2,489
Long-term liabilities	5	**2,699**	5,820
Deferred income taxes	9	**15,150**	7,787
		164,582	126,515
Commitments and Contingencies	7		
Stockholders' Equity			
Capital stock			
Common shares (2000 – 86,657,578; 1999 – 86,850,568)	10, 15	**106,936**	91,985
Retained earnings		**114,601**	79,341
Other accumulated comprehensive items		**(6,233)**	(8,712)
		215,304	162,614
		$379,886	$289,129

(see accompanying notes)

On behalf of the Board:

Douglas C. Cameron
Director

James M. Tory
Chairman

Consolidated Statements of Stockholders' Equity

(US$000s except share amounts, U.S. GAAP)

	(000s)				
Balances, February 28, 1997	87,178	$ 74,739	$ 46,122	$(4,949)	$115,912
Issuance of stock					
Stock option plans	3,316	8,557			8,557
Stock purchase plans	74	776			776
Business acquisitions	180	1,607			1,607
Repurchase of shares	(2,540)	(2,386)	(26,725)		(29,111)
Income tax effect related to stock options		2,425			2,425
	88,208	85,718	19,397	(4,949)	100,166
Net income			32,642		32,642
Other comprehensive items					
Foreign currency translation adjustments				(1,803)	(1,803)
Comprehensive income			32,642	(1,803)	30,839
Balances, February 28, 1998	88,208	$ 85,718	$ 52,039	$(6,752)	$131,005
Issuance of stock					
Stock option plans	1,054	4,141			4,141
Stock purchase plans	92	846			846
Business acquisitions	503	3,763			3,763
Repurchase of shares	(3,006)	(3,005)	(31,132)		(34,137)
Income tax effect related to stock options		522			522
	86,851	91,985	20,907	(6,752)	106,140
Net income			58,434		58,434
Other comprehensive items					
Foreign currency translation adjustments				(1,960)	(1,960)
Comprehensive income			58,434	(1,960)	56,474
Balances, February 28, 1999	86,851	$ 91,985	$ 79,341	$(8,712)	$162,614
Issuance of stock					
Stock option plans	**1,973**	**15,420**			**15,420**
Stock purchase plans	**120**	**1,095**			**1,095**
Repurchase of shares	**(2,286)**	**(2,458)**	**(23,555)**		**(26,013)**
Income tax effect related to stock options	**–**	**894**			**894**
	86,658	**106,936**	**55,786**	**(8,712)**	**154,010**
Net income			**58,815**		**58,815**
Other comprehensive items					
Foreign currency translation adjustments				**2,479**	**2,479**
Comprehensive income			**58,815**	**2,479**	**61,294**
Balances, February 29, 2000	**86,658**	**$106,936**	**$114,601**	**$(6,233)**	**$215,304**

(see accompanying notes)

Consolidated Statements of Cash Flows

(US$000s, U.S. GAAP)

	YEARS ENDED THE LAST DAY OF FEBRUARY		
	2000	1999	1998
Cash provided by (used in) operating activities			
Net income	$ 58,815	$ 58,434	$ 32,642
Non-cash items			
Depreciation and amortization	19,590	12,145	9,754
Write-off of acquired in-process technology	–	3,800	18,000
Deferred income taxes	7,165	(1,984)	543
Loss on disposal of fixed assets	148	185	403
	85,718	72,580	61,342
Change in non-cash working capital			
Increase in accounts receivable	(32,818)	(12,805)	(17,135)
Decrease (increase) in inventories	31	(267)	91
Increase in prepaid expenses	(1,328)	(2,852)	(837)
Increase in accounts payable	3,930	3,526	3,571
Increase in accrued charges	1,004	2,568	300
Increase in salaries, commissions, and related items	4,394	5,806	2,948
Increase (decrease) in income taxes payable	(3,993)	5,624	(2,603)
Increase in deferred revenue	26,280	10,438	8,208
	83,218	84,618	55,885
Cash provided by (used in) investing activities			
Maturity of short-term investments	138,796	96,860	131,340
Purchase of short-term investments	(146,238)	(116,093)	(151,141)
Acquisition costs	(2,146)	(9,174)	(16,915)
Additions to fixed assets	(28,096)	(21,147)	(12,068)
Proceeds from the sale of fixed assets	24	12	45
	(37,660)	(49,542)	(48,739)
Cash provided by (used in) financing activities			
Issue of common shares	17,409	5,509	11,758
Repurchase of shares	(26,013)	(34,137)	(29,111)
Repayment of long-term debt	(467)	(107)	(92)
	(9,071)	(28,735)	(17,445)
Effect of exchange rate changes on cash	2,331	(2,338)	(1,240)
Net increase (decrease) in cash and cash equivalents	38,818	4,003	(11,539)
Cash and cash equivalents, beginning of period	93,617	89,614	101,153
Cash and cash equivalents, end of period	132,435	93,617	89,614
Short-term investments, end of period	64,284	56,074	36,712
Cash, cash equivalents, and short-term investments, end of period	$196,719	$149,691	$126,326

(see accompanying notes)

Notes to the Consolidated Financial Statements

1___SUMMARY OF SIGNIFICANT ACCOUNTING POLICIES

NATURE OF OPERATIONS

The Corporation develops, markets, and supports computer software products for data access, exploring, reporting, and analysis, and for application development on a wide range of open and proprietary platforms. The Corporation markets and supports these products both directly and through resellers worldwide.

BASIS OF PRESENTATION

These consolidated financial statements have been prepared by the Corporation in United States (U.S.) dollars and in accordance with generally accepted accounting principles (GAAP) in the U.S., applied on a consistent basis.

Consolidated financial statements prepared in accordance with Canadian GAAP, in U.S. dollars, are made available to all shareholders, and filed with various regulatory authorities.

BASIS OF CONSOLIDATION

These consolidated financial statements include the accounts of the Corporation and its subsidiaries. All but one of the subsidiaries are wholly owned. Intercompany transactions and balances have been eliminated.

ESTIMATES

The preparation of these consolidated financial statements in conformity with GAAP requires management to make estimates and assumptions that affect the amounts reported in the consolidated financial statements and the accompanying notes. In the opinion of management, these consolidated financial statements reflect all adjustments necessary to present fairly the results for the periods presented. Actual results could differ from these estimates.

COMPREHENSIVE INCOME

Comprehensive income includes net income and "other comprehensive income." Other comprehensive income refers to changes in the balances of revenues, expenses, gains, and losses that are recorded directly as a separate component of Stockholders' Equity and excluded from net income. The only comprehensive item for the Corporation relates to foreign currency translation adjustments pertaining to those subsidiaries not using the U.S. dollar as their functional currency.

FOREIGN CURRENCY TRANSLATION

The financial statements of the parent company and its non-U.S. subsidiaries have been translated into U.S. dollars in accordance with the FASB Statement No. 52, *Foreign Currency Translation*. All balance sheet amounts have been translated using the exchange rates in effect at the applicable year end. Income statement amounts have been translated using the weighted average exchange rate for the applicable year. The gains and losses resulting from the changes in exchange rates from year to year have been reported as a separate component of Stockholders' Equity. Currency transaction gains and losses are immaterial for all periods presented.

REVENUE

The Corporation recognizes revenue in accordance with Statement of Position (SOP) 97-2, *Software Revenue Recognition*, issued by the American Institute of Certified Public Accountants.

Substantially all of the Corporation's product license revenue is earned from licenses of off-the-shelf software requiring no customization. Revenue from these licenses is recognized when all of the following criteria are met: persuasive evidence of an arrangement exists, delivery has occurred, the fee is fixed or determinable, and collectibility is probable. If a license includes the right to return the product for refund or credit, revenue is recognized net of an allowance for estimated returns provided all the requirements of SOP 97-2 have been met.

Revenue from product support contracts is recognized ratably over the life of the contract. Incremental costs directly attributable to the acquisition of product support contracts are deferred and expensed in the period the related revenue is recognized.

Revenue from education, consulting, and other services is recognized at the time such services are rendered.

For contracts with multiple obligations (e.g. deliverable and undeliverable products, support obligations, education, consulting and other services), the Corporation allocates revenue to each element of the contract based on objective evidence, specific to the Corporation, of the fair value of the element.

CASH, CASH EQUIVALENTS, AND SHORT-TERM INVESTMENTS

Cash includes cash equivalents, which are investments that are generally held to maturity and have terms to maturity of three months or less at the time of acquisition. Cash equivalents typically consist of commercial paper, term deposits, banker's acceptances and bearer deposit notes issued by major North American banks, and corporate debt. Cash and cash equivalents are carried at cost, which approximates their fair value.

Short-term investments are investments that are generally held to maturity and have terms greater than three months at the time of acquisition. Short-term investments typically consist of commercial paper, Government of Canada Treasury Bills, and banker's acceptances. Short-term investments are carried at cost, which approximates their fair value.

INVENTORIES

Inventories are comprised principally of finished goods and are stated at the lower of cost, on an average cost basis, and net realizable value.

FIXED ASSETS

Fixed assets are recorded at cost. Computer equipment and software, and the building, are depreciated using the straight line method. Office furniture is depreciated using the diminishing balance method. Leasehold improvements are amortized using the straight line method over either the life of the improvement or the term of the lease, whichever is shorter.

Assets leased on terms that transfer substantially all of the benefits and risks of ownership to the Corporation are accounted for as capital leases, as though the asset had been purchased and a liability incurred. All other leases are accounted for as operating leases.

INTANGIBLE ASSETS

This category includes acquired technology and goodwill associated with various acquisitions, and deferred software development costs.

Acquired technology represents the discounted fair value of the estimated net future income-producing capabilities of software products acquired on acquisitions. Acquired technology is amortized over five years on a straight line basis. The Corporation evaluates the expected future net cash flows of the acquired technology at each reporting date, and adjusts to net realizable value if necessary.

Goodwill represents the excess of the purchase price of acquired companies over the estimated fair value of the tangible and intangible net assets acquired. Goodwill is amortized over five years on a straight line basis. The Corporation evaluates the expected future net cash flows of the acquired businesses at each reporting date, and adjusts goodwill for any impairment.

Software development costs are expensed as incurred unless they meet generally accepted accounting criteria for deferral and amortization. Software development costs incurred prior to the establishment of technological feasibility do not meet these criteria, and are expensed as incurred. Research costs are expensed as incurred. For costs that are capitalized, the amortization is the greater of the amount calculated using either (i) the ratio that the appropriate product's current gross revenues bear to the total of current and anticipated future gross revenues for that product, or (ii) the straight line method over the remaining economic life of the product. Such amortization is recorded over a period not exceeding three years. The Corporation reassesses whether it has met the relevant criteria for continued deferral and amortization at each reporting date.

Income Taxes
The liability method is used in accounting for income taxes. Under this method, deferred tax assets and liabilities are determined based on differences between financial reporting and income tax bases of assets and liabilities, and are measured using the enacted tax rates and laws.

2__ACCOUNTS RECEIVABLE

Accounts receivable include an allowance for doubtful accounts of $4,734,000 and $4,430,000 as of February 29, 2000 and February 28, 1999, respectively.

3__FIXED ASSETS

		2000		1999	
		Accumulated Depreciation		Accumulated Depreciation	Depreciation/ Amortization
	Cost	and Amortization	Cost	and Amortization	Rate
	($000s)		($000s)		
Computer equipment and software	$ 63,334	$43,370	$ 46,795	$32,665	33%
Office furniture	21,602	11,317	15,877	9,230	20%
Leasehold improvements	8,160	3,726	5,404	2,754	Lease Term
Land	820	–	788	–	–
Building	7,198	1,243	6,916	967	2.5%
Construction in progress *	3,377	–	–		
	104,491	$59,656	75,780	$45,616	
	(59,656)		(45,616)		
Net book value	$ 44,835		$ 30,164		

* See Note 7

Depreciation and amortization of fixed assets was $13,898,000, $10,760,000, and $8,766,000 in each of fiscal 2000,1999, and 1998, respectively.

4__INTANGIBLE ASSETS

Intangible assets as at February 29, 2000, and February 28, 1999, include acquired technology and goodwill, and are disclosed net of amortization.

The Corporation recorded $2,352,000 of goodwill in fiscal 2000 and $21,604,000 of acquired technology and goodwill in fiscal 1999. Amortization of intangible assets was $5,692,000, $1,330,000, and $558,000 in each of fiscal 2000, 1999, and 1998, respectively (see Note 5).

The Corporation did not capitalize any costs of internally-developed computer software to be sold, licensed, or otherwise marketed in each of fiscal 2000,1999, and 1998, and recorded $0, $55,000, and $430,000 of corresponding amortization, respectively.

5__ACQUISITIONS

FISCAL 2000 ACQUISITIONS

On May 28, 1999, the Corporation completed the acquisition of Information Tools AG, the Corporation's distributor in Switzerland. The shareholders of Information Tools AG are to receive total consideration of approximately $657,000 of which $458,000 was received in cash during fiscal 2000. The remainder of the consideration ($199,000) is payable equally on the first and second anniversaries of the closing of the transaction. An amount not to exceed $500,000 could also be paid in contingent consideration. Of that amount, approximately $120,000 will be paid in fiscal 2001 relating to fiscal 2000 results and has been recorded as additional purchase price.

On July 15, 1999, the Corporation completed the purchase of the entire outstanding minority interest in the Corporation's subsidiary in Singapore, Cognos Far East Pte Limited. The former minority shareholders of Cognos Far East Pte Limited received approximately $1,688,000 in cash upon completion of the purchase. No further consideration is due to the former minority shareholders of the subsidiary.

Both acquisitions have been accounted for using the purchase method. The results of operations of both acquired companies prior to the acquisition were not material, and thus pro forma information has not been provided. The results of both acquired companies have been combined with those of the Corporation since their respective dates of acquisition.

Total consideration, including acquisition costs, was allocated based on estimated fair values on the acquisition date: ($000s)

	Information Tools AG	Cognos Far East Pte Limited	Total
Assets acquired	$ 683	$ –	$ 683
Liabilities assumed	(570)	– (570)	
Net assets acquired	113	–	113
Goodwill	664	1,688	2,352
Purchase price	$ 777	$1,688	$2,465
Consideration			
Cash	458	1,688	2,146
Deferred payment	319	–	319
	$ 777	$1,688	$2,465

FISCAL 1999 ACQUISITIONS

On December 3, 1998, the Corporation completed the acquisition of substantially all the assets of Relational Matters including DecisionStream software. DecisionStream aggregates and integrates large volumes of transaction data with multidimensional data structures. Relational Matters will receive approximately $7,555,000 over three years and 250,980 shares of the Corporation's common stock valued at $1,823,000 over the same time period. The shares, all of which were issued, are being held in escrow by the Corporation and will be released on the second (40%) and third (60%) anniversaries of the closing of the transaction. For valuation purposes, the deferred payments and shares were appropriately discounted. An independent appraisal valued the in-process research and development at $2,400,000. In the opinion of management and the appraiser, the acquired in-process research and development had not yet reached technological feasibility and had no alternative future uses. Accordingly, the Corporation recorded a special charge of $2,400,000 ($0.02 per share on a diluted basis) in the fourth quarter ended February 28, 1999, to write off the acquired in-process technology.

On February 24, 1999, the Corporation completed the acquisition of LEX2000 Inc., a developer of financial data mart and reporting software, for a combination of cash and the Corporation's common stock. The shareholders of LEX2000 Inc. will receive approximately $7,444,000 over three years and 252,118 shares of the Corporation's common stock valued at $1,940,000 over the same time period. Approximately 14,200 shares were issued at closing; the remainder, all of which were issued, are being held in escrow by the Corporation and will be released equally on the second (50%) and third (50%) anniversaries of the closing of the transaction. For valuation purposes, the deferred payments and remaining shares were appropriately discounted. An independent appraisal valued the in-process research and development at $1,400,000. In the opinion of management and the appraiser, the acquired in-process research and development had not yet reached technological feasibility and had no alternative future uses. Accordingly, the Corporation recorded a special charge of $1,400,000 ($0.02 per share on a diluted basis) in the fourth quarter ended February 28, 1999, to write off the acquired in-process technology.

The scheduled aggregate annual payments for the long-term liabilities related to these two acquisitions are $3,501,000 and $2,599,000 in fiscal 2001 and 2002 respectively. Amounts due within twelve months are included in accrued charges.

Both acquisitions have been accounted for using the purchase method. The results of operations of both acquired companies prior to the acquisitions were not material, and thus pro forma information has not been provided. The results of both acquired companies have been combined with those of the Corporation since their respective dates of acquisition.

Total consideration, including acquisition costs, was allocated based on estimated fair values on the acquisition date: ($000s)

	Relational Matters	LEX2000	Total
Assets acquired			
In-process technology	$2,400	$ 1,400	$ 3,800
Acquired technology	3,600	13,165	16,765
Other assets	25	1,501	1,526
	6,025	16,066	22,091
Liabilities assumed	(37)	(2,869)	(2,906)
Deferred tax credits	—	(5,267)	(5,267)
Net assets acquired	5,988	7,930	13,918
Goodwill	3,385	1,454	4,839
Purchase price	$9,373	$ 9,384	$18,757
Consideration			
Cash	$4,419	$ 4,755	$ 9,174
Deferred payment	3,131	2,689	5,820
Shares	1,823	1,940	3,763
	$9,373	$ 9,384	$18,757

FISCAL 1998 ACQUISITIONS

On April 9, 1997, the Corporation completed the acquisition of Right Information Systems Limited (RIS) of London, England. RIS was the provider of 4Thought™, business modeling and forecasting software. The shareholders of RIS received $4,500,000 and 180,000 shares of the Corporation's common stock, valued at $1,607,000. These shares, all of which were issued, are being held in escrow by the Corporation until April 9, 2000. An independent appraisal valued the in-process research and development at $5,000,000. In the opinion of management and the appraiser, the acquired in-process research and development had not yet reached technological feasibility and had no alternative future uses. Accordingly, the Corporation recorded a special charge of $5,000,000 ($0.05 per share on a diluted basis) in the first quarter ended May 31, 1997, to write off the acquired in-process technology.

On October 24, 1997, the Corporation completed the acquisition of Interweave Software, Inc. (Interweave) of Santa Clara, California, U.S.A. Interweave was the developer and marketer of the Interweave software product line, which allows information technology organizations to deploy intranet- and extranet-based business intelligence applications more broadly within and across enterprises. The acquisition agreement called for the Corporation to pay $12,415,000 to the shareholders of Interweave, the majority of which was paid upon completion of the acquisition. An independent appraisal valued the in-process research and development at $13,000,000. In the opinion of management and the appraiser, the acquired in-process research and development had not yet reached technological feasibility and had no alternative future uses. Accordingly, the Corporation recorded a special charge of $13,000,000 ($0.14 per share on a diluted basis) in the third quarter ended November 30, 1997, to write off the acquired in-process technology.

Both acquisitions have been accounted for using the purchase method. The results of operations of both acquired companies prior to the acquisitions were not material, and thus pro forma information has not been provided. The results of both acquired companies have been combined with those of the Corporation since their respective dates of acquisition.

Total consideration, including acquisition costs, was allocated based on estimated fair values on the acquisition date: ($000s)

	RIS	Interweave	Total
Assets acquired			
In-process technology	$ 5,000	$13,000	$18,000
Other assets	239	390	629
	5,239	13,390	18,629
Liabilities assumed	(1,050)	(4,544)	(5,594)
Net assets acquired	4,189	8,846	13,035
Goodwill	1,918	3,569	5,487
Purchase price	$ 6,107	$12,415	$18,522
Consideration			
Cash	$ 4,500	$12,415	$16,915
Shares	1,607	–	1,607
	$ 6,107	$12,415	$18,522

6__LONG-TERM DEBT

	2000	1999
	($000s)	
Mortgage at 12.5% per annum, repayable in blended monthly installments of principal and interest of Cdn $45,200 to October 2000	$ 2,142	$2,160
Other	34	452
	2,176	2,612
Less current portion	(2,176)	(123)
	$ –	$2,489

Interest expense on long-term debt was $264,000, $271,000, and $301,000 in fiscal 2000, 1999, and 1998, respectively.

7__COMMITMENTS

Certain of the Corporation's offices, computer equipment, and vehicles are leased under various terms. The annual aggregate lease expense in each of fiscal 2000,1999, and 1998 was $12,205,000, $9,219,000, and $8,599,000, respectively.

The aggregate amount of payments for these operating leases, in each of the next five fiscal years and thereafter, is approximately as follows: ($000s)

2001	$12,939
2002	10,261
2003	7,501
2004	4,915
2005	4,200
Thereafter	8,770

In August 1999, the Corporation announced plans for the construction of a second building on the site of its corporate headquarters on Riverside Drive in Ottawa — *Riverside II*. The total cost of Riverside II and related improvements is estimated to be $21 million. The Corporation is currently committed to approximately $15 million of the total cost and as at February 29, 2000, had incurred capital expenditures of approximately $3.4 million. Construction is expected to be substantially complete before the end of fiscal 2001.

8__FINANCIAL INSTRUMENTS

OFF-BALANCE-SHEET RISK

The Corporation's policy with respect to foreign currency exposure is to manage its financial exposure to certain foreign exchange fluctuations with the objective of neutralizing some of the impact of foreign currency exchange movements. To achieve this objective, the Corporation enters into foreign exchange forward contracts to hedge portions of the net investment in its various subsidiaries. As a result, the exchange gains and losses recorded on translation of the subsidiaries' financial statements are partially offset by the gains and losses attributable to the applicable foreign exchange forward contracts. Realized and unrealized gains and losses from the applicable foreign exchange forward contracts are recorded as part of the foreign currency translation adjustments included in the Consolidated Statements of Stockholders' Equity. The Corporation has foreign exchange conversion facilities that allow it to hold foreign exchange contracts of Cdn $130,000,000 (US $89,730,000) outstanding at any one time. The Corporation enters into foreign exchange forward contracts with major Canadian chartered banks, and therefore does not anticipate non-performance by these counterparties. The amount of the exposure on account of any non-performance is restricted to the unrealized gains in such contracts. As of February 29, 2000, the Corporation had foreign exchange forward contracts, with maturity dates ranging from March 30, 2000 to May 25, 2000, to exchange various foreign currencies in the amount of $6,239,000. As of February 28, 1999, the Corporation had foreign exchange forward contracts, with maturity dates ranging from March 25, 1999 to May 27, 1999, to exchange various foreign currencies in the amount of $3,862,000.

CONCENTRATION OF CREDIT RISK

The investment of cash is regulated by the Corporation's investment policy, which is periodically reviewed and approved by the Audit Committee of the Board of Directors. The primary objective of the Corporation's investment policy is security of principal. The Corporation manages its investment credit risk through a combination of (i) a selection of securities with an acceptable credit rating; (ii) selection of term to maturity, which in no event exceeds one year in length; and (iii) diversification of debt issuers, both individually and by industry grouping.

Included in cash, cash equivalents, and short-term investments as of February 29, 2000 and February 28, 1999 were corporate debt amounts of $73,805,000 and $46,941,000, respectively. The corporate debt amounts as of February 29, 2000 and February 28, 1999 were with two distinct issuers. These amounts were repaid, in full, at maturity in March of their respective years. All the Corporation's short-term investments as of February 29, 2000 and February 28, 1999 had maturity dates before the end of June of their respective years. The Corporation's cash, cash equivalents, and short-term investments are denominated predominantly in Canadian and U.S. dollars.

The Corporation has an unsecured credit facility, subject to annual renewal, that includes an operating line and foreign exchange conversion facilities. The operating line permits the Corporation to borrow funds or issue letters of credit or guarantee up to an aggregate of Cdn $15,000,000 (US $10,353,000), subject to certain covenants. As of February 29, 2000 and February 28, 1999, there were no direct borrowings under this operating line.

There is no concentration of credit risk related to the Corporation's position in trade accounts receivable. Credit risk, with respect to trade receivables, is minimized because of the Corporation's large customer base and its geographical dispersion (see Note 12).

FAIR VALUE OF FINANCIAL INSTRUMENTS

For certain of the Corporation's financial instruments, including accounts receivable, accounts payable, and other accrued charges, the carrying amounts approximate the fair value due to their short maturities. Cash and cash equivalents, short-term investments, long-term debt, and long-term liabilities are carried at cost, which approximates their fair value.

9 INCOME TAXES

Details of the income tax provision (recovery) are as follows: ($000s)

	2000	1999	1998
Current			
Canadian	$ 4,909	$ 5,313	$ 1,360
Foreign	9,943	9,228	8,550
	14,852	14,541	9,910
Deferred			
Canadian	8,201	(1,370)	2,459
Foreign	(180)	(37)	(1,252)
	8,021	(1,407)	1,207
Income tax provision	$22,873	$13,134	$11,117

The reported income tax provision differs from the amount computed by applying the Canadian rate to income before income taxes. The reasons for this difference and the related tax effects are as follows: ($000s)

	2000	1999	1998
Expected Canadian tax rate	44.0%	44.0%	44.0%
Expected tax provision	$ 35,943	$ 31,490	$ 19,254
Foreign tax rate differences	(10,422)	(10,906)	(8,740)
Net change in valuation allowance and other income tax benets earned	(6,688)	(9,142)	(10,759)
Non-deductible expenses and non-taxable income	2,876	193	643
Non-deductible in-process R&D write-off	–	560	7,400
Withholding tax on foreign income	1,179	987	822
Reorganization costs	–	–	2,426
Other	(15)	(48)	71
Reported income tax provision	$ 22,873	$ 13,134	$ 11,117

Deferred income taxes result principally from temporary differences in the recognition of certain revenue and expense items for financial and tax reporting purposes. Significant components of the Corporation's deferred tax assets and liabilities as of February 29, 2000 and February 28, 1999 are as follows: ($000s)

	2000	1999
Deferred tax assets		
Net operating tax loss carryforwards	$ 4,460	$ 5,507
Investment tax credits	1,404	4,499
Deferred revenue	2,490	2,702
Other	2,186	1,912
Total deferred tax assets	10,540	14,620
Valuation allowance for deferred tax assets	(4,460)	(5,507)
Net deferred tax assets	6,080	9,113
Deferred tax liabilities		
Book and tax differences on assets	9,489	6,969
Reserves and allowances	7,484	5,415
Income tax credits	5,346	4,502
Other	(1,089)	14
Total deferred tax liabilities	21,230	16,900
Net deferred income tax liability	$ 15,150	$ 7,787

The net change in the total valuation allowance for the years ended February 29, 2000 and February 28, 1999 was a decrease of $1,047,000 and $7,309,000, respectively.

Realization of the net deferred tax assets is dependent on generating sufficient taxable income in certain legal entities. Although realization is not assured, management believes it is more likely than not that the net amount of the deferred tax asset will be realized. However, this estimate could change in the near term as future taxable income in these certain legal entities changes.

As of February 29, 2000, the Corporation had tax loss carryforwards of approximately $10,027,000 available to reduce future years' income for tax purposes. These losses expire as follows: ($000s)

2002	$ 294
2003–2010	425
Indenitely	9,308
Total	$10,027

Income before taxes attributable to all foreign operations was $41,548,000, $42,152,000, and $23,546,000 in each of fiscal 2000, 1999, and 1998, respectively.

The Corporation has provided for foreign withholding taxes on the portion of the undistributed earnings of foreign subsidiaries expected to be remitted.

Income taxes paid were $18,658,000, $8,201,000, and $11,273,000 in each of fiscal 2000, 1999, and 1998, respectively.

10 __STOCKHOLDERS' EQUITY

CAPITAL STOCK
The authorized capital of the Corporation consists of an unlimited number of common shares, without nominal or par value, and an unlimited number of preferred shares, issuable in series. No series of preferred shares has been created or issued.

Share Repurchase Programs
The share repurchases made in the past three fiscal years were part of distinct open market share repurchase programs through the Nasdaq National Market. The share repurchases made in fiscal 2000 were part of two open market share repurchase programs. The program adopted in October 1998 expired on October 8, 1999. Under this program the Corporation repurchased 3,161,800 of its shares; all repurchased shares were cancelled. In October 1999, the Corporation adopted a new program that will enable it to purchase up to 4,200,000 common shares (not more than 5% of those issued and outstanding) between October 9, 1999 and October 8, 2000. This program does not commit the Corporation to make any share repurchases. Purchases will be made on The Nasdaq Stock Market at prevailing open market prices and paid out of general corporate funds. All repurchased shares will be cancelled.

The details of the share repurchases were as follows:

	2000		1999		1998	
	Shares	**Cost**	Shares	Cost	Shares	Cost
	(000s)	*($000s)*	*(000s)*	*($000s)*	*(000s)*	*($000s)*
July 1996 program	–	$ –	–	$ –	170	$ 1,931
October 1997 program	–	–	2,030	23,463	2,370	27,180
October 1998 program	**2,186**	**24,689**	976	10,674	–	–
October 1999 program	**100**	**1,324**	–	–	–	–
	2,286	**$26,013**	3,006	$34,137	2,540	$29,111

The amount paid to acquire the shares over and above the average carrying value has been charged to retained earnings.

Stock Option Plans

As of February 29, 2000, the Corporation had stock options outstanding under two plans: 4,421,000 pertain to the 1997–2002 Stock Option Plan and 2,849,000 pertain to the 1993–1998 Stock Option Plan.

There were 14,000,000 shares of common stock originally reserved by the Board of Directors for issuance under the Corporation's 1997–2002 Stock Option Plan ("the Plan"), which was approved by the Corporation's shareholders in June 1997 and replaced the 1993–1998 Stock Option Plan. Options may be granted to directors, officers, employees, and consultants at such times and under such terms as established by the Plan. Options may be fully exercisable on the date of grant or may be exercisable in installments. Options will expire not later than 10 years from the date of grant or any shorter period as may be determined. All options are priced at the market price of the Corporation's shares on The Toronto Stock Exchange on the trading day preceding the date of grant. In June 1999, options were awarded to employees, executive officers, and directors. These options vest equally in April 2000, April 2001, April 2002, and April 2003, and expire in April 2007. There were 9,381,000 options available for grant under the Plan as of February 29, 2000.

Under the 1993–1998 Stock Option Plan, options were awarded to directors, officers, and employees. For the options outstanding as of February 29, 2000, the vesting dates extend to September 2001 and the expiry dates range from April 2000 to September 2005. In April 1996, options were awarded to certain key officers under an executive option award. These options vest equally in April 1999, April 2000, and April 2001, and expire in April 2003. All options were priced at the market price of the Corporation's shares on The Toronto Stock Exchange on the trading day preceding the date of grant. The 1993–1998 Stock Option Plan expired on January 1, 1998.

Employee Stock Purchase Plan

This plan was approved by the Corporation's shareholders in July 1993 and was amended on May 19, 1999. The amended plan was approved by the Corporation's shareholders on June 22, 1999, and will terminate on November 30, 2002. Under the plan, 3,000,000 common shares were reserved for issuance. A participant in the Employee Stock Purchase Plan authorizes the Corporation to deduct an amount per pay period that cannot exceed five (5) percent of annual target salary divided by the number of pay periods per year. Deductions are accumulated during each of the Corporation's fiscal quarters ("Purchase Period") and on the first trading day following the end of any Purchase Period these deductions are applied toward the purchase of common shares. The purchase price per share is ninety (90) percent of the lesser of The Toronto Stock Exchange average closing price on (a) the first five trading days of the Purchase Period or (b) the last five trading days of the Purchase Period. All full-time and part-time permanent employees may participate in the plan.

Accounting for Stock-Based Compensation

The Corporation applies APB Opinion 25 in accounting for its stock option and purchase plans. The exercise price of all stock options is equal to the market price of the stock on the trading day preceding the date of grant. Accordingly, no compensation cost has been recognized in the financial statements for its stock option and stock purchase plans.

If the fair values of the options granted since fiscal 1996 had been recognized as compensation expense on a straight line basis over the vesting period of the grant (consistent with the method prescribed by FASB Statement No. 123), stock-based compensation costs would have reduced net income by $9,096,000, $8,239,000, and $6,824,000; reduced basic net income per share by $0.11, $0.09, and $0.08, and reduced diluted net income per share by $0.10, $0.09, and $0.07 in fiscal 2000,1999, and 1998, respectively.

Because Statement No. 123 is applicable only to options granted subsequent to February 28, 1995 and the Corporation's amortization period for compensation expense approximates four years, the above pro forma disclosure for fiscal 1998 is not indicative of pro forma amounts that will be reported in future years. The pro forma disclosure for fiscal 2000 and 1999 includes the full extent of amortization expense for four years of option grants.

The fair value of the options was estimated at the date of grant using a Black-Scholes option pricing model with the following weighted average assumptions for fiscal 2000, 1999, and 1998, respectively: risk-free interest rates of 5.8%, 5.5%, and 6.5%, expected life of the options of 2.8 years, 2.9 years, and 3.0 years, expected volatility of 55%, 56%, and 56%, and for all years, a dividend yield of zero.

Activity in the stock option plans for fiscal 2000, 1999, and 1998 was as follows:

	2000		1999		1998	
	Options	Weighted Average Exercise Price	Options	Weighted Average Exercise Price	Options	Weighted Average Exercise Price
	(000s)		(000s)		(000s)	
Outstanding, beginning of year	6,769	$ 9.72	6,571	$ 8.29	7,940	$ 5.33
Granted	2,772	11.18	1,935	13.33	2,190	11.48
Exercised	(1,973)	7.81	(1,054)	3.94	(3,316)	2.60
Cancelled	(298)	11.73	(683)	9.52	(243)	9.54
Outstanding, end of year	7,270	11.17	6,769	9.72	6,571	8.29
Options exercisable at year end	1,234		1,460		1,077	
Weighted average per share fair value of options granted during the year calculated using the Black-Scholes option pricing model		$ 4.59		$ 5.54		$ 4.84

The following table summarizes significant ranges of outstanding and exercisable options held by directors, officers, and employees as of February 29, 2000:

	Options Outstanding			Options Exercisable	
Range of Exercise Prices	Options	Weighted Average Remaining Life	Weighted Average Exercise Price	Options	Weighted Average Exercise Price
	(000s)			(000s)	
$ 3.55–$ 5.52	26	0.4 years	$ 4.22	25	$ 4.22
$ 8.76–$10.69	1,801	4.2	8.95	407	8.96
$10.70–$11.04	3,612	6.5	10.93	449	10.94
$11.05–$13.86	1,660	6.2	13.37	353	13.17
$17.58–$23.56	158	7.8	18.65	–	–
$27.95–$28.06	13	7.9	28.03	–	–
	7,270	5.9	11.17	1,234	10.78

NET INCOME PER SHARE

The dilutive effect of stock options is excluded under the requirements of FASB Statement No. 128 for calculating net income per share, but is included in the calculation of diluted net income per share.

The reconciliation of the numerator and denominator for the calculation of net income per share and diluted net income per share is as follows: (000s, except per-share amounts)

	2000	1999	1998
Net Income per Share			
Net income	**$58,815**	$58,434	$32,642
Weighted average number of shares outstanding	**85,972**	87,416	88,414
Net income per share	**$0.68**	$0.67	$0.37
Diluted Net Income per Share			
Net income	**$58,815**	$58,434	$32,642
Weighted average number of shares outstanding	**85,972**	87,416	88,414
Dilutive effect of stock options *	**2,128**	1,524	3,130
Adjusted weighted average number of shares outstanding	**88,100**	88,940	91,544
Diluted net income per share	**$0.67**	$0.66	$ 0.36

* All anti-dilutive options have been excluded. The average number of anti-dilutive options was 1,580,000, 1,980,000, and 542,000 for fiscal 2000, 1999, and 1998, respectively.

11__PENSION PLANS

The Corporation operates a Retirement Savings Plan for the parent company and also operates various other defined contribution pension plans for its subsidiaries. The Corporation contributes amounts related to the level of employee contributions for both types of plans.

The pension costs in fiscal 2000,1999, and 1998 were $3,839,000, $2,744,000, and $2,327,000, respectively.

12__SEGMENTED INFORMATION

The Corporation operates in one business segment—computer software tools. This segment engages in business activities from which it earns license, support, and services revenue, and incurs expenses. Within this business segment, the Corporation develops, markets, and supports two complementary lines of software products that are designed to satisfy enterprise-wide business-critical needs. The Corporation's business intelligence products give individual users the ability to independently access, explore, analyze, and report corporate data. The Corporation's client/server application development tools are designed to increase the productivity of system analysts and developers. Cognos products are distributed both directly and through resellers worldwide.

Revenue is derived from the licensing of software and the provision of related services, which include product support and education, consulting, and other services. The Corporation generally licenses software and provides services subject to terms and conditions consistent with industry standards. Customers may elect to contract with the Corporation for product support, which includes product and documentation enhancements, as well as telephone support, by paying either an annual fee or fees based on usage of support services.

The Corporation operates internationally, with a substantial portion of its business conducted in foreign currencies. Accordingly, the Corporation's results are affected by year-over-year exchange rate fluctuations of the United States dollar relative to the Canadian dollar, to various European currencies, and to a lesser extent, other foreign currencies.

No single customer accounted for 10% or more of the Corporation's revenue during any of the last three fiscal years. In addition, the Corporation is not dependent on any single customer or group of customers, or supplier.

The accounting policies for the segment are the same as those described in the Summary of Significant Accounting Policies. The required financial information for segment profit and segment assets is the same as that presented in the Consolidated Financial Statements. Geographic information is as follows: ($000s)

	2000	1999	1998
Revenue to external customers*			
U.S.A.	$204,730	$153,827	$123,774
Canada	30,120	24,040	22,328
United Kingdom	44,972	41,563	38,257
Europe	77,778	60,502	43,189
Asia/Pacific	28,040	21,193	17,286
	$385,640	$301,125	$244,834

* Revenues are attributed to countries based on location of customer

	2000	1999
Fixed assets		
Canada	$31,055	$20,148
U.S.A.	8,659	6,078
Other countries	5,121	3,938
	$44,835	$30,164
Intangible assets		
Canada	$ 8,264	$ 7,966
U.S.A.	13,599	17,237
	$21,863	$25,203

13__NEW ACCOUNTING PRONOUNCEMENTS

In June 1998, the FASB issued Statement No. 133, *Accounting for Derivative Instruments and Hedging Activities* which establishes standards for derivative instruments and hedging activities. It requires that all derivatives be recognized as either assets or liabilities on the Balance Sheet and be measured at fair value. This Statement is effective for fiscal years beginning after June 15,2000, which is the fiscal year beginning March 1, 2001 for the Corporation. Prior periods should not be restated. The Corporation has not yet quantified the impact, if any, of this pronouncement on its consolidated financial statements.

In December 1999, the Securities and Exchange Commission (SEC) issued Staff Accounting Bulletin (SAB) No. 101, *Revenue Recognition in Financial Statements*, which was amended in March 2000 by SAB 101A. The SAB summarizes certain of the SEC staff views in applying generally accepted accounting principles to revenue recognition in financial statements. This SAB is effective beginning the Corporation's second quarter of fiscal 2001. The Corporation does not expect the adoption of this SAB to have a material impact on its results of operations or financial position.

14 __COMPARATIVE RESULTS

Certain of the prior years' figures have been reclassified in order to conform to the presentation adopted in the current year.

15 __SUBSEQUENT EVENT

On April 6, 2000, the Board of Directors of the Corporation authorized a two-for-one stock split, effected in the form of a stock dividend, payable on or about April 27, 2000, to shareholders of record at the close of business on April 20, 2000.

All share and per-share amounts in the accompanying financial statements, and notes thereto, have been adjusted for the split.